NEWSPAPER LAYOUT & DESIGN

A TECHNICAL ION

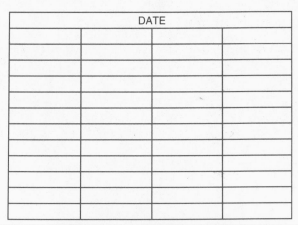

★ ★ ★ **THIRD EDITION**

NEWSPAPER

LAYOUT & DESIGN

A TEAM APPROACH

DARYL R. MOEN

IOWA STATE UNIVERSITY PRESS / AMES

Daryl R. Moen is director of Professional Programs and professor in the School of Journalism, University of Missouri, Columbia.

This book was produced from camera-ready copy designed and supplied by the author.

♾ Printed on acid-free paper in the United States of America

First edition, 1984
    Second printing, 1985
    Third printing, 1986
Second edition, 1989
    Second printing, 1990
    Third printing, 1994
Third edition, 1995

Library of Congress Cataloging-in-Publication Data

Moen, Daryl R.
    Newspaper layout and design / Daryl R. Moen.—3rd ed.
        p.   cm.
    Includes bibliographical references and index.
    ISBN 0-8138-1225-9
    1. Newspaper layout and typography.   I. Title.
Z253.5M63   1995
070.5'722—dc20   94-15567

CONTENTS

This book is dedicated to the concept of visual journalism. The chapters that follow explore how visual journalists working in teams rather than as individuals can ask not only "why?" but "why not?" not only "how?" but "what's the best way to tell the story?" Only then will journalists begin to achieve the potential of the medium.

Author

I.

GETTING READY: TRAINING FOR A NEW WORLD

II.

Segmenting is explained in Chapter 3.

GETTING STARTED: NEWSPAPER LAYOUT

v

Most of the decisions about how the paper looks *are journalistic ones.*
Dale Peskin
AME
Detroit News

The distribution map is one of several explained in Chapter 6.

We don't invent information; we allow it to reveal itself as it marches past. The parade must be encouraged, so that we can develop marvelous new organizational patterns that spark new understandings.

Richard Wurman
AUTHOR
Information Anxiety

III.

THE TEAM EFFORT

College papers have the opportunity to explore new dimensions in design. See Chapter 14.

IV.

APPLYING THE LESSONS: SPECIALIZED APPLICATIONS

Newspapers such as the **Detroit Free Press** are developing special sections to appeal to segmented audiences. See Chapter 18.

V.

BEYOND THE BASICS: NEWSPAPER DESIGN

PREFACE

The days of Lone Ranger journalism are over. The best journalism is being produced these days by teams of journalists who step beyond their specialties to offer and listen to suggestions. That's why this edition of *Newspaper Layout & Design* is subtitled, *A Team Approach*. Brilliant reporting and writing, exceptional photographs and startling designs aren't enough. To entice the scanner to read and make sense of the content, newspapers must offer coherent packages. The brilliant writing and exceptional photographs must complement each other in order to illuminate. Headlines, pullouts and cutlines that are written to supplement each of the other elements in the package help turn mere data into information.

That's why this book is based on the premise that the new generation of journalists must be cross-trained. Reporters must know the value and role of photography and graphics. Designers must know the value of good stories told well. Photographers must recognize that the pictures and words must work in tandem. Designers are the only cross-trained specialists now in the newsroom, and that's not the way it should be.

All of us in the newspaper business have a challenge ahead. The philosophers Fritz Machlup and Theodore Rusik have eloquently made the case that the quantity of information does not correlate with understanding. Richard Saul Wurman popularized the theory in *Information Anxiety*, in which he talks about the need to help readers sort through the avalanche of data to find meaning. Journalists working in teams asking the right questions and presenting the information intelligently can offer understanding. This book shows you how.

But first, it starts with the points and picas. It shows you how to fit elements on a page, how to show the relationship among them, how to determine headline sizes, how to change the width of copy and photographs and still make them all fit. These chapters illustrate the nuts-and-bolts approach taken throughout the book. This book doesn't just talk about layout and design; it gives you the information you need to do it. In a sense, you have two books here. The first is for the beginner; the second is for the advanced designer.

Much is new in this edition. Nearly 90 percent of the illustrations are new. For the first time, chapters are devoted to accuracy in charts, making words and visuals work together, designing college newspapers and designing advertising. The need to have minorities represented in our photography and graphics is also emphasized. The section on ethics in photo manipulation and selection has been expanded.

What's new

■ Chapters on accuracy in charts, making words and visuals work together, designing college papers and designing advertising

■ Ninety percent of the illustrations

■ A focus on the importance of teamwork

■ Hundreds of new ideas

━━━ " ━━━

Our focus group leader asked non-readers to describe our newspaper as if it were a person at a party. I watched the color drain out of my colleagues' faces as the descriptions spewed forth: Fat, arrogant. A beauty-parlor gossip. "I'm not sure what he'd look like," one woman said, "but I sure wouldn't take him home to meet my parents."

Tom Brooker
SPECIAL PROJECTS MANAGER
Appleton (WI) Post-Crescent

This is the first edition produced on a PC-based pagination system. That means the grid is more flexible and illustrations are located with the appropriate copy. As a result, the book is more usable and interesting. To make future editions even more useful, I'd like to hear from you. Write me at the Missouri School of Journalism, P.O. Box 838; Columbia, MO 65205.

This book is the work of many people. Through my teaching at the University of Missouri and in seminars from British Colombia, Canada, to Madras, India, I have learned a great deal from students and professionals, much of which I have shared with you. Thanks for the special contributions from Nanette Bisher of the Orange County Register; Kevin Boyd of the San Jose Mercury News; Tim Atseff of the Syracuse Newspapers; Bruce Kabat of the Waco Tribune-Herald; John Humenik of The Times in Munster, Ind.; David Fuselier of the La Crosse (Wis.) Tribune; Rueben Stern of the Journal and Constitution in Atlanta, and Lyle Boone of the Des Moines Register. A special thanks to Melissa Nagy, a Missouri student who produced most of the graphics for the book, Myra Ferguson, who paginated the book, and Jessie Dolch, who edited it.

Most of all, thanks to my wife, Nancy, and Chad, Mia and Marisa, whose support is the most valuable thing I have.

I.

GETTING READY: TRAINING FOR A NEW WORLD

1. THE VISUAL JOURNALIST

A child is kidnapped, a plane crashes, interest rates rise. The GATT talks conclude. NAFTA passes. The city council asks for a tax increase. Guns kill. Guns don't kill. The Soviet Union dissolves. East and West Germany reunite. IBM struggles to survive. Microsoft becomes a blue chip company. Health care. Deficits. Hurricanes, floods, fires and earthquakes. Data, data everywhere, and not a drop of understanding.

We are awash in a sea of news—unconnected bits of information that used to float ashore daily but now pound the shore minute by minute. Wars are televised live. Television news snippets beget Headline News Snippets. The amount of information doubles every six years, then five years. Like cholesterol shutting down the blood flow, information clogs the neural system. The question T. S. Eliot asked years ago remains unanswered: "Where is the knowledge we have lost in information?"

The information explosion

The expanding media mix is producing information in incomprehensible amounts at instantaneous speeds. The age is gone when Will Rogers could say, "Well, all I know is what I read in the newspaper." Newspapers, radio, television and electronic information systems jockey for position. Newspapers are too slow for sports enthusiasts, who call 900 numbers. Television is too slow for traders, who monitor business news on computers. Newspaper companies buy cable companies. Cable companies buy entertainment companies. A bigger company al-

1.1 Believing that extinction is not inevitable, the industry is examining its content and the way it produces information.

ways appears to gobble a smaller company in an effort to roar into the next Information Age. But the Information Age becomes the Information Anxiety Age, the black hole, according to Richard Saul Wurman, between data and knowledge. We wire the world to spread information, and the world uses the access not to read what the great companies are reporting but to create an underground communication system. The Russians describe the fall of communism on E-mail. Scientists trade research results long before the journals can publish the studies. Journalists monitor E-mail to find out what's really happening. Newspapers, it has been said metaphorically, should engage the community in a conversation with itself. However, the community is literally having that conversation without the benefit of traditional mass media.

Re-examining journalists' roles

So where does that leave newspapers? Newspaper penetration peaked in the mid-1940s, but the companies still enjoyed record profits for another 30 years. In 1920 there were more than 2,000 daily newspapers; by 1992 there were 1,570. The sight of the last Shreveport (La.) Journal was all too familiar (Fig. 1.1). Whether publishers, advertising managers and editors want it to or not, the role of the newspaper is changing. But extinction is not inevitable. Newspapers do not have to disappear like dinosaurs; they may adapt and survive like shrews. Radio didn't make newspapers disappear. Television didn't make radio disappear. Newspapers can evolve if they can find their way out of the morass of information and start sharing knowledge. Newspapers such as the phenomenally successful Orange County Register offer not only new blood but new thinking (Fig. 1.2). Quantity is not the answer. A common complaint that The Wall Street Journal heard when it added a third section was that the paper was too big. One of many publishers trying to engineer the new newspaper is Reid Ashe of the Wichita (Kan.) Eagle. "We have to recognize," he says, "that raw information is cheap, understanding is valuable and something you can act on is precious."

The best newspapers are fighting back by using some of the same technology that is assaulting them. Managers are ordering new presses to print papers with more and more color for smaller and smaller zones. They are developing data bases to help the sales staff help advertisers. Desktop publishing systems are putting power into the hands of journalists and saving newspapers money at the same time. The best newspapers are also re-examining content, redefining news

Design time line

Gutenberg goes broke printing the Bible	Publick Occurence, first American newspaper, appears	Publisher of first daily in English language, London's Daily Courant, is a woman	First drawing appears in newspaper	Baskerville type introduced
1455	1690	1702	1707	1750

values and inviting readers into the process. Now some American newspapers have reporters covering malls, commuting, day-care and fitness programs. Food coverage has moved from the magnificent meal to microwaves. We are counting calories and nutritional benefits with health-conscious readers. We are following readers into video rental stores and health clubs. We are writing about relationships. We are offering readers time-saving tips. We are telling readers how to take action with instructions and addresses, phone and fax numbers. We are offering readers an opportunity to take command of the campaign agenda by asking them what they want the candidates to address rather than simply reporting what the candidates want to say. We are opening our phone lines to readers for story suggestions and opinions. We are reaching out to ethnic communities.

The best of us are also re-examining how we gather, process and present the news. In Norfolk, Va., education beat reporters who were once scattered from the main newsroom to bureaus were teamed to look for patterns, to bring understanding from the fragments of coverage. In Logansport, Ind., as in dozens of other newspapers, teams have replaced individuals.

Welcome to journalism by design.

The assembly-line process that has produced raw information is changing in some newspapers and must in the rest. We are moving from a system that segregates journalists by their specialties—reporters, copy editors, photographers and designers—to a holistic system. Newspapers are a visual medium. The words, pictures and numbers all are visual. They work together synergistically, and the people who produce them separate themselves at the risk of fragmenting the message. If reporters intend to convey meaning rather than raw information, they must know the value of charts and pictures, photographers must know the value of words and charts, and graphic journalists must know the value of words and pictures. All must know that the presentation is part of the message. Individuals produce fragments of information; teams produce packages of knowledge. Together they can ask, "What is the best way to tell the story?" When they know what the whole is going to be, they can ask the specialists to produce the parts. On the best papers today, reporters are suggesting layouts, photographers are suggesting headlines, designers are suggesting photographs, copy editors are suggesting stories. You have reporters who understand that a zoning story needs a map, photographers who understand that a nutrition story needs a table, designers who understand that a good story told well needs space. The artificial and self-

1.2 The Register has been successful, in part, because they have been willing to be innovative.

Bodoni type introduced	First daily newspaper appears in America	Gutenberg era ends when The Times in London uses steampower to produce the first machine-printed newspaper	William Caslon IV introduces the first typeface without serifs	First machinery-produced type	America's first steam-driven cylinder press installed
1760	1784	1814	1816	1822	1825

1.3 The Miami Herald didn't stop at reporting the news of destruction...

defeating distinction between word people and visual people must disappear.

Designers are the engineers who are making it happen. Designers are the only newsroom specialists who have a holistic view of the newsroom. The best of the designers understand that the product is more than the sum of the parts, that we can tell stories using words, numbers and pictures only when the words, numbers and pictures work together. When all journalists recognize that symbiotic relationship and contribute to it, the designers will be no more or no less important than the others.

Contrast these scenarios:

In the traditional system, the city desk reacts to police scanner traffic about a drive-by shooting. The city editor dispatches two reporters to the scene. She sends another reporter to the police station, another to the files for background. Working feverishly against the deadline, they produce multiple stories.

In the team system, the city desk alerts other members in the newsroom—photographers, graphic journalists and the news desk. A photographer and graphic journalist join the reporters at the scene. The reporters write a narrative account filled with suspense. The photographer gets action shots. The graphic journalist produces a diagram showing the sequence of events. The news desk monitors their progress and clears the space. The presentation takes advantage of the best ways to tell parts of the story to present a coherent whole. The team has asked "what is" before answering "how to."

Learning the lessons

The big news event starts an adrenaline rush in journalists, who perform marvelously and creatively under deadline pressure. When a hurricane flattens South Florida, a fire blackens Southern California or a flood engulfs the Midwest, journalists find ways to tell stories with meaning. Fiefdoms disappear and teams appear. We can learn from these events and apply the lessons to our work daily.

In Miami, for instance, Hurricane Andrew tested the Miami Herald as well as the citizens of South Florida. Journalists were victims as well as observers. The newspaper had to find ways to print and then to re-create its distribution system. Through it all, the newspaper understood that to the thousands of people who had lost homes and jobs and who needed water and medical attention, something you can act on is precious. So in addition to the stories of heroes and villains, in addition to the photographs of devastation, in addition to the maps

Telegraph first used to transmit news	Newspapers begin using decks during Mexican War	Philadelphia Public Ledger uses first-ever rotary press	New York Journal of Commerce is 3-feet x 5-feet		First web-perfecting press installed	Newsprint soars to $440 a ton	New York Evening Telegram begins using cartoons regularly
1844	**1846**	**1847**	**1853**		**1863**	**1865**	**1867**

1.4 ...it offered solution journalism to help readers cope with the tragedy.

1.5 Special events require special measures. The Register used a wrap-around section to cover the local fires in depth. The regular front page was inside.

1.6 Good labeling helped readers in Orange County through a mass of information telling readers how to get help.

and charts, the newspaper told readers how and where to get help (Figs. 1.3 and 1.4). They didn't just do it once; they did it every day. No longer just the town crier, the paper offered solution journalism.

With the most destructive wildfires in California history within sight of its office, the Orange County Register created a wrap-around section devoted to the fire (Fig. 1.5). The newspaper used scores of photographs and dozens of maps. It ran a box across the top of each page with information such as how to help children, how to file an insurance claim, and where to turn for shelter, help and legal aid. Most of all, it organized the reams of material to create not just quantity but also coherence (Fig. 1.6).

Applying the lessons

The teamwork and creativity shouldn't subside with the adrenalin. Big news sells newspapers to occasional readers. Everyday news made

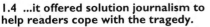

First photo, "Shantytown," appears in New York Daily Graphic

New York World introduces "ears" in nameplate

Hoe press prints 48,000 copies of a 12-page paper an hour

American Type Founders is created

New York World prints first color pictures on newspaper presses and runs front-page illustration of the sinking of the battleship Maine

1880   **1881**   **1890**   **1892**   **1893**

1.7 The Morning Call created information out of data by looking at the big picture rather than drowning readers in details of the Shah of Iran's attempt to find medical care.

useful may convert them to frequent readers. The publisher Reid Ashe reminds us that traditional ways of delivering traditional news aren't working. "The problem with newspapers is that we've grown too good at the wrong things, and neglected the things our readers and society value most," he says. "We've honed the art of compiling and delivering information—and convinced ourselves that's our principal function—at a time when information has grown cheap and abundant" (Ashe 1992).

Here are some ways to create knowledge, to communicate excitement daily and to give readers information on which they can act.

1. Make everyone in the newsroom understand that he or she is a visual journalist. Make specialists part of a team responsible for the package rather than the parts.

2. Make sure stories include a "this is important because..." paragraph. Some newspapers call it the "so-what" or "why should I care" paragraph. Answered properly, the question helps transform data into knowledge.

3. Look for patterns. Show connections. Explain. Long before most newspapers began thinking visually, the Morning Call in Allentown, Pa., offered readers coherence by pulling together the story of the Shah of Iran's journey around the world looking for cancer treatment. No country wanted to admit him because all were afraid of irritating Iran's new rulers. Besides, the rulers were holding Americans hostage. Readers had been bombarded for days with the odyssey. Each piece was part of the puzzle. The Call gave form to the puzzle by letting readers look at the big picture with a world map and copy blocks tracing the Shah's journey (Fig. 1.7).

Everyday the wire is full of fragments. Fires. Shootings. Wars. Revolutions. Traditional categories of news don't always show the patterns. A plane crash in the United States runs on the national page. A plane crash in Germany runs on the world page. Gasoline prices in the United States run on the national page. OPEC decisions run on the world or business page. When we scatter pieces of the puzzle throughout the paper, the news is data. When we recognize patterns and present information coherently, we create knowledge from the data. The useful newspaper adds value to the news.

One of the most useful additions to journalists' ability to find patterns is computer-assisted reporting. The computer allows us to find patterns in reams of data. Newspapers have used computers to show which banks discriminate against minority borrowers, to show that some judges deal more harshly with minority than with majority defendants, to show patterns in state bid-letting and to identify cam-

Cheltenham type introduced	Rotogravure sections introduced	Garamond type introduced	Leica introduces 35-mm camera	AP News Photo Service inaugurated	Times New Roman type introduced	AP sends black-and-white photos in only 10 minutes
1902	**1914**	**1918**	**1924**	**1927**	**1932**	**1935**

1.8 Photo manipulation used properly produces better understanding. The Hartford Courant created a skyline based on developers' plans.

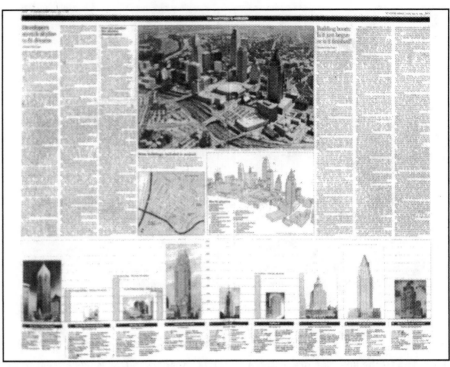

1.9 The paper explained its techniques and used text and information graphics to continue telling the story.

paign contributors who try to hide behind facades. The computer provides the data; it's up to the journalist to give it meaning through words, numbers and pictures.

4. Use the newspaper's potential as a visual medium. When the Hartford Courant asked, "What's the best way to tell the story about the city's changing skyline?" the answer was to use the computer to create the skyline by filling in the proposed buildings (Figs. 1.8 and 1.9). Words could describe the new skyline, but the picture did it better. On the eve of a national television debate, the Globe and Mail (Toronto) created a full-page table of the candidates' positions that readers could use as a scorecard (Fig. 1.10). The Dallas Morning News eschewed the traditional text round-up preview to the National Basketball season to create an intriguing graphic (Fig. 1.11). These solutions to story telling combine the work of reporters, photographers and graphic journalists.

5. Anticipate. Newspapers traditionally tell what happened. That

Washington Daily News prints nation's first perfumed advertisement	AP distributes first spot color picture of President Roosevelt welcoming King George VI	Photographic typesetting introduced	Helvetica type introduced	International Typeface Co. formed	Scanners introduced to make color separations	Daily newspapers in U.S. hit 1,774
1937	**1939**	**1954**	**1955**	**1970**	**1970s**	**1974**

1.10 The Globe and Mail presented a traditional subject in an untraditional— and effective—way.

1.11 Readers in Dallas were treated to an innovative, entertaining, informative and easy-to-read advance on the NBA season.

continues to be important, but so is telling readers what will happen. The La Crosse (Wis.) Tribune devotes the top of its business page to what's coming up (Fig. 1.12). Most newspapers already offer lists of government meetings, entertainment and sports events. When they also preview important meetings, they are empowering readers to take action. Readers can write or call officials, they can protest, they can attend meetings and be heard.

6. Practice service journalism. Tell people what they need and want to know and how they can act. Give times, dates and places. Give phone and fax numbers and addresses. List the questions readers should ask to get help with their taxes. Newspapers traditionally write about the ups and downs of the stock market. Money magazine analyzes stocks and mutual funds, ranks them by various indicators, gives phone numbers and addresses. Newspapers publish unconnected bits of data; Money offers the information in a form that makes it useful and usable.

7. Offer solutions. Don't just write about the problem of crime. Do a data base search and find communities that have had success fighting crime. Don't just write about your city's lousy bus system; visit cities with successful systems and report why they work. Don't just chortle over

1.12 Newspapers must do a better job of anticipating the news. The LaCrosse Tribune offers a look ahead each Monday in Business.

1979	1980	1982	1984	1986	1987	1991
Society of Newspaper Design founded	Pocahontus Times in Marlinton, W. Va. still sets type by hand	National Geographic electronically moves a pyramid in a cover photo	Daily U.S. circulation peaks at 63,081,740	Editor of A Day in the Life of America electronically manipulates cover photo	Dow Jones average drops 508 points. Newspapers react by printing more front-page graphics than on any day in history	AP completes switch to digital transmission

catching your city's comptroller with a hand in the cookie jar; tell what the city should do to make sure it doesn't happen again.

8. Invite readers to participate. When Oregon's legislators were debating how to balance the budget, the Oregonian in Portland asked readers for suggestions. Not only did it get readers involved, the paper received several interesting solutions (Fig. 1.13). Other newspapers routinely seek readers' opinions and ideas on all kinds of issues. The Kansas City Star invites readers to participate in daily telephone polls and offers readers audio supplements to the news.

9. Reinvent the newspaper. Richard Saul Wurman facetiously suggests in Information Anxiety (1990) that the newspaper could be divided into three categories: hope, absurdity and catastrophe. That may be too radical for some, but we should be willing to examine everything we do from the readers' viewpoint. As we enter the 21st century, what do readers want from our newspapers and how do they want it? Newspapers used to be the dominant information medium; now for too many, they are a supplement. Readers say they don't have time, but they are spending more time watching television. Newspapers aren't important enough to them, especially to the younger generation. How can we change that?

Our front pages are static except for Big Events. Should they be? Should they offer an expanded table of contents? The News in 5 Minutes? A page of pictures? A diagram of the day's events? Should they be devoted to the topic of the day? Some journalists are asking these questions. The prototypes may someday appear on the streets (Fig. 1.14).

Should the news continue to be divided into geographic categories—region, state, nation and world—or do other categories make sense in this "global village"? If not Wurman's "absurdity," how about hunger? If not "hope," how about good news? If not "catastrophe," how about natural disasters? Does it make sense to treat the national debate about health care in the United States separately from the debates in other countries? Does it make sense to treat U.S. trade problems separately from Germany's or Mexico's? Does it make sense to report on economic problems in the United States without linking them to Japan's or Canada's? Do traditional categories of news facilitate or impede understanding?

Reinventing the newspaper goes far beyond dealing with the great issues. It forces us to question everything we do. When we publish recipes, do we format them so readers can easily clip and save them or do we wrap them from one column to the next or even jump them? Are school lunch menus formatted to be clipped? Obituaries? Weddings and engagements? Do readers want us to organize our entertainment listings by day or type of entertainment? Should sports agate be organized alphabetically?

The now-defunct St. Louis Sun published an innovative daily full-page television grid with color and advertisements built into it. Many other newspapers liked it so much they immediately adopted the idea. The Sun also published a weekly TV guide. One week when editors accidentally repeated the same grid two days running, they didn't receive a single call from their 100,000 subscribers. The readers obviously

1.13 Readers contributed ideas for dealing with Oregon's budget crisis, thanks to an invitation from the newspaper.

1.14 Prototypes such as this, prepared at the Syracuse newspapers, get journalists thinking about innovative ways of presenting the news.

But as we expanded, we hired people with a more sophisticated background—not just communications or fine arts, but journalists with design skills, people who understand the importance of content.

Ed Kohorst
EDITORIAL ART DIRECTOR
Dallas Morning News

were ignoring the daily grid and using the weekly booklet, but no one at the newspaper knew.

Should advertisements be organized by content? Should all the clothing ads be run together so readers can compare? Should advertisements appear in dedicated spaces on page 1? On section fronts? Should every newspaper have an advertising index? Should advertisements be offered only in modular units? The News in Boca Raton, Fla., asked readers how they used the classified ads to shop for used cars, new homes and apartments. Readers responded that they didn't like searching through columns of small text for the items that interested them. As a result, the News created an innovative grid that organizes apartments by geographic location and price. It did the same with homes and cars. Readers reinvented that classified section. Your readers can help you reinvent the newspaper.

Conclusion

The playwright George Bernard Shaw once wrote, "You see things and you say 'why?' But I dream things that never were; and I say 'why not?' " This book is dedicated to the concept of visual journalism. The chapters that follow explore how visual journalists working in teams rather than as individuals can ask not only "why?" but "why not?," not only "how?" but "what's the best way to tell the story?" Only then will journalists begin to achieve the potential of the medium.

II.

GETTING STARTED: NEWSPAPER LAYOUT

2. THE LANGUAGE OF LAYOUT & DESIGN

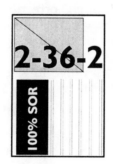

"I need a 3-36-2 jump head."

"Should I squeeze it or take it down a couple of points?"

"Get me cutlines for these pix."

Sound Greek to you? If it does, you're not alone. This jargon is a shorthand version of the vocabulary of layout and design editors. It is sometimes logical, sometimes illogical, and often inconsistent from newspaper to newspaper. To complicate matters, the vocabulary is a mixture of hot and cold type production systems, of dedicated terminals and of PCs. You may be more familiar with "template" than "grid," with "tracking" than "letterspacing," but you should learn all the terms.

Regardless of the production system, there is a basic layout and design vocabulary; this chapter defines some of these terms. Others are defined throughout the book, and all appear in the glossary. This chapter also teaches you how to work in picas, how to count and size headlines and how to size photographs. When you're done, you'll be ready to lay out a newspaper page.

Measurements

Although feet and inches are the basis for most measurements in the United States, designers work with picas and points. Your pagination software allows you to work in inches, but picas and points are more exact.

Type size is measured in points; copy widths are measured in picas

15

2.1

2.2

and points (Fig. 2.1). You see that there are 12 points to the pica. Although the decimal point in math indicates tenths, the decimal point in typography represents twelfths. That is why it may be easier for you to express the measurement as 13p6 rather than 13.6. Thus, 13.6 is 13 1/2, but 13.5 is slightly less than one-half. Working in twelfths also means that you can have 13.10 and 13.11; 13.12 would be 14 picas.

Picas and points are also used to measure the gutters, the white space between columns of type and between pictures. The gutters between columns usually range from 9 points to 2 picas. In the mid-1980s, most newspapers adopted a standard width of 78 picas to make it easier for national advertisers to place their ads. Before, advertisers had to make ads of many different widths or permit newspapers to reduce or enlarge them, sometimes with disastrous results. Standard widths also make it easier to verify billings. These uniform dimensions are known as SAUs, or standardized advertising units.

While the industry, especially the dailies, adopted the 78-pica width, newspapers subdivided the space differently. Most adopted a six-column grid with column widths of 12p2 with 1-pica gutters. There are several variations.

In layout and design, the editor must determine horizontal widths within a couple of points (Fig. 2.2). Elements that do not fit horizontally must be corrected, copy must be reset, and illustrations must be trimmed or resized. Such corrections take too much time. When fitting items vertically, however, the editor has more flexibility. Because copy that is too long can be trimmed quickly, vertical problems are solved more easily.

Newspaper pages range in size from approximately 20 to 22 1/2 inches in depth. Most newspapers are 21 or 21 1/2 inches deep.

The elements

The six basic tools that editors use are text type, display type, rules and borders, photographs, artwork and white space. Each, except white space, has its vocabulary.

TEXT TYPE

Text type is used to set the stories. It is measured in points, and most newspapers use sizes of 8 to 10 points. By comparison, books are often set in 10- to 12-point type. This book is set in 10-point type. Variations in size and legibility are discussed in more detail in Chapter 9.

The space between the lines of type is called leading, a term from hot metal days when a piece of lead was inserted between lines. It is often expressed as 9/10, which means 9-point type with 1 point of leading. Text can even be set with negative or minus leading (less than the size of the type being used). For example, the following copy is set with negative leading:

This is possible because type is measured from the top of the ascender (the upper parts of letters such as d and b) to the bottom of the descender (the lower parts of letters such as p or y). Even when a descender is aligned directly over an ascender, the two do not touch, as this example, set in 10-point type with 9 3/4 points of leading, illustrates.

Most newspapers have 1/2 to 1 full point of leading between lines; there are 2 points in this book. The type size and amount of leading affect the number of lines that can be printed in a newspaper column and the legibility.

Most text copy is set flush left and flush right, or justified. That is, the copy lines up evenly on both the left and right margins. To accomplish this, the line is justified by placing small amounts of space between words and hyphenating words at the end of a line when necessary.

Type can also be set ragged right. Instead of hyphenating words, the computer leaves white space at the end of the line and starts a new one. Despite the irregular space at the end of the lines, ragged right does not take up more room. It simply transfers the extra space between words to the end. A few newspapers set all their text type ragged right.

Computers can also be programmed to set type in a modified ragged right. That is, the computer will hyphenate words to ensure a minimum width. An editor might want to program the computer to hyphenate only when a line of type would not exceed 50 or 60 percent of the potential line length. This eliminates inordinately short lines. Newspaper text is set in columns, legs, or wraps of type. A story that extends across five columns of a newspaper page is said to have five legs or wraps.

DISPLAY TYPE

Display type or headlines are the larger version of text type. They too are measured vertically in points. Headline type starts at 14 points and extends over 100 points. Normal headline schedules—a list of type sizes available to the editor—include 14-, 18-, 24-, 30-, 36-, 42-, 48-, 54-, 60-, 72-, 78- and 84-point type (Fig. 2.3). The increments after 18 points are 6. That's because when type was metal, the increments between available sizes were 6 points. Now, you can set type in increments of 1 point or less. However, most newspapers retain the traditional 6-point increments to ensure a hierarchy of type sizes on the page.

The shorthand for headline instructions varies from newspaper to newspaper. One of the common systems is to designate width, size and number of lines by writing 2-36-3. This means the headline is two columns wide, 36 points, and three lines.

Various newspapers use different rules of capitalization in headlines. The least legible is all caps, or HEADLINES WITH ALL THE LETTERS CAPITALIZED. Many newspapers still use the traditional uppercase style of capitalizing the first letter of each word except articles and prepositions. The lowercase style capitalizes only the first letter of the first word of the headline and proper nouns. The lowercase style also permits more to be said in the same space.

Most newspapers position the headlines flush left; that is, the headline begins at the left margin of the copy. Other styles include flush right (the white space appears to the left of the headline), centered (the headline is centered above the story), and stepped down (the second and all subsequent lines of a head are written shorter than the

Type Sizes

Size	
14	a
18	b
24	c
30	d
36	e
42	f
48	g
54	h
60	i
66	j
72	k
78	l
84	m

2.3

2.4 A few newspapers, including the News & Observer, center all headlines.

preceding one and indented under the one above it). The stepped-down style is archaic. A few newspapers, including the Providence Journal Bulletin and the Raleigh (N.C.) News & Observer, center all heads (Fig. 2.4).

Headlines, regardless of where they are placed or their format, must fit. The writers can count the letters, but at most newspapers, computers are doing that work quickly and accurately. However, at newsrooms where letters must still be counted, a standardized method is needed. There are several formulas, each equally good if used consistently.

A headline "schedule" is established, in which each letter is assigned a unit of width, some letters being wider than others. The easiest, though not the most exact, way to make a headline chart is to set at least three headlines in all the sizes you will be using. Place the headlines across a full newspaper page marked off by columns. Determine the number of units, or counts, that will fit in each column width, or establish the number of counts per pica. Sometimes a headline will count shorter because it has an unusual number of l's t's, or f's, which are thinner than other letters. Here's a typical system:

Lowercase letters	1 unit
Uppercase letters	1 1/2 units
Spaces	1/2 unit
Punctuation	1/2 unit
Numbers	1 unit

EXCEPTIONS
Lowercase f, i, l, t, j	1/2 unit
Lowercase m, w	1 1/2 units
Uppercase M, W	2 units
Uppercase I, L and 1	1/2 unit

Not all the vocabulary that refers to special uses of headline type is standardized. However, here are the most common (see Fig. 2.5 for examples):

Banner: a large headline that extends across the top of the front page above the most important story of the day.

Deck: one or more lines that are subordinate to the main headline and give the reader additional information about the story. They commonly are half the size of the main head.

Conversational deck: a deck usually written in complete sentences and run in sizes usually ranging from 14 to 18 points. Also called summary or nut graph deck.

Kicker: three or four words that are set half the size of the main headline and usually appear flush left above the main headline. Generally, the main head is indented under the kicker, which should not be smaller than 24 points. Kickers have limited usefulness because they are easily overlooked. They also add white space.

Hammer: a one- or two-word headline in large type. It is effective in attracting attention and adding white space to the page but needs a deck to further explain the story. The hammer should be 6 to 12 points larger than a headline in the same location. The deck usually is half the size of the hammer. Hammer heads can be set flush left or centered. They are most effective in two- and three-column formats. Beyond that width, hammers usually create too much white space.

Sidesaddle: also called a side head, the type is placed at the left of the copy rather than over it. Sidesaddles are usable only in tight spaces above ads when there are no other stories on the page or in boxes.

Read-in: similar to the kicker in size and placement, the read-in is a conversational approach to headline writing and needs the main title or headline to complete the sentence. The main head, a label or title, should be able to stand alone. It is best used when you have adequate white space around the head; readers' eyes will go first to the larger type and may never see the read-in unless it gets special treatment.

Blurb: also called a pullout or pullquote, it is a short piece of interesting or alluring information pulled from the body of the story and set in display type, usually 14 to 18 points. It is either tucked under the headline or placed somewhere in the body of the copy.

Overline: a headline for a photograph. It appears above the photograph.

Catchline: a headline between the photograph and the cutline.

BORDERS AND RULES

Sometimes borders and rules are used to set off headlines; they are also used around illustrations and copy. A rule usually refers to a plain line, whereas borders are ornamental, but the terms are of-

---

Headlines tell and sell

Headlines need elaboration. One way to do this is in a summary or conversational deck. This is sometimes called a readout or dropout.

Kicker

This headline is usually indented

This format can be used to tell the story. It is called a

Read-in

Hammer head

These attract attention

This is a sidesaddle headline

Sidesaddle heads are useful devices in certain circumstances. For instance, they can be used on inside pages where the space for stories is shallow. If advertisements fill all but two or three inches at the top of the page, a sidesaddle headline can be used to good advantage. A traditional headline run over the copy would consume nearly all the space and leave room for only a couple lines of text in each column.

Sidesaddle heads can also be used on a page with other stories above it. However, to keep from confusing the reader, the story with the sidesaddle should be boxed or a heavy rule should be placed above the story.

2.5

Borders and rules

2 pt.

4 pt.

6 pt.

8 pt.

Oxford

Ben Day

2.6 There are several types of rules available to designers.

ten used interchangeably. A selection of both is shown in Figure 2.5. When a rule or border is used around copy, it is called a box. Different newspapers use different-sized rules for boxes, and sometimes the same newspaper uses more than one size. Most, however, use rules rather than borders to box stories. In earlier times, vertical rules were used in the gutters to separate columns; now white space commonly performs this function. Cutoff rules are lines below or alongside an illustration to separate it from unrelated material.

PHOTOGRAPHS

Photographs are also called cuts, pic (singular) or pix, and sometimes, mistakenly, art. Photographs come from staff photographers, wire services and free-lancers (people who sell pictures to a publication). The text that accompanies a photograph is most commonly called a cutline, but it is also known as a caption or legend.

ARTWORK

Artwork is any illustration other than a photograph. Photographs used for special effects, such as silhouetting or screening to produce a different image (Fig. 2.7), are properly classified as art. Art that is black and white, such as a chart or a simple line drawing, is shot without a screen and is called line art. If it is the correct size, it can be affixed directly to the page from which the plate is to be burned. If it has gray tones, it must be screened (shot as a halftone).

Almost all photographs and artwork need to be reduced or enlarged before they are printed. The proportions are established by the layout editor or designer. A proportion wheel or calculator is used to determine the proper percentage of enlargement or reduction (discussed below). Artwork shot at 100 percent will reproduce at the same size as the original. Anything shot at larger than 100 percent results in an enlargement; less than 100 percent provides a reduction.

Structures

Most newspapers use a combination of vertical and horizontal shapes to package the information. Some rely primarily on vertical or horizontal. Each has its advantages and disadvantages.

The Wall Street Journal is structured vertically. A vertical newspaper runs few headlines more than two columns wide. Stories start at the top of the page, and many run all the way to the bottom. On the inside, the vertical structure is not as pronounced because the vertical copy flow is interrupted by ads.

2.7 Halftones can be shot with screens that produced special effects, such as this one, which produces a mottled or overexposed effect.

The Journal has been so successful for so long that it has imbued the vertical structure with a personality that is conservative, reliable and traditional. In that sense, the Journal is a well-designed newspaper. Vertically structured newspapers are also quicker to lay out and compose because there is little for the layout editor to do but fit the stories in the holes.

Because one- and two-column headlines take up less space than larger multicolumn headlines, it is possible to get more stories on a vertically structured page. Consequently, the vertical format is the best choice for newspapers seeking a high story count on page 1.

For some newspapers, however, the advantages of the vertical structure are also disadvantages. Newspapers that do not want a conservative, traditional image or are more concerned with the visual excitement and photo display than the count on page 1 see the vertical structure as a disadvantage. This structure also works against a page design that tries to move the reader around the page. Vertical papers usually are top-heavy; the bottom half has little or nothing to attract the reader's attention, and it is difficult to keep the page from looking gray and dull.

On the other hand, the horizontal structure has several advantages, the most prominent being that most readers perceive it as more modern and pleasing (Siskind 1979). Stories laid out horizontally take advantage of the reader's inclination to read from left to right. The horizontal structure also permits the layout editor and designer to be more flexible when balancing the page and offers better photo display. The larger, multicolumn headlines used in horizontal makeup not only attract attention but also add weight to the page (Click and Stempel 1974).

Another important advantage is the optical illusion that results when a story is laid out horizontally. A 20-inch vertical story would extend from the top of the page to the bottom. It looks long, and because of the limited number of things a designer can do in one column, it looks dull. Readers who wear bifocals have difficulty reading a vertical story because they must fold or raise the broadsheet page as they proceed down the column. The same 20-inch story run horizontally across six columns would be 3 1/2 inches deep. Consequently, it looks shorter and may attract more readership.

One of the few disadvantages of the horizontal structure is the additional time required for layout or design. A purely horizontal page (Fig. 2.6), however, is as dull as purely vertical makeup. A combination of the two is needed. A good horizontal structure needs strong vertical elements to provide contrast. Monotony is the enemy of any structure. To the editor working on a horizontal page, nothing is more welcome than a strong vertical photograph.

How to size photos and art

Pictures and art usually need to be resized for publication. Here are two ways.

First you can use the standard proportion formula. You know the width and depth of the picture as is, and you know the width of the resized photo. (Occasionally, you size to the depth; the formula is the

Points to decimal conversion

1pt. = .06
2pts. = .17
3pts. = .25
4pts. = .33
5pts. = .42
6pts. = .50
7pts. = .58
8pts. = .67
9pts. = .75
10pts. = .83
11pts. = .92

2.8

2.9. Measure the original illustration. In our example, the photograph is 45 by 30 picas after cropping. Always express the width first.

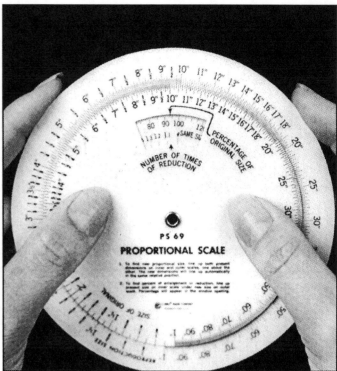

2.10. Determine the most important measurement needed to fit your dummy. Usually that is the width. The known measurement of the reproduction is three columns wide (42 picas in this case). Most wheels are expressed in inches, but you can assign any label, including picas, to the numbers without converting them. Thus in our example, 45 inches on the wheel becomes 45 picas. Place the number showing the original size (45) under the reproduction size (42).

same.) You need to determine the depth. This the formula: Original width is to new width as original depth is to new depth. Here's an example. Original width is 24 picas; new width is 28 picas. Original depth is 30 picas; new depth is x, the unknown. Therefore, 24 is to 28 as 30 is to x, or, $24x = (28 \times 30)$. Complete the calculation as shown:

$$24x = 840$$
$$x = 840 \div 24 = 35$$

The resized photograph will be 28 picas wide by 35 picas deep. If you use a calculator, you need to convert decimals to points (Fig. 2.8). To size photographs or art with a proportion wheel, follow the cutlines in Figures 2.9 through 2.12.

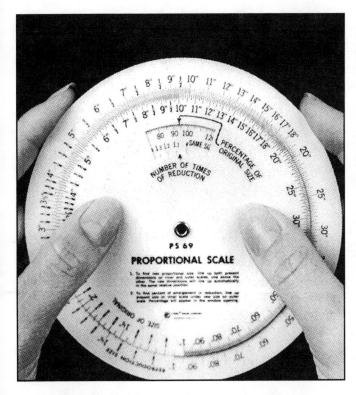

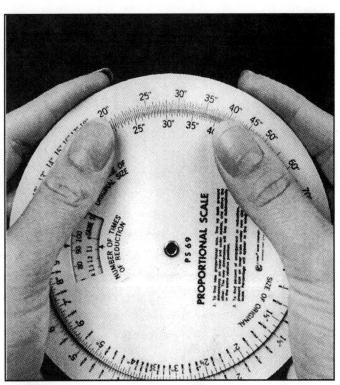

2.11 Without moving the wheel, look at the window showing the reduction ratio. The arrow points to 94, which means that the photograph will be shot at 94 percent and will be reduced 6 percent from its original size. When an illustration is enlarged or reduced, its size is changed proportionally in all directions. Consequently, while the width is decreasing 6 percent, from 45 to 42 picas, the depth will be shrinking by the same percentage.

2.12. Again, without moving the wheel, look at the 30 (depth of the present photograph) on the inside wheel, which is marked original size. The number above 30 is 28, the depth of the reproduced picture. In every case, you have three known measurements and one unknown.

3. LAYING OUT PAGES

Journalism, as it refers to the reporting and writing process, has been described as literature in a hurry. Layout is design in a hurry.

Dummying is the technique of placing elements on a page. The dummy is a blueprint when it is done on paper. When layout editors work on pagination systems, all or most of the elements are placed on the page, and the editor can view the result on a computer screen. Normally, layout is done under deadline pressure. A designer might do one page in two or three hours, but a layout editor may need to do several. Journalists doing layout need to know how to work in modules (discussed in the next chapter), show relationships and display photographs. They must also understand basic design principles. Because speed is essential for most pages in a newspaper, there is and will continue to be a need for people who know the basics of layout. Designers may work on page 1, section fronts and special projects, but most pages will continue to be drawn by layout editors.

Before you lay out the page, you must make several decisions.

Pre-layout decisions

Before your cursor touches the template or your pencil touches the dummy, you must make the following decisions within the philosophy of the publication on which you are working, and, hopefully, with other members of a team:

━━━━━━━━━" ━━━━━

Em dashes are also available in virtually all fonts. They are accessed by typing the hyphen key while holding down the option and shift keys. Two hyphens do not equal an em dash—and they are not part of typographic communication.

Allan Haley
TYPOGRAPHER

1. Determine the number and size of the various stories, pictures and pieces of art that will be placed on the page.

2. Decide which elements are related and how to group them.

3. Select the major display element (or elements) for the page and build the page around it.

4. Select the second major display element (or elements) for the page and put it as close to the bottom as possible and on a diagonal line from the major display element.

5. Identify the lead story. If the lead story is related to the main photograph, show the relationship. If not, disassociate them.

If you are a beginner, this list is like the formula you used when learning to write an inverted pyramid story. When you began, you mechanically went through the process of identifying the who, what, where, when and why in each story and ranking them in order of importance. For the beginner in layout, it is helpful if you use these five steps. With a little experience, the process will become second nature to you. Let's take a look at each of the steps.

The number of elements goes a long way toward determining the look of a page. Traditionally, that decision has been made by managing editors, and the layout editors were left to find a way to make all the pieces fit. However, this method is increasingly recognized as unsatisfactory. The problem and a proposed solution are discussed further in Chapter 12. Regardless of who makes the decision, story count is critical to what can be done with the page.

The newspaper's jump policy is also critical. If the paper is willing to continue stories from page 1 or from one inside page to the next, the story count can be higher. If the paper does not jump stories or sets a maximum number of stories that can be continued, stories will have to be shorter, there will be fewer of them or writers will have to write to front page space and then start another story for inside display. Within the confines of the newspaper's policy, then, you determine the number of elements that must appear on the page and their size or length.

The second decision involves related elements. Which picture or pictures go with which story? Do any of the stories have sidebars? Is there more than one story on the same general topic, such as health or education? The process of grouping related elements forces the editor to think in terms of packages rather than individual elements. Sometimes this can result in elevating two or more less important stories to a larger package that is more significant because of its combined message, makes more sense to the reader and is easier to handle graphically. Grouping related stories turns facts into information. Packaging puts stories in context.

The next step is to determine which element (or elements) will be the major display item. This is not always the same as selecting the most important story. The major display element consists of the dominant visual element. If the lead story does not have any photographs or artwork, the major display element may consist of a secondary story that has visuals. However, even if the most important story does not have any visuals, it still can be the major display element. The editor can use type and other graphic devices to create a package that adds to the information in the story and attracts attention to it.

Usually, the major display package consists of text and illustrations. If the major display element is also the most important story, the editor's job is simplified. If it is not, the editor must lay out the page so that the most important story attracts the attention it deserves even though the page is built around the visual elements. In most cases, the page is built around the major display element, which should be placed at or near the top of the page.

The next decision is identification of the second major display element, which will anchor the bottom of the page. That package, which usually includes illustrations, is needed to balance the weight at the top of the page and attract the reader's eye (Fig. 3.1). This creates motion on the page. The reader's eye will move from the major display elements at the top to those at the bottom. In the process, most readers scan the headlines on the page as they go. If the stories are interesting and the headlines are well written, readers may stop or return after reading other stories. If no major display element is placed at the bottom, the editors have conceded that half of the page to dullness.

The last step in preparing to lay out the page is to identify the lead story. If it goes with the major display element, the editor then determines how to show the proper relationship between the story and the photo or art element. If the lead story is not related to the major display element, the editor then must determine how to disassociate them while placing both at the top of the page (Figs. 3.2 and 3.3).

You should always keep the following basic principles in mind when dummying a page (note exceptions):

1. Avoid most tombstoning, or the practice of bumping headlines against each other. You should not bump heads because the consumer might read from one head into the next. Tombstoning also concentrates type in one area and can create clutter and unbalance the page.However, there here are four ways to prevent the negative effects of tombstoning and still bump heads (Fig. 3.4):

a. Run a large, one-line, multicolumn head against a small, one-column head. It is reasonable to assume that a consumer would not read from a one-line, four-column, 48-point headline into a one-column, two- or three-line, 24-point headline.

3.1 A secondary display element appears in an story unrelated to the dominant display element. It anchors the bottom of the page.

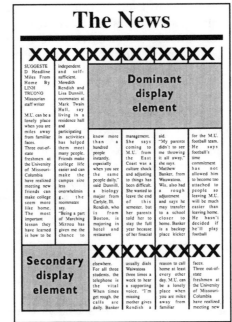

3.2 The headline over the story and picture shows the relationship.

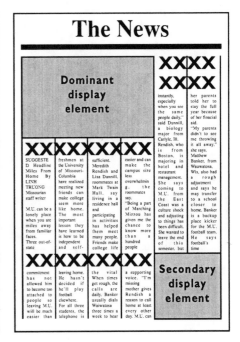

3.3 When the dominant picture does not go with the lead story, you must be certain to show readers the correct relationship. The lead story is in a separate module to the right of the picture.

How to tombstone

This is a large, one-line head

Use a bold headline

Write a headline short

Against a small, two-line head

Against an italic head

The extra space buffers the bump

3.4

This is a sidesaddle headline

3.5

b. Vary the typeface. Using regular type against italic or bold against a lighter weight can prevent the reader from inadvertently going from one head to the other. Such techniques, however, may not avoid clutter or clustering of too much type in one place.

c. Write the headline on the left intentionally short. White space provides the buffer.

d. Dutch wrap the copy under the related photo or artwork or box the stories. A Dutch wrap refers to copy that comes out from under its headline.

2. Do not tombstone unrelated photographs or artwork. Again, there are two reasons: bumping photos or artwork concentrates too much weight in one place on the page, and the reader may think the photographs or artwork are related because they are adjacent to one another.

3. On inside pages, avoid placing art, photographs or boxes next to advertisements because they usually have a high noise level; that is, they contain their own large type, photographs or artwork. Similar editorial material placed next to ads also unbalances the page. Because many inside pages have little news space, it is not always possible to avoid bumping editorial art against advertising art. As a general practice, however, it is better to speak with a softer voice on inside pages dominated by ads. The contrast is likely to attract more attention than if both the news and advertising are competing with the same type of materials. Boxed news stories on top of ads, which also are boxed, look like advertising copy. If it is necessary to box a story adjacent to an ad, the box should extend into the news space instead of running flush with the advertising.

4. Try to avoid Dutch-wrap copy situations. Readers are not accustomed to having the text width exceed that of the headline. However, if there is no possibility that the reader will become confused by the layout, it is permissible, even advisable, to wrap the copy from underneath the head. This most often occurs on inside pages where advertising takes up all but the top few inches of the page (Fig. 3.5). If there is only one story, the reader can easily follow the path of the copy. If there are two or more stories above each other, the material must be separated. Sometimes this is done with a heavy 4- or 6-point rule or by wrapping copy underneath a related photograph. A similar situation exists when editors use a sidesaddle head with a story on a tight inside page. The head sits alongside the story rather than over it.

Dummying the page

The industry is in transition between electronic pagination and the traditional paste-up system. In electronic pagination, the editor can see all the elements on the page. In the traditional paste-up system, editors work on paper dummies. Here is how the traditional system operates.

Inside pages arrive at the layout desk with the advertising space already indicated on the grid. In Figure 3.6, the grid shows three ads on the page. At some newspapers, the name of the advertiser may be shown on the dummy. Even when editors know the name, they seldom know the content of the ads. Consequently, it is best to avoid placing illustrations adjacent to the ads because there might be too much competition for the reader's attention. When the ads are stacked in a pyramid, the editor should work off the edges to create modules, which are square or rectangular copy blocks.

The story slugged "Argentina" has a 3-42-1 headline (Fig. 3.7). That means the headline is three columns wide, 42 points high, and one line deep. The headline over "Surrender" is 1-24-3, which means one column wide, 24 points high, and three lines deep. Such a designation is common, but many newspapers do it differently. Some use numbers. A #4 head, for example, might mean a 36-point head over two columns. Others give headline directions by writing only 6-48, which indicates the number of columns and the point size. At some papers, the number of lines in the headline is indicated by marking x's on the dummy. At others, the number of vertical lines underneath the

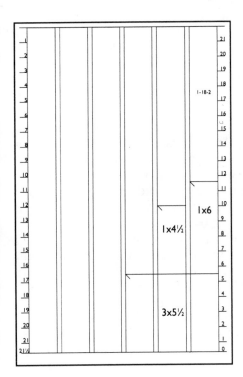

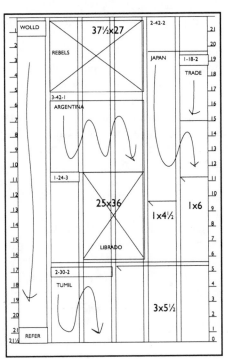

3.6 This is a typical dummy or grid showing spaces for advertising already blocked out.

3.7 The page might look like this when it leaves the newsroom. Grid markings are not standard in the industry.

3.8 This is what results from the layout shown in Figure 3.10.

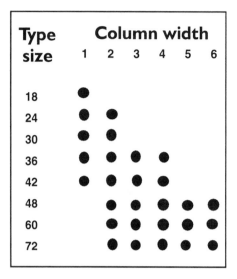

Type size	Column width					
	1	2	3	4	5	6
18	●					
24	●	●				
30	●	●				
36	●	●	●	●		
42	●	●	●	●		
48		●	●	●	●	●
60		●	●	●	●	●
72			●	●	●	●

3.9 You can use this guide for sizing headlines with a bold headline face in columns 12-14 picas wide.

How to figure headline depths
1. Divide the head size by 12
2. Multiply by no. of lines
3. Result is picas deep
Example for 2-line, 48-pt. head:
1. 48 ÷ 12 = 4
2. 2 x 4 = 8 picas deep
Example for 3-line, 30 pt. head:
1. 30 ÷ 12 = 2.5
2. 3 x 2.5 = 7.5 picas deep

3.10

type size indicates the number of lines. Figure 3.8 shows the result of the drawing in Figure 3.7.

Regardless of how headlines are marked on the dummy, size selection is important. The best way to get a feel for it is to learn to recognize headline sizes. Go through a newspaper and try to identify the size of the type in the heads. Then take a pica ruler and measure the heads from the top of the ascender to the bottom of the descender (for instance, from the top of the h to the bottom of the y). The headlines may not come out in traditional sizes because of the variety of type designs, because most phototypesetters can produce type in 1-point increments and because some newspapers reduce their pages slightly before printing them, but you should be within a couple of points.

The proper size for the headline depends on the type design and the column width. The bolder the headline, the smaller size needed. At newspapers that use the regular weight as the standard head and have column widths of 12 to 14 picas, Figure 3.9 can be used as a guide.

The x's indicate, for instance, that you can use a 30-point headline for one- and two-column stories but not for three columns and larger. The chart is based on the number of characters it takes to fill the space in a given column width. Type set at 36 points in a one-column width looks large, but spread over four or five columns, it looks small. Type set at 48 points in two or three columns looks large and makes the story look more important; however, used across six columns, it looks smaller. Type set at 24 points looks small over 25 to 29 picas but will work on a two-column news summary.

At newspapers where headlines are set separately from the copy, it is important to mark the depth of the headlines on the grid (Fig. 3.10). This permits the composing room employees to paste in the copy even before the copy arrives. In most newspapers, copy and heads are set together, even if a pagination system is not being used.

If you know points and picas, you won't have any trouble determining how much space to leave for headlines. Because 72 points equals 1 inch, you know that a two-line, 72-point headline is approximately 144 points or 2 inches deep. The precise depth depends on how much space you leave between lines of type and between the headline and copy. Most newspapers set headlines solid, that is, with no extra space between the lines. That means you can add the points in the lines of type, then add 12 to 24 more for the space between headline and copy.

Copy flow directions on the grid vary widely among newspapers. Some depend on the grid to indicate where the copy begins and ends. Some do not have any copy flow marks. Each newspaper has its own set of easily learned symbols. As the industry completes the move to electronic pagination, those symbols will be relegated to history books. Pagination systems transfer this work to the computer screen. Editors learn how to place the items themselves rather than writing the symbols that direct the composing room to place them. The advantages are enormous. Editors no longer have to visualize what will be; they can see problems such as clutter, uneven distribution of weights and improper sizing. Editors can make everything fit exactly. Most importantly, they can make changes quickly.

Copyfitting problems

Regardless of whether you are working on paper or computer, you should know how to make the copy fit horizontally. You may be working on a four-, five-, six-, or even nine-column grid, but there will be many occasions when you want to change the copy width. Here's how. You must know three measurements of your newspaper: the standard column width, the gutter width and the width of your story or package. With these measurements, you can determine the correct copy settings for a boxed story by doing the following:

1. Subtracting a set amount of space for the box. For instance, many newspapers subtract 2 picas to accommodate the rule and to leave a sufficient and standardized amount of space between the rule and the copy.

2. Subtracting the space for gutters. The gutter space occurs only between columns of type or between a column of type and a picture. The space between the type or picture and the box is already accounted for in step 1. There is always one fewer gutter than legs of type.

3. Dividing by the number of columns of type. The result should be a copy setting adjusted for the box. Assume that the columns are 12.2 picas, or 12p2, and the gutters are 1 pica. To put a box around a four-column story and still run four columns, we must first determine the amount of horizontal space we are going to occupy. You can look at the newspaper's chart, which will immediately tell you the width of four columns. But you still need to know how to determine width because, especially in feature packages, you may be working in spaces that donot coincide with columns. Here's what you do to find the width of four columns: 12p2 (width of column) x 4 (number of columns) = 48p8 + 3 (number of gutters; always one less than columns) = 51p8 (width of four columns and gutters). Now follow the three steps outlined above: 51p8 - 2 (box) = 49p8 - 3 (gutters) = 46p8 (space for type). This type space, 46p8, divided by 4 is 11p8.The copy boxed should be set 11 picas, 8 points. Many beginners would have made it 11 picas, 7 points. That's because they often forget that 46p8 is 46 picas, 8 points. When you divide 4 into 46 picas, you get 11 with 2 picas remaining. You cannot bring down the 2 because you would be combining apples and oranges. You have 2 picas and 8 points remaining. Here, you must convert the picas to points. Because there are 12 points in each pica, you have 24 points plus 8 points remaining. First, add the two sides of the decimal: 24 points + 8 points = 32 points. Then divide by 4. The result is 8 points. Let's try again. This time, assume you are going to box a three-column space, but you are going to run only two columns or legs of type in the remaining space. Again, your columns are 12p2, and your gutters are 1p. Here are the steps:

1. Total space for the package: 38p6
2. Subtract 2 for the box: 36p6
3. Subtract 1 for the gutters: 37p6
4. Divide by 2: 18p9

In step 4, the division again forces you to convert picas to points: 1p6 = 18 points. Now you are dividing 2 into 18.

Here's a copyfitting situation that requires you to determine the width of the picture first. If you wish to run a picture and story alongside each other and the picture is to be a bastard (nonstandard) size, you must figure the text settings after you size the picture. The picture determines the text width. For example, in a five-column, 64p10 space, you might have a picture that you want to run 31 picas wide. You would then proceed this way:

1. Total space for the package: 64p10
2. Subtract width of picture (31 picas): 33p10
3. Determine how many columns of type you want in the remain ing space. Let's use two.
4. Subtract the gutter space (1 between columns of type and 1 be tween the type and the picture): 31p10
5. Divide by the number of columns (two): 15p11

Again, during division, it is necessary to convert 1 pica, 10 points to 22 points before arriving at the 11 points in the setting of 15p11.

There is one more copyfitting situation. It occurs when you want to run copy alongside and under a photo. In the previous example, you had to determine the width of the picture before you determined the copy setting. In this situation, you need to determine a copy setting first and then size the picture to the column widths. Otherwise, you would have one column width running alongside the picture and a different copy setting for the copy underneath the picture. Obviously, the copy would not be the same width as the picture. In this example, we will use a four-column, 51p8 space. Here are the steps:

1. Total space for the package: 51p8
2. Subtract 2 for the box: 49p8.
3. Determine the number of columns. In this example, let's run three.
4. Subtract the gutter space (2): 47p8
5. Divide by 3: 15p10
6. Size the picture to your new column settings. If you run the picture across two columns, it would be 32p8. When multiplying 15p10 by 2, again you have to convert points to picas: 2 x 15.10 = 30 picas, 20 points. Because there are 12 points in a pica, you convert that to 31 picas, 8 points. Then add 1pica for the gutter because the picture crosses the gutter. Now when you run the copy underneath the picture, it aligns with the picture exactly.

Now that you know how to place the material on the page, it's time to look at some of the applications.

Segmenting the package

Some stories are like a huge banquet: There doesn't seem to be an end to the amount of food. Although we may think we can't eat it all, we might be surprised how much we can take in when it is presented

3.11 The fire story is broken into seven parts: two stories, two pictures and three graphics. All appear in the same module.

3.12 The story on how to stay fit is segmented into a story, a list and two pictures. The smaller bites give readers more entry points and invite more readership.

3.13 One picture, two stories and a series of lists combine to create a reader-friendly package. Run as a single piece, the story would scare many readers away.

in attractive courses. Breaking banquet stories into digestible courses is called segmenting. People who would not read a 40-inch story might read four 10-inch stories. People who would not read a 100-inch story might look at pictures and information graphics and read three 15-inch stories.

Segmenting begins at the stage that the story is proposed. Reporters must recognize that they are not writing for a super-reader; most people are not willing to consume reams of text in a single sitting. However, readers unwilling to commit themselves to start reading a 25-inch story may be willing to start a 10-inch story. The reporter must understand that unless the story is especially compelling, it should be broken into shorter takes.

3.14 This special tabloid on weather was organized by the 12 months.

3.15 The segmentation permitted better integration of words and visuals and was more inviting to readers.

The first step in segmenting is to ask the question essential to all stories: What is the best way to tell the story? One long text piece? A

Legislative report

XXXXXXXXXXXXXXXXX XXXXXXXXXXXXXX XXXXXXXXXXXXXXXXX XXXXXXXXXXX
XXXXXXXXXXXXXXXXX XXXXXXXXXX XXXXXXXXXXXXXXXXX

3.16 Packages such as this and derivations of it allow editors to break stories into smaller bites and still show the relationship among them.

One great Kidd

But the question is: how long before Cal's Jason Kidd jumps to the pros?

3.17 Avoid breaking over more than one column of your setting. Some readers will bounce to the top of column two when they hit the rule.

Spice adds zest to your plate, palate

Jenny Hofherr began "cooking low fat" two years ago when she met her future husband John, who ate a low-fat diet. "He was into it, and I got caught up in it," she said.

While low-fat foods may not always taste as good, Hofherr uses spices to improve the flavor.

> **"He was into it, and I got caught up in it," she said.**

"I cook low fat all the time." she said, "I just add more spices to make it taste better."

At her bridal shower six months ago, Hofherr got a spice rack with 16 spices. "We've used almost all of them," she said.

3.18 Readers won't get lost if the copy wraps around the copy. The quote also adds color contrast to the text.

Privacy— think again

Not a moment too soon. Consider how abuses of power are proved by insiders versus outsiders.

This past summer, a couple of Clinton State Department appointees wrongfully searched the files of their predecessors in the Bush administration; the subsequent dishing of dirt was done from the Washington private line of Warren Christopher's top aide, who was off in Singapore. State's inspector general sent a report to the secretary of state, who fired the culpable appointees, and a "prosecutive summary of potential Privacy act violations" to Justice. Time-servers there gave the blatant, politically motivated intrusion a desultory look-see and declined to prosecute.

Contrast that inaction with the

> **Privacy invaded all over the lot in the Department.**

3.19 A quote with a picture is even stronger than a quote by itself in stopping scanners.

shorter story with sidebars? Pictures? Charts and tables? Illustrations? Diagrams? Segmenting is using all the best tools available to tell the story. The St. Petersburg (Fla.) Times used information graphics, pictures, a story and a sidebar to tell about the California wildfires (Fig. 3.11). The graphics show how the winds drive the fires. The pictures show the impact, the main story reports the news, and the sidebar offers readers a glimpse of the effect of the fires on one person's life. The Norfolk (Va.) Virginian-Pilot used photos, a story and a useful "how-to" takeout to tell how a family can stay fit together (Fig. 3.12). The Oregonian in Portland used a picture, a sidebar story and a sidebar pullout listing rewards by age groups (Fig. 3.13). All illustrate the range of segmenting approaches available to journalists.

Segmenting works on larger packages, too. The Wichita Eagle used segmentation when it produced its innovative "Weather Book," a tabloid combining text and information graphics. Editors organized the information by months. Although 28 pages long, the story is really 12 smaller stories, each of which is broken into text and graphics (Figs. 3.14 and 3.15).

Segmentation should also extend to spot news stories. City council or school board stories should not automatically be 20 inches. Working from an agenda, reporters can anticipate natural subdivisions, and editors should plan two or more stories in addition to a box summarizing the action. Every state's legislature is worth several stories a few times during the session. Editors can design a format for segmenting and packaging the information. Figure 3.16 shows one such approach. Such a package does not preclude a major legislative story from running on page 1 as long as there is a refer line to the package. On some days, there would be no package; on others it might be three columns wide and on yet others, six columns. The format forces the reporters to break the information into segments.

Relieving grayness

If you segment, you will have few problems with grayness because you are working with multiple elements. However, there are times when you have to present long text blocks in an interesting way. Only a complacent designer would pour long stories into the column troughs without providing visual relief.

Even without pictures and graphics, editors' toolboxes are full of tones ranging from white to black and of contrasting shapes and techniques to make long stories look shorter. Let's examine the options.

3.20 The pullout quote serves as a headline on this page of a continued story in a magazine or tabloid format.

ANow you need someplace comfy to sit. Since there is no soft grass in your home, a blanket spread on the floor will give the illusion and provide some cushioning.

Beaches which are located in Florida provide a great way to relax and get a tan. Some favorites are located in Miami and along the Gulf of Mexico. If you are tired of the surf, you can take a trio into Orlando and visit Epcot Center.

3.22 Inset cap letters (top) break up the text and can be used to tie the story to the headline when the same typeface is used. Rising cap letters perform the same function but also add white space, which is useful in longer stories.

3.21 The generous use of white space frames and directs attention to the package on mammograms.

3.23 Subheads offer visual relief and break the story into shorter segments. They also offer readers an exit point.

3.24 Screens provide a graphic weight where pictures and information graphics aren't available.

1. Blurbs. Used primarily to tease the reader, blurbs also provide visual relief. They are usually set in 14- to 18-point type and often set off by rules. The weight depends on the overall design of the paper. Blurbs, which can be interesting lines or quotes from the story, normally are placed at the top of the leg of type because some readers will bounce from the top of the quote to the top of the next column if they encounter a pullout in copy. An even worse error, however, is running a pullout over more than one column of your setting (Fig. 3.17). That almost ensures that the reader will make a mistake. One solution is shown in Figure 3.18. Readers can continue around the quote. Type combined with a photo or graphic is even more powerful in attracting attention to the page and transferring that attention to the story (Fig. 3.19). The pullout can even be elevated to a major display element on the page (Fig. 3.20). strong quote can entice readers into the text.

2. White space. White relieves gray just as much as black does. Newspapers traditionally have packed material onto the page. White space is thought to be wasted space, but it serves a purpose, especially in special displays and longer stories. The Ft. Lauderdale Sun-Sentinel used white space to air out its package on mammograms (Fig. 3.21).

3. Inset and rising capital letters. When the first line of copy comes off the top of the capital, it is called an inset cap; when the first line comes off the bottom of the capital, it is called a rising cap. Inset caps add black tone to an otherwise gray mass; rising caps add black tone and white space where the letter extends above the copy. The size of the caps depends on the design of the package. A modest size for caps is 30 to 36 points. Some designs, usually poster sectional fronts, include caps at much larger sizes (Fig. 3.22). The caps provide visual relief but do not add any information.

4. Subheads. Subheads can make long stories look like a series of shorter stories. Some scanning readers start a story at a subhead and then, if interested, go back to the beginning. Subheads should be larger than the text (11 or 12 points with 9-point text) and placed at logical transitions in the copy (Fig. 3.23). The old method of placing them every four paragraphs does not increase reader comprehension. Subheads, like headlines, should be written to attract attention. Leaving a line of space above the subhead and none below it establishes relationship and airs out the text.

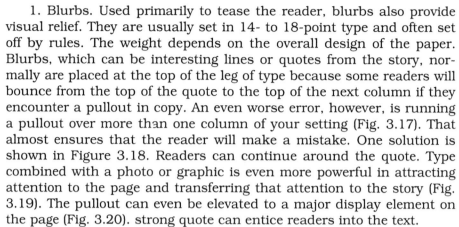

3.25 The designer used formal balance on the layout on hats.

3.26 The Times used type in an unusual way to move readers around the page and give it balance.

5. Varying settings. A page that is text-heavy benefits from the relief that different column widths provide.

6. Ragged right setting. Like slightly open venetian blinds letting light filter into a darkened room, a ragged right setting permits white space to lighten the textual gray.

7. Rules. With the proper amount of white space above and below them, rules as heavy as 12 points bring black or a spot color to the page and can help organize the material.

8. Screens. A light gray screen over copy provides a different tonal quality. Be careful to preserve the legibility of the copy (Fig. 3.24).

9. Invent your own. The possibilities are endless. One enterprising graphics editor who was working with a story that had five steps designed a series of numbered copy breakers that not only relieved the grayness but also served as a map for the reader. Chronology lends itself to the use of dates or times as copy breakers.

Principles of design

To know the principles of design is to know why you are doing what you are doing. No designer carries the list around consciously. Beginners, however, use the principles as guides until they are comfortable with the concepts. Although the names may be forgotten, the lessons never are. The five principles are balance, contrast, focus, proportion and unity.

BALANCE

A square is perfectly balanced, but it is also monotonous. Similarly, formal balance in newspapers is dull and predictable, as were the people described as "square" in the 1960s. Formal balance is also the ultimate victory of form over content.

Although a formal balance format does not suit a newspaper's daily needs, any given design package can use formal balance successfully. The fashion spread on hats in Figure 3.25 is attractive, easy to read and perfectly balanced. So is the interesting typographic treatment in the Los Angeles Times (Fig. 3.26).

Formal or symmetrical balance may be useful when building arches, but asymmetrical balance is more flexible and useful to newspaper designers. Balance is not achieved merely by using identical elements. Optical weights result from tones ranging from black to white. Tones, in turn, are provided by type in its various weights from light to bold, photographs and art, reverses and screens, rules, borders and white space.

When two people are on a teeter-totter, they find the right balance by moving closer to or farther from the fulcrum. The weight is defined in measurable terms. Optical weight is not measured; it is observed. A small, dark shape balances a larger, lighter shape; white space in the margin balances the grayness of text type. (Fig. 3.27).

Designers balance the right against the left and the top against the bottom. To achieve this, the designer places the major display element close to the optical center, which is slightly above and to the left or right of the mathematical center.

Dividing the page into quadrants is useful only if the design does

3.27 Optical weights should be arranged as if you are worked off a teeter-totter.

3.28 Contrast is available by using different weights, forms and families of type.

3.29 The large picture dominates the page and gives the reader a starting point.

not divide itself into four equal parts. Each of the four divisions should have some graphic weight to balance the page, but the weight should not be confined to the quadrant. It should extend vertically, horizontally or both into other quadrants, just as the heavier of the two people on the teeter-totter moves closer to the fulcrum.

Designers working in modules have more control over weights on a page because their boundaries are defined. Meandering, irregular copy wraps make it more difficult to weight the elements visually.

CONTRAST

Designers balance a page by contrasting weights. A three-column photograph at the upper right can be balanced with a three-column photograph at the lower left. The photograph can also be balanced with a large, multicolumn headline or white space. An 8-point rule can balance a block of text type.

Designers use type to provide contrast. For instance, bold type in the main head contrasts with light type in a deck; sans serif type in the cutlines contrasts with roman type in the stories; ragged right contrasts with justified; all caps contrasts with lowercase; 90-point type contrasts with 24-point type; and sans serif type contrasts with serif type (Fig. 3.28).

Designers also contrast forms. Strong verticals give the impression of taller space and longer stories; horizontals appear to make space wider and stories shorter.

Dimension is an aspect of contrast too. A small photograph placed next to a larger one provides a contrast in size and adds dimension. To help children see this principle, Johannes Itten of the Bauhaus told them to draw an outline of their hand on a sheet of paper and next to it pieces of fruit and a gnat. But when he asked them to draw an elephant, they objected. Elephants were too big for a sheet of paper. So Itten encouraged them to draw an elephant so it looks big by having smaller things next to it: "Draw an old, big elephant—a young elephant next to it—the keeper...stretches his hand out to the elephant—in the hand lies an apple—on it sits a gnat" (Itten 1964, p. 98). From that exercise, the children learned to contrast size by using relatively large and small shapes. Publication designers use the same device.

FOCUS

Pages with focus clearly define the starting points and also show that an editor is not afraid to make decisions. To achieve focus, an editor has to decide which element or elements are most important or visually interesting and have the courage to let the design reflect the decision. Indecision confuses the reader and results in a meek or, worse, cluttered page.

Focus usually is provided by a dominant photograph (Fig. 3.29). Three-column pictures on a six-column page are just average and have little visual impact, but pictures wider than three columns provide both focus and impact.

Type can also be used effectively to provide focus. Readers move from large to small (large photograph/headline to small photograph/headline), black to white, color to black and white and top to bottom. It all begins at the dominant element.

PROPORTION

Proportion, or ratio, has fascinated mathematicians, architects and artists for centuries. Fibonacci, an Italian mathematician of the late 12th and early 13th centuries, observed that starting with 1 and adding the last two numbers to arrive at the next created a ratio of 1:1.6 between any two adjacent numbers after 3 (1, 1, 2, 3, 5, 8, 13...). Fifteenth-century architect Leon Battista Alberti believed that there was a relationship between mathematics and art because certain ratios recurred in the universe.

3.30 Le Corbusier worked out the classic proportions with the human body, known as the golden ratio.

3.31 The advocates of breast screening effectively used the principle of proportion to make a point.

Leonardo da Vinci, who was not only an artist but also a mathematician, collaborated with a friend on a book titled On Divine Proportion. To da Vinci, proportions were of basic importance "not only...in numbers and measurement but also in sounds, weights, positions and whatsoever power there may be."

The classic definition of proportion was worked out by the architect-designer Le Corbusier in the early 1900s. He drew the human form with the left arm raised above the head. He then divided the anatomy into three uneven parts: from the toes to the solar plexus, then to the tip of the head, and finally to the tip of the raised hand (Fig. 3.30). From this he developed what is known as the golden ratio. The ratio is 1:1.6, the same as Fibonacci's ratio. In nature, we see the same proportion in, for instance, a daisy, a pine cone and a pineapple. The double-spiraling daisy has 21 spirals in a clockwise direction and 34 in a counterclockwise direction—a 3-to-5 ratio. The ratio of the printed surface of a newspaper page is 1:1.6.

Consciously or unconsciously, designers use this ratio when working with copy shapes on a page. The wider the story runs horizontally, the deeper it can go vertically and still maintain aesthetic proportions. On a six-column page, a four-column story 56 picas wide could be 30 to 35 picas deep from the top of the headline to the bottom of the story. As it goes deeper, it approaches the shape of the less-pleasing square. Stories of one and two columns should be proportioned vertically in the same manner.

No designer actually measures the depth of the stories to determine whether the ratio is correct. The eye recognizes what the calculator confirms. A sense of proportion is necessary for every designer.

Proportion helps convey the message in Figure 3.31. The advocates of breast screening show rather than merely tell the effectiveness of the technology they use.

In graphic design, proper use of proportion means avoiding

Proportion

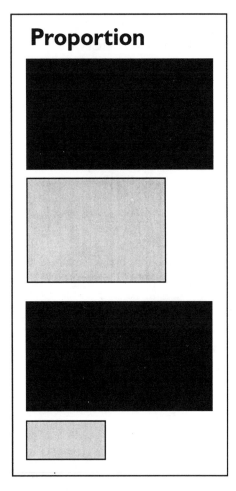

3.32 Although both the black boxes are the same size, the second one looks larger next to the smaller of the two subordinate elements.

squares unless they are required by the content. It also means being consistent about placing proportionally greater amounts of white space between unlike elements than between related elements. For instance, the designer might specify 18 points between the end of one story and the top of the next headline but only 12 points between the headline and the related story. The larger amount of space between the copy and the headline below disassociates the two when they are viewed against the lesser amount of white space between the headline and its related copy.

A good grasp of the concept of proportion is essential to anyone dealing with photographs. First, there is the proportion of the photo to the page. To dominate a page, a photograph must occupy more than half the width of the page or be proportionally sized vertically. The key is the size of the page. A broadsheet page requires one minimum size, a tabloid page another and a magazine page such as National Geographic still another. Smaller pages require smaller visuals, a truism that many editors have not grasped. A 40-pica picture that runs margin to margin on a tabloid would not dominate a broadsheet page. In fact, 40 picas is a modest width on a broadsheet page, but visual impact is still possible with smaller sizes.

Pictures should also be sized in proportion to each other. The 40-pica picture that looks so modest on a broadsheet page looks large when paired with one or more significantly smaller pictures. The smaller the subordinate picture, the larger the dominant picture appears. When two or more pictures are close in size, neither dominates, even if both are relatively large (Fig. 3.32).

Type also looks larger as the horizontal space it occupies grows smaller. A 48-point headline appears larger in a two-column setting than in a six-column format because it is larger in proportion to the space occupied. Type size is selected in part on the basis of the length of the story. Putting three lines of 24-point type over a 3-inch story would look odd because the headline would be one-third the depth of the story. Proportionally, there would be too much headline type. Conversely, a three-line, 24-point headline over a story 18 inches long would also look odd.

UNITY

The designer must unify the work on two levels: the sections of the publication and the content and form of the individual packages. Creating unity for the publication is discussed further in Chapter 18. Designers use unifying devices in series or special packages. They should make certain that readers recognize the package whether it jumps to the inside or appears again the next day. Unifying devices include logos, consistent use of inset or rising caps, repetition of the title in smaller type with the jump and a consistent grid.

On one level, the principles of design are esoteric; they cannot be subjected to quantitative analysis. On another level, they all have specific applications to the day-to-day operations of a newspaper. The better you understand the principles, the more confidence you will develop in your own judgments about design.

4. WORKING IN MODULES AND ESTABLISHING RELATIONSHIPS

 This is the age of modules—modular homes, schools, furniture and electronics. This, too, is the age of modular page design.

A module is a unit, a subdivision of the whole. As applied to page design it is a rectangular or square unit. It contains anything from a single story to a package that includes a story, sidebar and illustrations. Pages are formed by assembling modules. If they are put together in a pleasing arrangement, the page is well designed.

The Seattle Times is one of many newspapers whose editors work in modules. The front page shown in Figure 4.1 has six modules and 13 elements. In Fig. 4.2 you can see the modules in a blueprint of the page. The page is clean and organized. Most readers probably will look first at the large photo then move to the story underneath it. Photos draw the most attention, followed by headlines and pullouts. Most people scan a page before stopping to read, although a story of particular interest to them may stop them at any time.

An alternative to the modular page is one in which copy wraps irregularly around related or unrelated stories and pictures. Copy in irregular shapes is said to dogleg. Few newspapers still use this method. Beginning in the early 1960s, many newspapers went to the simplified modular style and eliminated column rules, fancy borders and decorative type. By 1974, when the Louisville (Ky.) Times sponsored a watershed experimental newspaper design seminar, nearly all the proposed redesigns were modular. Newspapers did not suddenly invent the con-

41

4.1 Although there are 13 elements on the page, they are displayed in six modules.

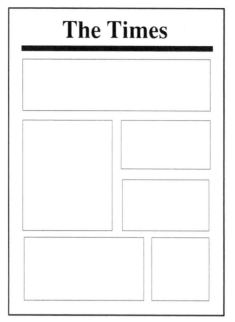

4.2 This blueprint of the page shown in Figure 4.1 identifies the modules. Pages arranged in modules are less cluttered.

cept of working in modules. Magazines had been doing it for years, with good reason. Most of them sold advertising in quarter, half and full pages. The result was an editorial space blocked off in squares or rectangles. Most newspapers still do not have that advantage. The Standard Advertising Unit (SAU) system permits 56 advertising sizes for the broadsheet page.

Advantages of modular layout

In addition to its clean, simple look, modular layout saves time in the production process, adapts quickly to technological changes, permits better packaging of related elements, provides the opportunity for contrast on the page and serves reader preferences. Irregular wraps are more time-consuming in both traditional paste-up and electronic pagination systems. Corrections are also more quickly accomplished on modular layouts because lines can be added or subtracted more easily in modules than in irregular wraps.

Production time is also saved when editors have to substitute stories on a modular page. A layout editor can easily pull out a module and substitute another without disturbing the entire page or a large section of it. Such changes are more difficult on a page with several uneven wraps. If the new story is shorter, the editor can insert two stories; if it is longer, the editor can eliminate two or more modules. In either case, the editor does not have to disturb a substantial portion of the page to make a change. This flexibility is especially attractive to papers with multiple editions.

Working in modules also forces the layout editor to group related stories, pictures and artwork for the reader's benefit. The basic principle is that all related material should be in the same module. Readers want to know which stories are related and prefer to have similar stories grouped by subject matter (Clark 1979, p. 30). Proper use of modules accomplishes this in a strong visual message.

Modules also make it easier for the editor to provide balance and break up the grayness that results from unrelieved areas of textual matter. Dividing the page into modular units forces the editor to work in specified subdivisions of the page, and the final product usually has better contrast throughout. Breaking up the broadsheet into smaller, more manageable areas allows the reader's eye to deal more effectively with the space.

The last and most important advantage of the modular format is the favorable reaction of the readers. Respondents to a survey in the early 1970s told researchers they preferred newspapers with a modern design, which is characterized by modules, an optimum six-column format and horizontal layout. In fact, the authors concluded that the findings were a "ringing endorsement" for such newspapers (Click and Stempel 1974).

Sissors (1974) sampled young, college-educated readers to determine format preferences. Reactions to the four front pages were mixed, and even though a traditional page edged out a more modern design, the clearest finding was the extremely low rating given to the only page not done in a modular format.

Until research is done using modules as the only variable, it is impossible to say flatly that modular layout is preferred over irregular wraps. It is unlikely that people in all communities will prefer one over the other. Most of the research, however, lends support to modular formats. Designers who are trying to achieve a clean, uncluttered appearance and are conscious of legibility research prefer to use the modern formats.

Advertising arrangements

It is a challenge for editors to accommodate the reader's desire for uncluttered design on pages that contain both news and advertising because some advertising formats work against good design. There are three basic advertising configurations: the well or U-shaped layout, the pyramid stack and the modular layout.

From the reader's standpoint, the well advertising arrangement is the most annoying because news copy is stuck between overpowering advertisements. Figure 4.3 illustrates how copy is trapped between advertisements in the well format. Because the well uses advertisements in both the upper right and left, it is impossible to design a page with a strong editorial focus. Seldom is there enough room to display photographs or artwork adequately. In fact, it often is preferable to use only headlines and text. Advertisements often have such large headlines and artwork that the editor may attract more attention to the stories on the page with a scaled-down design that offers a contrast.

Few newspapers still use the well arrangement; most use the pyramid, in which ads are stacked toward the top left or top right (Fig. 4.4). This permits the news department to use either the top right or left of the page for a package that will attract readers as they look through the publication. A modified pyramid stack is one in which ads of various sizes are stacked to decrease the number of advertising ledges jutting into the editorial space (Fig. 4.5). Instead of running more ads up the right side of the page, the Seattle Times has stacked two ads on the right and three on the left. The modified pyramid stack creates only one ledge.

The well and pyramid arrangements both are designed to place news copy adjacent to the advertisements. Newspaper advertising departments have long sold the idea that readership of advertising that touches editorial copy is higher than readership of advertising that does not touch editorial copy, such as a shopper. However, a 1989 study did not support this contention. In addition, the author reported

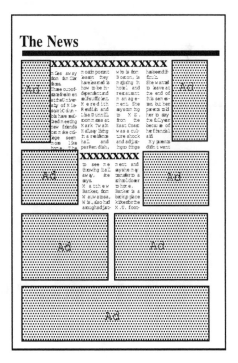

4.3 A well-advertising format is the most intrusive on good page layout of all advertising arrangements.

4.4 In this typical pyramid advertising stack, the ads are run like stair steps to the left.

4.5 This modified pyramid stack creates only one ledge and lets editorial and advertising work together better.

4.6 The modular ad stack contributes to better display space and less-cluttered pages. Ads in modular stacks receive as much attention as those in pyramid stacks.

that readers found the pages with modular advertising stacks and modular layout to be more attractive (Lewis 1989, p. 73). Although the intent of the advertising arrangement is to serve the reader, the arrangement of the news and advertisements may be counterproductive. As one reader told a researcher, "I was reading this story and it was interesting, but then I turned to where it was continued and all I could find was a big ad for discount drugs or liquor or something which occupied most of the page" (Clark 1979, p. 19).

From both economic and readership standpoints, advertisements are important. A newspaper without advertising sells far fewer copies than a newspaper with ads. Papers that do not have a good selection of grocery ads, for instance, are harder to sell than papers that do. Classified ads attract strong readership because advertisements carry information that readers want. Consequently, it is important that advertisements and editorial copy work in tandem (Fig. 4.6). Although readers object to searching for copy buried among the ads, they also object to editors using space alongside large ads for uninteresting stories. A well-designed advertisement can attract readership on its own and does not need the perfume of news copy.

In the 1970s, modular advertising formats were adopted by many newspapers, including Newsday (a tabloid), the Chicago Tribune and the Los Angeles Times. Smaller newspapers may have trouble selling the concept to local advertisers because a purely modular advertising system restricts ad sizes to an eighth, a quarter, a half or a full page. However, smaller papers can adopt a modified modular system by selling all the traditional sizes and stacking the ads so that they are blocked off.

Working with advertisements

Editors of newspapers that do not use modular advertising stacks must learn to work with advertisements instead of against them. The pyramid stack poses problems, but they are not insurmountable. The editor can create modular units with the space remaining on the page by working off the corners of the ads. In Figure 4.7, lines are extended from the corner of the stacked ads. The letters A through C indicate the modular units created. Each of these units can be subdivided into more modules. The lines represent either headlines or the edges of

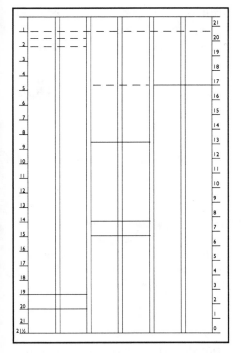

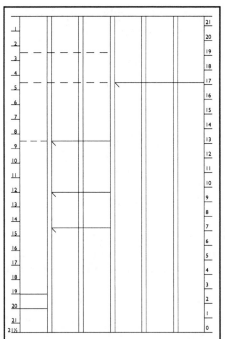

4.7 The dotted lines indicate locations to place headlines or photographs. That placement creates modular spaces on a page that has advertising ledges.

4.8 The designer has several options with the same advertising arrangement. This shows how a designer might create a different layout using the same ad stack as in Figure 4.7.

4.9 And this is how one newspaper actually worked off that ad stack. It created six modular units.

photographs or artwork. The number and shape of possible modules are limited only by the editor's imagination. Figure 4.8 shows a different modular arrangement with the same ad stack, and Figure 4.9 shows how one newspaper actually handled the problem and produced a clean, orderly page.

Any reasonable designer and editor would be quick to acknowledge that the content cannot always be accommodated in a modular unit on an inside page. Often this is not possible because there is room for only one story, and the editor cannot break off the ad stack with headlines for secondary stories. In all cases, logic must temper layout decisions.

Modular open pages

Although it is much simpler to work in modules on pages with no advertisements, editors are obligated to arrange the elements on these open pages in a pattern that enhances readability.

The designers at the Herald-Sun in Durham, N.C., worked in modules on the "hometown" page (Fig. 4.10). Five modules containing nine elements fill the page. The page features contrasting vertical and horizontal modules. Boxing each element on the page, the Chicago Tribune defines each of the four modules on its page (Fig. 4.11). It, too, offers vertical and horizontal shapes. Both of those pages have a low story count, a function of the page content, not of modules.

In comparison, the Atlanta Journal and Constitution Saturday edi-

4.10 This page, which has five modules, works, in part, because of the vertical column. The other modules play off it.

4.11 The Chicago Tribune also uses a column played vertically to create contrast of shapes on the page of modules.

tion is much livelier because it is a front page (Fig. 4.12). Its six modules contain 22 elements. The related elements appear in the same module. For instance, the "Edgy parents" package consists of a headline, deck, photograph, story and graphic. All are in a vertical module. The Clinton package consists of a headline, deck, story and a highlights pullout in a vertical module. Modular layout does not define the number of stories or elements.

Establishing relationships

Working with a modular layout is relatively easy, but using modules to communicate relationships can be complicated. The effort is necessary, however, if publications are to serve the best interests of readers. Grouping elements in an orderly fashion adjacent to each other helps the reader understand the relationships, but putting all the elements into a single module makes it easier for the reader to see the relationships. When related elements are not in the same module, the reader may still make the connection but not without some effort. In Figure 4.13, two baseball stories and an unrelated picture of Martina Navratilova run under the baseball story. The heavy rule around the picture is a signal to readers that it is not related to the headline. There are no signals for readers to go from the picture to the story about Navratilova in the lower right hand corner. Readers can make the proper connections, but scanners don't have time to study pages. Properly establishing relationships among elements on the page saves readers' time and eliminates confusing ambiguities.

Working under deadlines, editors often unintentionally place unrelated elements together and create a funny or embarrassing package. That was the case when the headline about the sex education class ran over an unrelated picture of youths at a baseball party (Fig. 4.14).

Five ways to show relationships

When multiple elements are put into the same module, a relationship is established. That's not always enough. Editors have five ways to establish relationships even within the module: placing related elements in a vertical module; boxing related elements; running a headline over related elements; running the copy alongside and under a related story, picture or graphic; and using icons, color or some other unifying device to identify elements on

4.12 The high element count page is organized by modules to tone down the clutter while still giving the page a feeling of activity.

4.13 The relationship between the Navratilova picture and the copy around it is ambiguous, especially because USA Today usually runs a story related to the picture in that location underneath it daily.

the same topic.

1. Placing related elements in a vertical module. The natural order is photograph, cutline, headline and story. The eye is first attracted to the photograph. Most readers come out of the bottom of a picture to look for cutline information. The natural move is then to the large headline under the photograph. To successfully show the relationship, the headline should begin at the lower left hand corner of the picture and extend the width of the picture. The relationship between the apartment fire photo and story are clearly established using this method (Fig. 4.15).

2. Boxing related elements. Elements within a box must be on the same topic. The Chicago Tribune communicates the relationship among the three pictures and story on the unseen war by placing them all within a box (Fig. 4.11). The two stories on Yugoslavia (Fig. 4.16) are within a box; the sidebar is boxed within the larger box. The device pulls the main story and

sidebar together. The gray adds a graphic weight to the package to help attract attention.

A box that pulls elements together also separates. For instance, it is inappropriate to run a main story and box a sidebar outside the module of the main package. Short sidebars can be boxed if they are

4.14 Unintentional mistakes are sometimes embarrassing. The group looks as if it is cheering for the sex education class, but that story has no relationship to the photo. The headline of an unrelated story should not have been run over the picture.

4.15 The story and picture about the fire are in the same module arranged vertically. This is the easiest way to show the relationship between a picture and a story.

4.16 Boxes pull related elements together and also separate unrelated elements. The relationship of the story about the border control to the main story is preserved because the box appears within the larger box. If the large box were not there, the box around the sidebar would separate it from the main story.

4.17 In similar fashion, the screened sidebar appears within the box around the larger package. The large box preserves the relationship.

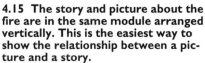

4.18 Running the copy in an "L" helps establish the relationship between the story and the picture.

4.19 The box around the postal error story helps disassociates it from the story on the Japanese cabinet, which appears in the same module.

contained within the larger unit, as it is in the "Car care" package (Fig. 4.17). But if the same story runs outside the package, the box disassociates the two stories.

3. Running the headline over related elements. We have already seen the confusion, and sometimes embarrassment, that can result when a headline runs over unrelated elements. That ambiguity occurs because readers have been taught that the headline creates relationships among the elements under it.

4. Running the story alongside and under related elements. Sometimes you do not wish to run a headline over a story and picture because of other elements surrounding it or because the story deserves only a one- or two-column headline. Your solution then is to "L" the story under the related picture (Fig. 4.18).

5. Using icons, color or other elements to show relationships. When you work in modules, stories stacked on or alongside each other are technically in the same module even when they are not related. To show the relationship of adjacent stories, you can use a repeating element. Icons, a small graphic representation, can be inset into the beginning of related stories. Same-color bars can be repeated with related stories. In fact, any repetition of design elements helps communicate relationships.

How to disassociate elements

Just as important as showing relationships is knowing how to signal readers when elements are not related. When you are trying to disassociate elements, first avoid putting elements together in the five ways described above. But additional steps need to be taken to disassociate elements. There are three ways: boxing, using vertical or horizontal rules and avoiding running headlines the width of pictures under unrelated pictures.

1. Boxes associate; they also disassociate. The postal error and Japanese cabinet stories are in the same horizontal module (Fig. 4.19). The box disassociates the stories.

2. Vertical and horizontal rules are like fences; they separate stories. The risk you run is having the reader overlook them. Look closely again at Figure 4.12. Notice the vertical rules between all the unrelated stories and elements. The rules are light, but if they are used consistently, regular readers will understand them. If they are used inconsistently, readers may not understand. Horizontal rules are called cutoff rules. That's because they are intended to cut off the reader from reading from one element into the next.

3. Almost all newspapers run stand-alone pictures. Unless the picture is sitting on the bottom of the page, it immediately creates a challenge to disassociate the copy that appears under it. Many newspapers properly box stand-alone pictures. That may not solve the problem. The rule may not be heavy enough. If you show a relationship between a picture and story by running a headline from the lower left hand corner of the picture the width of the picture, it follows that you should not run a headline the width of the picture if they are not related. In Figure 4.20, the two stories under the flooding picture are not related

to the picture. Fortunately, the editors did not run a headline the width of the picture. Running two headlines helps. It might have been even more effective to run the one-column story on the left. That's a stronger signal to readers that the headline doesn't go with the story.

Protecting copy flow patterns

Modular copy gives the reader a fixed starting point, a principle long prized by legibility experts. In Figure 4.21, even though there are four wraps of copy, readers return to the same height or starting point each time they finish a column of type. Little is lost with an L-shaped copy wrap (Fig. 4.22), where the jumps from the end of each column are the same. The L-shaped wrap also requires that the reader make less of a jump to columns B, C and D than many other alternatives, such as the reverse L (Fig. 4.23). The jump from column A to column B is longer, more difficult and more time-consuming.

Usually in an effort to break up the grayness of the text, editors sometimes create copy flow patterns that challenge readers to follow. In Figure 4.24, readers are required to make progressively higher jumps from each column. No two columns start at the same height. It might take a pogo stick to get through the story. Another kind of copy flow problem is illustrated in Figure 4.25. Readers have to jump the illustration five times to follow the copy trail. Reading shouldn't be as difficult as running a triathlon. If the illustration had been moved up an inch to prevent any copy appearing above it, the designer would have had a more successful page.

That problem could be avoided by following a simple rule: never break across more than two columns of your setting with anything.

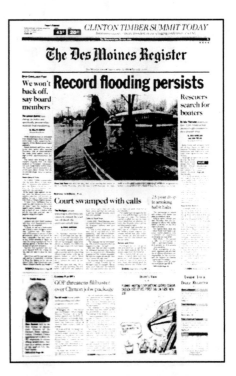

4.20 In an attempt to signal readers that the two stories under the flooding picture do not go with the picture, the designer has boxed the stories and broken the headline so it does not extend the width of the picture.

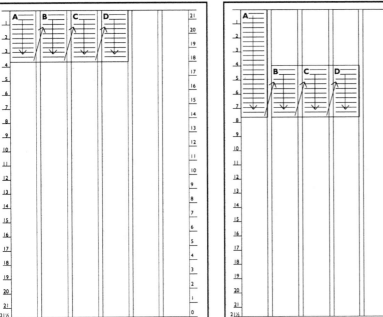

4.21 Modules bring readers to the same starting point in each column. That can increase reading speed.

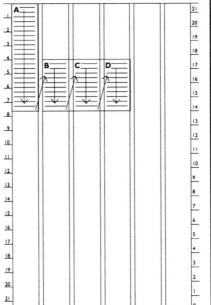

4.22 The L-shaped copy block helps connect the story and a visual.

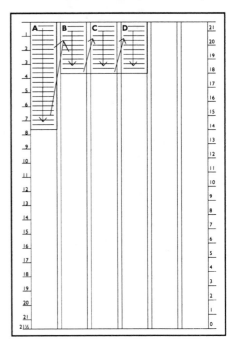

4.23 The reverse L does not create as effective a path for the eye as the regular L.

Don't run pullouts, maps or pictures through the middle of two or more columns. Place these elements on the top of columns or at the bottom of the package or wrap the type around them. When you break across columns, you invite some readers to detour to the top of the next column. There they discover they made the wrong turn, and they may not care enough to turn around.

4.24 At first glance the page looks easy to read but look at the complicated copy flow map. Each leg of type starts at a different height.

4.25 An even more complicated copy path is illustrated in this layout. The reader must jump over the bat three times.

> *Documentary photographs are most memorable when they transcend the specifics of time, place and purpose. When they invest ordinary events and objects with enduring resonance. When they illuminate as well as record.*
>
> **Naomi Rosenblum**
> **AUTHOR**

5. USING PHOTOGRAPHS

When newspapers and news magazines ran a photo of a wounded American being dragged through the streets of Somalia like a trophy, Americans reacted with outrage—as much at the publications for running the picture as at the Somalian mob (Fig. 5.1). A typical reader protest appeared in the Indianapolis News: "How would you react if he were your brother, father, son, husband or friend? I'm sure those pictures...will haunt the people who loved him for the rest of their lives. You are no more civilized than the desecraters. I'm appalled!"

The reaction testifies to the power, even in the video age, of still photography. The ability of photographs to attract readers' attention and report the news remains the great untapped resource of journalism at many newspapers. The successful use of photographs and words in tandem is a realization of the powerful potential of the newspaper as a visual medium. Photographs are the stop signs in the designer's traffic pattern. Photographs are the most-looked-at items in newspapers (Garcia and Stark 1991). Stories with pictures command better readership and hold the reader's attention longer than stories without pictures (Bain and Weaver 1979).

We have come a long way since 1893 when the editor of the respected magazine Nation asserted that pictures appealed chiefly to children and were beneath the dignity of good newspapers. Even though Look and Life magazines pushed the still photograph to new limits and National Geographic dramatized its potential as a reporting

51

THE IMAGE THAT BROUGHT THE TRAGEDY HOME

5.1 This Associated Press photograph created a firestorm of protest from U.S. readers. Does the reaction mean it should not have been printed?

tool, it was not until the 1960s that a significant number of newspapers started integrating the photograph into the news product instead of using it only as a decoration or to break up type.

Many editors still consider the photograph a supplement to words rather than a form of reportage. That is not surprising because most newspaper managers were trained to use words. Consequently, photographers are still fighting for first-class citizenship in too many newsrooms.

Once there is a willingness to use photographs, staff members must be trained to use them correctly. At large newspapers, a photo editor, usually a photographer by training, is responsible for the selection and display of all photographs and artwork. At small and medium-sized papers, that job often is done by the layout editor, who is usually a former copy editor. Editors who would be aghast at having a photographer run the copy desk think nothing of having copy editors edit, crop and display photographs. Photographers need to be photojournalists; copy editors need training in photography. Both need to know not just how to use photographs but also to recognize when an ethical line has been crossed. This chapter is a start in that direction.

Photography ethics

Ethical questions fall into two categories: definitions of manipulation and questions of taste.

MANIPULATION

It used to take time and effort to alter a photograph. All that has changed. Thanks to computers, photo editors now can change photos digitally, so the opportunity for mischief is greater and easier than ever. Hardly had the first computer photo software been installed than there were celebrated cases of questionable photo manipulation.

On its February 1982 cover, National Geographic moved a pyramid so the photo would fit better in a vertical format. Rich Clarkson, then director of photography, explained: "It's exactly the same as if the photographer had moved the camera's position. I have a hard time thinking that's a clear-cut issue. But people say, 'My God, you moved a pyramid! Then you can move anything!' Also in that picture was a camel train. There's suspicion that the photographer convinced them to move the camel train to that area. He also used a filter to change the sky. The scene you'd see if you were there is not the scene the photographer took. But it's a beautiful photo" (Reaves 1987, p. 32).

Many in the industry were disturbed at the Geographic's disclosure. But the word did not get to everyone.

In Edmonton, Canada, a staff member took pictures of a professional hockey player and his coach at a trapshooting range. In the lab, the negatives were flopped and printed as if the two were in the same frame. The coach and the player, who had been feuding, had guns pointed at each other's heads. Only after readers protested did the paper acknowledge the picture was a hoax. National Geographic used a computer to move a pyramid; the Edmonton Journal performed its mischief in the photo lab.

Where do correcting and manipulation intersect? Many newspapers used their computers to "correct" the blue in the historic Associated Press shot of the space shuttle Challenger exploding. Is that unethical? Photographers have always corrected color, burned and dodged in the darkroom. Should there be different standards for electronic retouching? Computer software permits us to alter far more than we could in the photo lab, and the computer enables us to do it quickly and with such attention to detail that it is difficult to detect. TV Guide, for instance, electronically placed Oprah Winfrey's head on Ann-Margret's body—and dress—for a cover photograph. Who blew the whistle? Not Winfrey. Not Ann-Margret, but Ann-Margret's dress designer.

News Photographer, the magazine of the National Press Photographers Association, does an excellent job of examining these issues (Fig. 5.2). Classic cases of electronic manipulation show up in the series of Day in the Life books. Editors used a computer to add water at the top of the photo on the Australia book; the editors changed a dull, gray sky to bright blue for the California book; they moved a tree down a hill to create a vertical cover picture for the book on America. These instances of electronic manipulation have received an enormous amount of attention in the industry because the work of some of the best photographers in the world are included. Rick Smolen, one of the organizers of the projects, has said that none of the pictures inside the books was manipulated.

Some editors say that although they would never manipulate news photos, they have different standards for feature photos. Some draw the line only at photo illustrations, which are a made-up situation anyway. Sheila Reaves of the University of Wisconsin gathered a cross section of views on the limits of photo manipulation. She concluded: "Will readers be able to make distinctions between a newspaper's handling of feature photography and news photography as easily as some editors do? If not, newspapers may risk losing the public's trust in all photography" (Reaves 1987, p. 32).

Some editors suggest that some manipulation could be done if it were noted in the caption. One problem is explaining to readers. Newsweek found in 1990 that less than 40 percent of the public had even heard of "digital enhancement." Newspapers in some Scandinavian countries use a small logo in the corner of a photo that has been changed electronically. The Associated Press's policy is clear: "The content of a photograph will NEVER be changed or manipulated in any way." In a survey that posed increasingly more intensive levels of manipulation or retouching, editors involved in photo selection were not unanimous in almost every situation (Reaves 1992). Here are five of them.

1. Okay to remove a telephone wire from the background? Yes, 29 percent; no, 70 percent.

2. Okay to zip up a child's pants? Yes, 27 percent; no, 71 percent.

3. Okay to move subjects closer together to fit a layout? Yes, 6 percent; no, 83 percent.

4. Okay to eliminate some extraneous people to improve the graphic effect of the picture? Yes, 11 percent; no, 87 percent.

5.2 The photographs in the three covers shown on this page were all manipulated electronically.

5.3 USA Today put Hill and Thomas together from separate photographs and ran it on its front page. Does the photograph deceive readers?

5.4 The Boston Globe also put Hill and Thomas in the same frame but made it look as if the picture were ripped.

5. Okay to eliminate a distracting person in the background? Yes, 10 percent; no, 89 percent.

Some editors also have no problem with combining photos to create a photo illustration. Is the combination in Figures 5.3 and 5.4 a photo illustration or news photography? Anita Hill accused Clarence Thomas, then a nominee to the U.S. Supreme Court, of sexual harassment. Neither USA Today nor the Boston Globe had a picture of the two of them together, so they created a composite. USA Today created a blue background grid, presumably to signal to readers that it was a composite (Fig. 5.3). The Globe created a rip (Fig. 5.4). Neither told readers how the pictures were produced.

At stake is the credibility of photographs. As readers realize what can be done with photographs, will they ever again trust what they see? As soon as they see a photograph they don't believe or don't want to believe, will they accuse the publication of lying? Each publication needs to address the issue and produce written guidelines.

TASTE IN EDITING

Designers must be sensitive to the issue of whether to use photos showing victims grieving, dead bodies, people in compromised positions and other instances of questionable taste. The profession has many examples of intense negative reader reaction when photos of victims or of grieving relatives have been published. More than 500 readers objected with phone calls, threats and letters when the Bakersfield Californian ran a photograph on page 1 of a family grieving over the drowning of a 5-year-old son and brother. The victim's face was visible from the half-open body bag (Fig. 5.5). Robert Bentley, then managing editor, said readers cited two reasons why the picture should not have been published: "They didn't want to be forced to visually intrude into what should have been a family's private time of shock and grief" and "they didn't think a newspapers photographer should have done so either" (Thornburg 1986). Bentley later apologized in a column for running the photograph.

5.5 Readers reacted strongly against the paper that printed this photograph, which was taken locally.

Sandra Rowe, then executive editor of the Norfolk Virginian-Pilot, reported a similar reaction from readers when her paper printed a page 1 photograph of three young victims of a car accident (Fig. 5.6). The father, a police detective, told the paper, "Three of my children were still in hospital beds. I had no idea a picture like that was going to be in the newspaper. I was hurt. I was upset" (Thornburg 1986).

Both photos won awards. Both photos evoked a public outcry. Journalists must be aware of community standards. The decision may be made to print regardless of the public's attitude because it serves a greater public good, such as intensifying a drive for safer swimming or driving conditions. Or the decision may be made that although the photograph is exceptional, it is not suitable for a general-circulation newspaper.

An even more complicated situation occurred when the Pennsylvania state treasurer called a news conference to respond to stories that he had accepted bribes. With video rolling and still cameras clicking, he shot himself. The pictures were extraordinary, sensational, repulsive and historic. The Associated Press moved pictures of the treasurer pulling out the pistol, handling it, placing it in his mouth, slumping to the floor after firing and lying dead on the floor. A survey of newspapers in New York, North Carolina and Pennsylvania found that only 17 percent of the 114 respondents ran the picture of him with the pistol in his mouth and only 5 percent ran the photo of him dead. In Pennsylvania, however, of the 57 respondents, 25 percent ran both pictures along with others (Kochersberger 1988).

Many memorable pictures are offensive. Lasting images of the Vietnam war include the photographs of a naked child running screaming down a street after her village was napalmed and of a South Vietnamese general shooting a prisoner in the head. These types of photographs are always tough calls. In hindsight, it is easier to make the call on classic photographs. However, no picture is a classic when it arrives at deadline. The soldier being dragged through Somalia's streets may be the lasting image of our involvement in that country, but at the time it arrived, it was just another dramatic picture that raised questions of taste. The photograph ran on page 1 of scores of newspapers. The Tennessean in Nashville circulates at Fort Campbell, Ky., where the soldier was based. It did not publish the picture. The Clarksville Leaf-Chronicle also circulates there. It ran it on page 1. The editor received at least 100 calls and had about 50 cancellations. The editor said as time passed, some people who were initially angry came to understand the reason for publishing it (Fitzgerald 1993).

There is no "right answer." As ethicist Deni Elliot says, "There always are pictures where reasonable people will disagree and both be ethical. The ethics is not that you print, but how you come to the decision" (Kalfus, p. 30). Here are some criteria against which to measure your decision.

5.6 The father of these children was upset when he saw the picture in the paper. Should that be a consideration when the editors decide whether to print?

1. Proximity. A picture of local people has more impact than showing the same incident miles away. That is why readers accept most pictures of war or starvation but react strongly to a picture of death at home.

2. Dead bodies. Dead bodies seem to be acceptable to readers in some instances. But when the face is showing, the reaction is usually stronger and longer.

3. Accident victims. A picture of an accident victim who will survive is accepted more readily than one of a victim who may later die. The problem is that the outcome often is not known at publication time. If the victim is in serious or critical condition, readers will normally react negatively, especially to a photograph showing the face.

4. Suffering. Many readers consider it an invasion of privacy to show the suffering of people.

5. Size. If a photo is exceptionally good, the first impulse is to run it large. Many readers accuse the paper of sensationalism when it runs large pictures of tragedy.

6. Location. It is natural to put such photos on the front page. The same picture is less offensive inside.

7. Purpose. Last, but most important, ask yourself whether there a real or only an imagined public benefit to be derived from publishing the photo.

None of these criteria is meant to suggest that controversial photographs shouldn't be run. Some should; some shouldn't. What is important is that journalists not make knee-jerk decisions. A newspaper should have written guidelines for handling pictures involving death, injury, suffering, nudity and offensive cultural elements. The discussion should include the photographer, a photo desk representative, the ranking news executive available and the section editor where the picture would run. If the decision is to run, editors should carefully write a cutline and headline and review the page proofs. In some situations, the editors may want to explain the decision to readers and invite their reactions. Whether the picture is published or not, steps should be taken to guard against future possible misuse of the photo if it is going to be placed in archives. The staff should also be informed of the decision.

Integrity of the photograph

Changing the facts in a photograph or deciding whether to publish pictures of victims involves ethical and legal questions. Techniques such as mortising, insetting, overprinting and silhouetting involve the integrity of the photo.

Mortising, which is the overlapping of two or more photographs or type and a photograph, is rarely effective. In Figure 5.7, the placement of the small head shot interferes with both the story and the larger picture. Another familiar technique is an inset, a picture placed entirely within another photograph. This technique is successful only when the inset adds information to the dominant photo and is effective in a small size. The inset does not work in Figure 5.8 because the background is too busy. The intention was to show the crowd watching the victory hug for the golf tournament winner, but the result was a cluttered background of heads sliced by the inset. This space-saving effort was not successful because there was no place to inset a photo in the larger photo without interfering with the content.

The use of insets in Figure 5.9 illustrates the potentials and dangers of this technique. The winners of the races are set into an excellent cross-country shot that was enlarged to 9 by 14 inches. By shooting when the runners were turning and descending a hill, the photographer was able to get a flow and feeling of motion. Do the insets work? The inset in the upper left cuts off a head and obviously interferes with the content of the photograph. Be careful with heads. Every head has a mother. Although the inset at the lower right appears to be

5.7 Mortising, the overlapping of two photos or a photo and type or art, usually detracts from all the elements.

5.8 Insets can work but not when they interfere with the content of the larger photograph, as this does.

in an empty space, there might have been a sign there indicating location. Even if the space were left empty, it could serve a purpose. Photographs with motion need space for the action to flow into. The presentation would have been more effective if the insets had been cropped to the heads—we already know what they are wearing—and run next to each other at the bottom right.

The guidelines for overprinting headlines, or occasionally text, on a photograph are similar to insetting: Overprint only if you don't interfere with the content of the photograph and overprint only if there is a continuous tone. Black type can be printed against a light area such as the sky, or type can be reversed to run against a black background. This guideline protects legibility. By reversing type over a time-exposure picture of coal mining at night (Fig. 5.10), the designer was able to echo the environment of the story without interfering with the message. However, the Saturn package (Fig. 5.11), although dramatic, is too difficult to read because there is so much small text type. (See Chapter 9 for legibility considerations.) Reversed display type works when there are few words and the type is large. Text type should be larger than normal (at least 11 points) and used in small amounts, as it is in Figure 5.12.

Silhouettes are effective when the contrast between the silhouetted object and the background is substantial (Fig. 5.13). For instance, a person wearing light clothes should never be silhouetted against a light background.

Editors who appreciate photographs for their informational content are not likely to destroy them with artistry. We have discussed some of the potential pitfalls. Some solutions come next.

5.9 These insets interfere with a beautiful cross-country picture. One solution is to run 6 x 9-pica head shots of the winners in the lower right-hand corner.

The photo request

One of the most important steps to getting better photography is to create a photo request form. It's a request instead of an order form when the photo editor has the authority to reject or negotiate the request. There are several reasons why a request might be denied; the most common would be that the situation will not yield good photographs. Ideally, the photographer and reporter would work together on a story. The photographer should be willing to include the people and places the reporter thinks are important; the reporter should be

5.10 The type does not interfere with the content, and it echoes the environment of the story—working at night.

5.11 It is difficult, if not impossible, to read the text, which is set in reversed type.

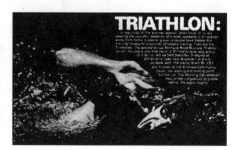

5.12 The smaller type block and large type size protects the legibility of the type.

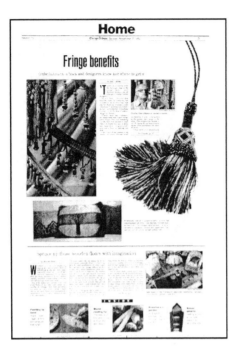

5.13 The silhouette of the broom is appropriate to the tone of the article.

5.14 In photography, one plus one equals three. The two different views of the subject create a third impression.

willing to include the people and places the photographer believes make good pictures. Sometimes the photographer shoots to the story; sometimes the reporter writes to the pictures. When journalists don't work as a team, it's impossible to produce a package. Once, when an early-morning fire raced through a barn and destroyed several valuable horses, a reporter and photographer were sent to the scene from their homes. Both worked alone. When they returned, the photographer didn't have a picture of the dejected owner who led the story. And the reporter didn't have any quotes from the dejected owners the photographer had interviewed and shot. Words and pictures can't work together if journalists don't work together.

When the reporter and photographer can't work together or when there is no story planning conference, a photo request is necessary. The story, even if only in rough draft, should accompany the request. If no writing has been done, the request should include a synopsis of the story. It should also include other basic information: when, where, the reporter's name and phone number, the source's name and phone number, time and date the photos are due and whether they are to run in color or black and white.

Using two or more photographs

The one-frame mentality that dominates the thinking of many editors inhibits good photo selection and use. Although a reporter can cover several disparate topics in a single story, a photographer can usually capture only one segment of a story in a single frame. Much of the drama is left in the photographer's discarded contact sheets when the editor says, "Give me your best picture to go with this story." However, the best picture may be a two-picture package. Here are some common situations.

1. Contrast. Look for dissimilarities in like subjects and subtle similarities in unlike subjects (Hurley and McDougall 1971, p. 5).

2. Close-up and context. When the photographer has to back up to show where the action is occurring, the picture makes a general statement. A second shot can give a close-up look at a small portion of the overall scene.

3. Sequence. One frame captures just one moment in the series; two or more frames permit the action to unfold. However, when displaying sequences, keep the same vantage point in the cropping.

In photography, one and one make three. Although each photo has its own story, pairing offers a third story that results from the interplay of the two photos. That happened when the Portland Oregonian ran two pictures on a swimmer (Fig. 5.14). The swimming picture shows her strength and grace in water; the secondary picture shows her figure. Combined, they visually report the point of the story.

Properly used, the pairing principle tells a story quickly and dramatically. However, when the words say two and there is only one picture, there is an obvious hole in the package. That was the case in the package on a woman who is both a belly dancer and a Sunday school teacher (Fig. 5.15). The story needs two pictures to show her in both roles.

A feature story on a rail transient is told through an environmental shot of the subject far down the tracks and a close-up that shows him smoking a cigarette (Fig. 5.16). The larger picture communicates the loneliness and solitary nature of his life. The close-up permits readers to see him.

The pictures in both examples are adjacent, complement each other and are dominant-subordinate. Those three points are important to remember whether two or several pictures are being used. The first ensures that the reader immediately grasps the relationship between the pictures. The second ensures that there is focus to the package in the same way that a writer must focus on one aspect of the story. And the last, the dominant-subordinate guideline, ensures that one picture is significantly larger than the other.

If a package contains three or more pictures, there are four additional guidelines: interior margins should be consistent, excess white space should bleed to the outside of the package, sizing should be proportionate to the space of the total package, and there should be a variety of shapes. Figure 5.17 shows the use of these guidelines. One photo clearly is dominant, and it provides focus for the spread. There are a variety of shapes, and the interior margins are kept consistent by allowing the excess white space to bleed to the outside of the pictures.

To be dominant, a picture must be large in proportion to the page or portion of the page it occupies. For instance, in National Geographic, a picture 20 picas wide will dominate the page. In a tabloid newspaper, however, a dominant picture needs to be 40 picas wide, and in a broadsheet newspaper, 50 picas wide. The size of the dominant picture should be proportionate to the total space available, but the size of the subordinate pictures should be proportionate to the dominant picture. The difference in size between the dominant and subordinate pictures should be obvious to the reader's eye.

Experience in the use of photos permits possibilities beyond these guidelines. Some situations require two large photos of equal size. A sequence or story about a man who is a banker by day and a farmer by night might have more impact with two equal pictures. Knowing how to handle these exceptions comes with experience.

A common exception occurs when newspapers are printing weddings and engagements, which usually run the same size. In these and similar situations, follow the principle of clustering and alignment. To help the reader, it is important to place the copy with the picture. But to organize the page, it is also important to run the photos in groups and use common alignment (Fig. 5.18). Whenever you print two or more headshots in the same package, make the heads the same size.

5.15 The deck immediately tells you there is a picture missing.

5.16 The simple but strong package features proportional sizes and contrast in shapes.

5.17 This page illustrates the basic multiple-picture package guidelines: one picture is dominant, the interior margins are consistent, the additional white space bleeds to the outside and there are a variety of shapes.

5.18 When running multiple head shots, create clusters and keep the heads the same size.

The picture page

A page of pictures does not make a story, but a page of pictures with continuity does.

Selecting and displaying a group of photographs is similar to writing a major story. When the material is selected and arranged in a coherent and entertaining manner, it has impact. If poorly done, the information is submerged in the resulting clutter.

The difference between a picture story and a picture essay is like the difference between a news article and interpretive reporting (Hurley and McDougall 1971, p. 69). The picture story is a narrative. The essay expresses a point of view. Both require focus, a strong opening and a strong closing. Unfortunately, too many groupings of pictures are just collections of related events. Such groupings are similar to stories that ramble, and they should be rejected.

A photographer made pictures of the last weeks of a baby's life (Figs. 5.19 and 5.20). The result is a story organized by chronology. It starts with a picture of a healthy-looking baby and ends with the funeral. In between, we see the parents prepare for their child's death. The baby had spinal muscular atrophy, a rare genetic disease. This is a photo story.

When lawmakers debated whether to close a hospital for the mentally retarded, a photographer talked to some of the residents (Fig. 5.21). She made the pictures and let the residents create their own essay.

When doing picture pages, remember the following:

1. The telling of a story through pictures begins before the shooting when the photographer and reporter plan the project. Even if the photographer is doing both pictures and text, planning is important. It makes the difference between a story and a collection of facts.

2. The pictures and text must work together. If the text is going to tell a story by focusing on one person, the photos should too.

3. The title of the page must capture the essence of the story. The display type is essential to the success of the page because the title is the quick explanation of all the pictures and text. The title and dominant picture should hook the reader.

When selecting and displaying pictures, include these steps:

5.19 When a photographer gained the confidence of a family whose baby was dying, she was granted access to many private moments.

5.20 The story was organized chronologically and the pictures were presented in clusters.

1. Select as few pictures as possible (most picture pages have too many pictures) so that the ones that are used can be sized adequately. Do not use a full page if the material is not worth it. Skilled photo editing saves space.

2. Omit redundancies. If the story is told with as few pictures as possible, redundancy will not be a problem. Unfortunately, we are always tempted to repeat ourselves photographically, both in full pages and lesser packages.

3. Run one photo significantly larger than the others. That photo should be the dramatic moment or emotion, the essence of the story.

4. Maintain consistent interior margins. White space is trapped when the margins are not consistent, and the reader notices it for itself rather than as a feeling of airiness. Let the extra white space bleed to the outside of the package.

5. Write a cutline for each picture and place it under the picture. Ganged cutlines make readers work extra hard.

6. After you have selected the pictures and determined the length of the text, set the photos before you. The story line and the flow of action should determine the arrangement of the pictures on the page.

7. Place the copy in a modular block. The title doesn't necessarily have to go directly over the copy, but if it doesn't, a subhead over the copy is useful.

8. Write a title or headline that plays off a photograph and place the title directly over or, preferably, under that photograph.

No list of guidelines can prescribe the proper way to produce a successful page. Such guidelines can only steer the beginner away from pitfalls that others have experienced.

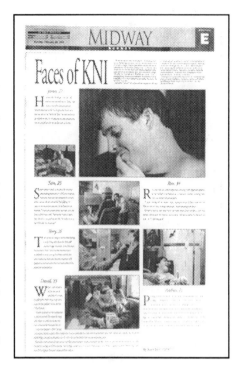

5.21 This essay is a series of pictures centered on a theme. It contrasts with a picture story, which has a beginning, middle and end.

Editing photos

The best photo editors have a sense of news as well as balance and flow. Like reporters, photographers often are the best judges of their own work. They do some physical editing while shooting and some mental editing on the way back to the office. However, also like reporters, they occasionally are too close to the story to see the significant or the unusual. Sometimes a second editor can catch the overlooked frame.

Picture selection depends on the space available and whether there is an accompanying story. Photos that stand alone must capture the essence of the story; photos with text can concentrate on a part of the story. The successful wedding of pictures and words sometimes requires that photos be selected to follow the text and sometimes that the text be written to focus on the dramatic angle developed by the photographers. Consequently, it is important that the photographer and reporter work together on assignments. Such teamwork can produce startlingly good journalism.

Photo editing can be an enormous job. Two photographers can shoot hundreds of frames at a football game. Normally, only two or three would be used, and they must be selected in minutes. Photographers at the Lexington (Ky.) Herald-Leader shot as many as 10,000 frames of the Kentucky Derby and then used approximately 60 of them in a special section.

A former photo editor for National Geographic compiled the following list of questions to ask when selecting a photograph (Terry 1980):

1. Can you justify your selection on a sound editorial basis?

2. Are you looking for a record or snapshot of the event, or do you want the pictures to add depth to the story?

3. Is the photograph more than just technically acceptable and editorially useful?

4. Does the photograph have a mood? (Fig. 5.22)

5. Does the picture have photographic qualities that make it appealing, such as strong graphics, interesting light and forceful composition?

7. If the photograph is unusually good, have you reconsidered the space allotted to it?

A good photo editor is like a strong city editor who can find the story line in a reporter's notes and help the reporter organize the story. A good photo editor recognizes possibilities in the photo that others may not see. Photo editors can turn tepid shots into red-hot drama by cropping tight for impact and backing off for content and form or by cropping to eliminate distractions in order to focus attention on the point of the picture. Such techniques may sometimes require close-ups (Figs. 5.23 and 5.24). Other times, you have to know when to back off (Fig. 5.25).

5.22 **Photographs convey moods and emotions—and humor. Photographer Brian Kennedy captured humor when a deer eased behind tourists looking for wild game.**

Cutlines

Cutlines, or captions, may be the most overlooked element in the paper. Journalists, not readers, are ignoring them. Readership of cutlines is 10 to 15 percent higher than that of stories. This figure alone suggests we should write better cutlines and use them to attract readers to stories.

Writing better cutlines requires changing the system in most newspapers so that the person who edits the story and writes the headline also writes the cutlines. At some newspapers, people write cutlines without even seeing the photographs.

The goal should be to create a package whose parts complement each other. The photograph and headline both tell and sell part of the story; these are the two elements most readers see. The cutline should not only tell readers what they need to know about the photograph but also include something from the text to tease them into reading the story. What we pull should not already appear in the headline or pullouts.

One-line cutline formats usually are too restrictive. A few photographs need only a line, but every newspaper also needs a text cutline format. A text cutline is used when a photograph needs a longer explanation. Here are 14 things to consider when writing cutlines (for more details, consult McDougall and Hampton [1990], who have excellent instructions and examples on cutline writing).

1. Cutlines can convey non-visual senses better than photos: hearing, touch, smell, taste.

2. Cutlines can tell time, temperature and size better than photos.

3. Cutlines can identify people and their relationships. Photos can't.

4. Cutlines can explain the causes or consequences of what the photos show.

5. Cutlines can prevent possible misunderstanding of photos.

6. Cutlines can call attention to something that might be overlooked in the photo.

7. Cutlines should explain any techniques used to create special effects. Even if it's a natural phenomenon, such as a light source, explain it.

8. Cutlines should entice people to read the accompanying story but should not repeat information in the headline or pullouts.

9. Cutlines should match the mood of the photo.

10. Cutlines should be accu-

5.23 **A loose crop fails to emphasize the key subject in the photo.**

5.24 **A tight crop emphasizes both the subject of the photo and the intensity of the discussion.**

5.25 The photographer included a dog in the picture. Assuming the dog is not a part of the story, where do you crop the picture? And why?

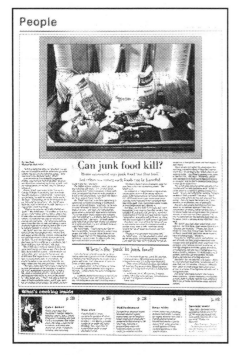

5.26 The humorous interplay between the photo illustration and the words adds to the message that is not a real situation.

rate. Check the names, address and numbers in cutlines against the story. Count the number of names in the cutline against the number of faces in the photo.

11. Crop the photo before you write the cutline. It will save you the embarrassment of identifying someone not in the photo.

12. Don't state the obvious: "kisses the trophy," or "grimaces."

13. Don't editorialize, don't attribute human characteristics to animals and don't put words into people's mouths or thoughts into their heads ("Jones must have been unhappy...").

14. Be succinct. Use "from left" instead of "left to right." Omit needless phrases, such as "pictured here" and "above."

Journalistic tradition calls for cutlines to be written in the present tense to convey a sense of immediacy. It may be time to question that tradition because it must be obvious to any reader that the action is over. It also leads to awkward and grammatically incorrect sentences when writers use the present tense with a date: "Jones scores a basket Sunday..." Writers are to use the past tense in the sentence in which the date is reported, but many forget. Even if they follow convention, the cutline becomes a mix of present and past tense. Perhaps it is time for the industry to re-examine the tradition.

When a picture stands alone, it often has a catchline or headline over the cutline. Depending on the newspaper's headline style, the catchline is either flush left or centered. Cutline text type should be larger than the text type and should offer contrast of race, serif or sans serif, for example, or at least form. Because text type in newspapers is usually serif, sans serif works well, but italic and boldface of the text font will also differentiate the story and cutline text.

The newspaper should have standardized text cutline settings for the width of the picture. Text cutlines in the 10- to 12-point range generally should not exceed 25 picas in width. Gutters should be the same as those used elsewhere in the paper. One way to build white space into the paper is to set cutlines narrower than the width of the picture. This permits extra white space at either side of the cutline.

A one-line format often is a larger version of the cutline text face; 13- or 14-point type works well. In this size, there are no gutters; the cutline can extend the width of the picture.

Although cutlines should appear underneath the related photo, occasionally they are placed to the right or left. In such cases, they should line up with the bottom of the photo to make it easy for readers to find it. Placing cutlines anywhere except underneath the photo should be an exception. Readers read out of the bottom of the photograph in search of the cutline. Grouped cutlines irritate readers because they have to work harder to match the text information with the appropriate photograph. Most won't work that hard.

Credit lines can appear at the end of the text cutline, but most newspapers anchor them at the lower right corner of the photo in 7- or 8-point type.

Photo illustrations

When a photographer can't get a literal representation to accompany a story, a decision must be made whether to order an artist's drawing or a photo illustration. For instance, a photographer can't always be at an undercover investigation, but an artist can effectively re-create a scene such as an exchange of drugs or money in the shadow of a doorway. Stories that discuss ideas, issues or sensitive legal or moral subjects may lend themselves to photographic illustrations, which are pictures staged with people and/or props that represent ideas rather than literal scenes.

To produce an illustration, a photographer needs time, props, facilities and a thorough under-

5.28 The hypodermic needle full of numbers makes a statement. The words help a scanner understand the illustration quickly.

standing of the story being illustrated. Ideas for illustrations are often produced in conferences involving the reporter, story editor, design editor and photographer. It is a time-consuming process, but it pays visual dividends. The photographer who received the assignment to illustrate an article on junk food (Fig. 5.26) brought two important elements to the job: a lively imagination and a casket, which she just happened to have in her van.

Sometimes there is more than one way to tell the same story visually, although one often works better than another. An example of this can be seen in Figures 5.27 and 5.28.

A photo illustration should not be used as a substitute for documentary photography because an illustration lacks immediacy, spontaneity and, to some extent, credibility. It is, after all, a made-up situation (Fig. 5.29). It should be labeled as a photo illustration. These days, photo illustrations are as likely to be created on a computer as they are in a studio. It becomes even more important that readers understand what is happening. It may not be enough to put "photo illustration" in small type under photo illustrations done on a computer because they look so real. If there is any chance readers will be deceived, information about how the illustration was produced should be included in the cutline.

5.29 What's the best way to tell the story? In this case, the answer was an illustration.

Mainstreaming minorities in photos

Designers and photo editors must reflect the entire community the newspaper serves and avoid dealing in stereotypes. A National Association of Black Journalists' study in 1991 of one week's papers from four cities showed that the number of minorities in photographs fell far below the representation of the minorities in the readership areas. Reporters, photographers and graphic journalists must consciously mainstream minority coverage. Ray Wong, design editor at the Nashville Tennessean, says his paper doesn't define mainstreaming as publishing pictures of African-American athletes or entertainers.

5.30 A fowl in formal wear and a play on a well-known line adds up to an effective photo illustration.

"However," he adds, "a successful African-American businessman (and we're not talking about just another minority success story), Asian-American triplets at college orientation, a Latina Girl Scout or an African-American mother who bakes bread as a food page feature are good examples of mainstreaming."

Avoiding stereotypes requires everyone in the chain to ask questions about the fairness of the photos and illustrations. Mike Martinez, deputy director of photography at the Detroit News, offers a typical example. His newspaper spent weeks working on a series on crack babies. Two days before the series was to run, an editor looking at the photographs asked, "Why are all the photos of black women?" The newspaper held the story for two weeks until the photographer produced pictures of black and white mothers of crack babies. That question needs to be asked often and routinely.

6. CREATING INFORMATION GRAPHICS

Nearly 50 years ago, Nelson Poynter, publisher of the St. Petersburg Times, asked why his newspaper wasn't printing maps and other information graphics like Time magazine. That question brought information graphics to daily journalism on a regular basis. Today, papers large and small are creating graphics daily. Since the early 1980s, newspapers have increased the use of graphs and maps dramatically, thanks to the influence of Time magazine, computers that automate part of the process, the example of USA Today and a growing understanding of the role of graphics in communicating information.

In October 1987, when the Dow Jones average fell 508 points, it's possible that more newspapers published more information graphics on front pages than on any day in history. Graphics were used to chart the fall of the Dow Jones average. Again, in January 1991, graphics dominated newspaper front pages when the United States attacked Iran to open the Gulf War. This time, it was because no action photographs were available.

In addition to locally produced graphics, there are several sources of syndicated graphics, such as the Associated Press, Gannett Graphics Network, Knight-Ridder and the Chicago Tribune Co. Information graphics are recognized for their ability to show visual relationships among numbers or locations and to attract more readership than text. Properly done, information graphics, like stories, convert data into information, information into understanding. Information graphics are here to stay.

Background

Information graphics encompass a wide range of story-telling devices. If used correctly, all of them show relationships between two or more items. Charts are pictures of numbers. Maps not only locate Peoria and New Delhi but also show elevations, underground rock formations and cancer clusters. Diagrams explain a space shuttle and how to play hockey.

The term "information graphics" may be confusing because it is a compound noun. Some people incorrectly use the term "informational graphics," but the adjective "informational" implies that some graphics don't have information in them. Journalists who produce graphics are often called artists or graphic artists. But most charts and tables don't, or shouldn't, have art. Perhaps a better name would be "graphic journalists." Regardless of the confusion surrounding the terms, information graphics are being used more than ever these days and often used well.

Technology and a willing industry came together at the right time. Not many people saw the St. Petersburg Times, but when USA Today began printing charts, journalists around the country jumped on the bandwagon. The Macintosh personal computer arrived to a willing audience and made it all possible. But newspapers had a problem: People who could figure out how to work the computer didn't necessarily know the difference between a good information graphic and a bad one. Unfortunately, many still don't.

The industry assumed that graphics were useful for communicating certain types of information, but it didn't really know. In the early 1980s, most of the research on information graphics had been done by statisticians and psychologists. Most of the material tested was too complicated to run in the mass media. Researchers at journalism schools are scrambling to catch up now, and the early returns support the initial enthusiasm. Several small tests have been conducted. In general, these are the findings (Ruel 1993; Stark, Poynter Report; Lott 1993; Vessey 1991; Ward 1992; David 1992):

1. Numerical data is comprehended better in graphics than in text.
2. Readers are more likely to read and remember data in graphics than in stories.
3. Information graphics attract slightly higher levels of readership than stories.
4. Readers have a low threshold for "chartjunk," the artwork some artists build into the data lines. Readers lose the data in the art, and the art sometimes distorts the data.
5. Charts allow readers to grasp trends among numbers more quickly, but comprehension of the numbers in tables is higher than that of charts.
6. People read charts on two levels. One is the visual level—a quick scan that picks up trends or relationships. The second level comes from those who examine the graphic closely, look at the numbers, the trends and second and third levels of information.

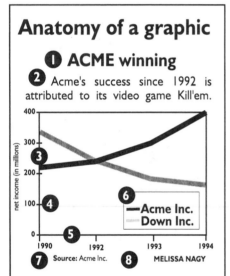

Anatomy of a graphic

❶ ACME winning

❷ Acme's success since 1992 is attributed to its video game Kill'em.

❶ **Headlines:** use a subject and a verb

❷ **Copy block:** explains the most important point in the graphic and tell us a reason

❸ **Y-axis:** dependent variable

❹ **Tick marks:** show values or years and must be evenly spaced

❺ **X-axis:** independent variable

❻ **Key:** identifies fever lines

❼ **Source line:** attribution

❽ **Credit line:** optional according to newspaper policy

6.1

Helping readers understand charts

To help readers understand charts, journalists have developed some aids. Two of the most important are the headline and copy block (Fig. 6.1). The headline tells readers and scanners the most important information in the graphic. Unlike a label or title, the headline has a subject and verb and completes a thought. "City budget" is a label that doesn't tell the reader the important news; "City budget up 10%" is a specific statement. The copy block should fulfill some or all of the following functions:

1. Add details to support the headline. "The City Council adopted a budget Wednesday that increases spending $500,000. Most of the increase is for police and fire protection."

2. Tell the reader what can't be or isn't contained in the graphic. "The budget will require a tax increase of 50 cents per hundred dollars evaluation."

3. In charts reporting poll results, not only support the headline but also give readers the information they need to evaluate the survey: how many polled, when and how the survey was conducted and the margin of error.

4. Call attention to something that might be overlooked in the graphic.

5. Tease or direct the reader to the story for more information.

6. In stand-alone charts, explain the causes or consequences of the information.

The headline and copy block serve the same purpose as the headline and lead paragraph in an inverted pyramid story. All information graphics also should contain a source line. Graphics need to acknowledge the source or sources of material in the same way as stories contain attribution.

Because of the emphasis on drawing in graphics, the first wave of people doing information graphics were artists. Now, the ideal graphics person offers a combination of art and journalism and understands numbers. Newsrooms are requiring that information graphics be sound journalistically. Chart journalists should not be compositors; they should be able to evaluate the information with the reporter, point out holes, suggest new angles, gather information for the graphic and explain why a graphic is or isn't appropriate. Often, chart journalists are experts on sources for statistics (see the list of sources at the end of this chapter) and can help reporters. In short, information graphics are becoming less a decorative element and more a story form. The industry still has a long way to go (see Chapter 7), but it is moving in the right direction.

Preparing to create a chart

Before you worry about what kind of information graphic you will create, you should ask the reporter, other editors or yourself these questions:

1. What is the point of the story? Some graphics are stand-alone

6.2 The headline refers to a falling index, but the chart shows the index rising. It is important for someone to look at the graphics and the stories together.

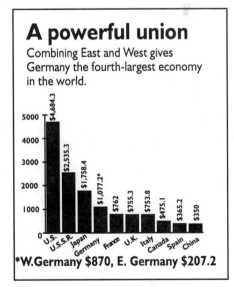

6.3 A little addition reveals that W. Germany had the fourth-largest economy even before the union. The chart gives the impression that the merger changed the rankings.

elements. Even when it accompanies and supplements a story, the graphic should also make sense by itself. Some readers who look at the graphic will not read the story.

2. Do the story and graphic agree? At design conferences, anecdotes abound about graphics that were created using a different time period than the reporter and about graphics with data that didn't agree with the reporter's data (Fig. 6.2).

3. Ask, "so what?" Just because it has numbers doesn't mean it's a graphic. If it can be explained in a couple of lines in a story, it's a waste of space and time to create a graphic (Fig. 6.3).

4. Ask, "compared with what?" Too often, reporters use a set of numbers in stories and expect them to be graphed when they haven't finished their reporting. For instance, when the local schools annually report the results of the ACT tests, among the first questions the reporter should ask is "compared with what?" That question could lead to ACT figures for the state, region and nation, and those figures would lead to a better story.

Check your charts

1. Are the right numbers used? For instance, if you were reporting on the performance of newspapers, would you compare circulation or penetration?

2. Are the tick marks on the line chart spaced equally and do they represent equal amounts or time periods?

3. Do the length of the bars and portions of the pie chart reflect the numbers?

4. If any of the lines or shapes are canted, are the data distorted?

5. Is the choice of chart appropriate for the content?

6. Is the headline specific?

7. Is there a copy block that explains the chart?

8. Is there a source line?

9. Does it use space efficiently? Charts do not have more impact when they get bigger. They ought to maintain the legibility of the type.

10. If art is included, does it obscure or distort the data?

11. Has the story been edited with the graphic in mind? Do the numbers agree? Is there unnecessary redundancy?

6.4

Now, you're ready to consider the most appropriate type of graph to convey the data. The four basic divisions of information graphics are charts, datelines, maps and diagrams. We will look at the attributes of each.

The four kinds of charts

There are four kinds of charts: column and bar, line, pie and tables. Both column and line charts have an x axis, or horizontal scale, and a y axis, or vertical scale. The x axis should contain the independent variable and the y axis, the dependent variable. Thus, when charting inflation rates over time, the rates would be the dependent variable appearing on the y axis, and time would be the independent variable appearing on the x axis.

You should ask a number of questions about each chart. The checklist appears in Figure 6.4.

COLUMN AND BAR CHARTS

A column chart has vertical columns and a bar chart has horizontal bars (Fig. 6.5). Journalists commonly refer to both as bar charts. Think of column and bar charts as still photographs. The format freezes and emphasizes the numbers. By comparison, a line chart is like a video; it maps trends, it shows action. Besides emphasizing the numbers, column and bar charts are useful when you have missing years in your data. A line chart requires an unbroken string of data at even intervals. When the data is missing or is not available in even intervals, the trend is interrupted.

Column and bar charts are strongest when they compare two or more items. For instance, you could compare the price of a steak, a gallon of gas and a movie ticket at intervals over several years. If you wanted to emphasize the specific numbers, you would use a column or bar chart rather than a line chart. If the y axis interval values are so large that it becomes difficult to determine the exact value of the bar, you may wish to print the numbers at the end of each bar. Bars can be arranged by size, alphabet and location, to mention a few ways. However, once you have established the order, each cluster should be consistent. Column charts, rather than bar charts, should be used when you are showing deficits because the vertical presentation is easier to understand.

One variation of the column chart is the two-layer column chart, which shows two layers on one column (Fig. 6.6). It's a space-efficient way to present data. Another variation is the hi-lo chart, used for such things as showing the high and low of stocks or temperatures on a given day (Fig. 6.7).

LINE CHARTS

A line chart shows variations in numbers over time (Fig. 6.8). It's the video showing numbers in action. This format is commonly used to chart Dow Jones averages and temperature fluctuations. It is also popularly known as the fever chart because it was used to chart hospital patients' temperatures. It doesn't show individual numbers as well as the bar chart. It doesn't work well when there is too little variation in the figures because the line appears flat. Sometimes, when there is too much variation in the numbers, the line may rise or fall so much that too much space is required and there are large gaps between numbers. A single line across the chart often indicates that the data could be told in a couple of sentences. A single line showing temperature fluctuations for the month or year is useful; a single line showing DWI arrests in five-year intervals for the last 25 years isn't complete. The arrests should be compared with something, such as ar-

6.5 This bar chart visually shows that it has been a snowy year all around the country. Bar and column charts are like still photographs; they freeze the numbers in time.

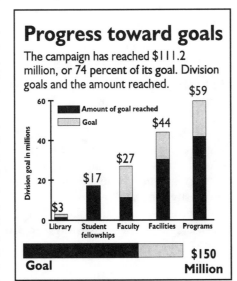

6.6 The layered column or bar chart saves space because two measurements are contained in a single bar. The darker color should be kept at the bottom of column charts.

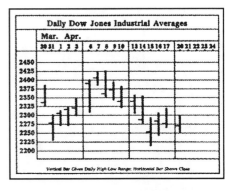

6.7 The hi-low chart also is an efficient and simple way of presenting ranges such as stock market prices and temperatures. The top of the bar charts the Dow Jones high and the bottom charts the low for each day. The horizontal line shows the closing average.

Prospective gains in U.S. grain exports to Mexico

If the North American Free Trade Agreement is approved, U.S. corn exports to Mexico are projected to increase 28 percent by 1995. Soybean exports are expected to increase 15 percent.

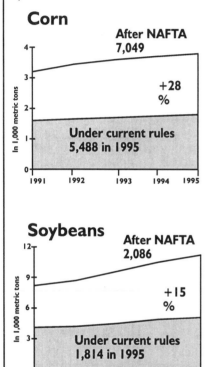

Corn

After NAFTA
7,049

+28 %

Under current rules
5,488 in 1995

In 1,000 metric tons

1991   1992   1993   1994   1995

Soybeans

After NAFTA
2,086

+15 %

Under current rules
1,814 in 1995

In 1,000 metric tons

1991   1992   1993   1994   1995

6.8 The line chart is like a video; it shows numbers over time. The visual message is the trend.

HMO IS TOP PLAN

The HMO is the top choice among the 5,496 city employees who chose a new health-care plan. The plan was chosen by 3,160 employees.

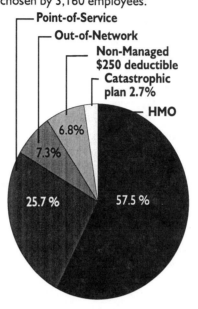

— Point-of-Service
— Out-of-Network
Non-Managed
$250 deductible
— Catastrophic plan 2.7%
— HMO

6.8%
7.3%
25.7 %
57.5 %

6.9 Pie charts show parts of the whole. Too many divisions can make the pie too complicated to read, however. And too few make the chart unnecessary. Three to eight divisions are a comfortable range.

6.10 Tables such as these effectively organize several different numbers into a coherent presentation.

rests in similar jurisdictions or other kinds of arrests. If the change is significant, the numbers should be adjusted for population changes.

Too many lines are confusing. Color permits you to use more lines because each can be identified more easily. When working in black and white, it is better to restrict yourself to two or three lines if they cross.

One variation of the line chart is the area chart, created when you fill in the spaces between the lines. The area chart emphasizes the vertical distance between the lines.

PIE CHART

The pie chart is used to show parts of a whole (Fig. 6.9). It is usually, though not always, circular. The divisions are usually expressed as percentages. The pie chart does not work well when there are too many divisions: They are hard to see, hard to label and hard to differentiate, especially in black and white. On the other hand, a pie chart showing only two divisions is often a waste of space; the numbers would take a single sentence in a story.

A first cousin of the pie chart would be any representation showing parts of a whole. Thus, to show market share for the automobile industry, a car could be divided into appropriate shares and labeled. Be careful though; the form can easily overwhelm the content. Pie charts are inflexible. They can show only parts of one number. Because pie charts show percentages, the number the percentages are based on should appear in the copy block. If you are using adjacent pie charts to show year-to-year changes, use the same key to identify the same categories and keep the categories in the same order.

TABLES

Like Rodney Dangerfield, tables can't get no respect. Yet they are easily understood and used more often than many journalists realize. Tables appear everyday as television grids. Sports agate is full of tables, from the standings to performance reports on players. Tables are columnar listings of names or numbers or both and can organize and relate several categories of information (Fig. 6.10). Tables should be used when there are too many numbers to chart, the data is too disparate (for instance, comparing a group of schools by more than one measurement, such as math and verbal scores), or it is necessary to see the exact numbers, such as in an income tax table. When there are few numbers or when the numbers show a definite trend, it would be better to use a chart.

Tables often are not used to their potential. The table in Figure 6.11 ranked 100 magazines by number of advertising pages published. That's fine for a short list,

Magazine ad page leaders

Rank	Magazine	Pages	% change	Dollars	% change
1	Forbes	3,763.84	5.4	173,351,101	11.0
2	Business Week	3,585.53	-4.0	211,073,967	-4.1
3	People	3,280.57	-0.5	368,179,491	6.7
4	Bride's & Your New Home	3,000.63	-1.2	58,803,774	3.5
5	The Economist	2,743.14	13.8	30,920,562	33.5
6	Modern Bride	2,580.53	-0.4	46,804,832	12.9
7	Vogue	2,370.21	1.8	106,695,989	3.7
8	Fortune	2,552.59	-13.5	133,761,772	-12.8
9	TV Guide	2,502.36	3.8	276,247,005	-1.1
10	Sports Illustrated	2,207.71	-8.8	314,149,507	-2.8

6.11 The problem with ordering the magazines by rank, as they are here, is that it is time-consuming to find any given magazine.

Magazine ad page leaders

Rank	Magazine	Pages	% change	Dollars	% change
21	American Way	1,706.66	2.9	25,199,864	5.1
4	Bride's & Your New Home	3,000.63	-1.2	58,803,774	3.5
2	Business Week	3,585.53	-4.0	211,073,967	-4.1
5	The Economist	2,743.14	13.8	30,920,562	33.5
1	Forbes	3,763.84	5.4	173,351,101	11.0
8	Fortune	2,552.59	-13.5	133,761,772	-12.8
6	Modern Bride	2,580.53	-0.4	46,804,832	12.9
3	People	3,280.57	-0.5	368,179,491	6.7
10	Sports Illustrated	2,207.71	-8.8	314,149,507	-2.8
9	TV Guide	2,502.36	3.8	276,247,005	-1.1
7	Vogue	2,370.21	1.8	106,695,989	3.7

6.12 By ordering the magazines alphabetically, readers can find the magazines that interest them and still get the ranking immediately.

but if you were looking for a specific magazine, you would have to scan until you found it. Obviously, the easiest way for readers to find specific magazines is alphabetically. We can do that and still list the ranking along with the other information (Fig. 6.12). You could highlight the top 10 ranking magazines with color type, tint or screens. Now the list is reader-friendly.

Adjusting for inflation

Whenever you are creating charts or tables and using money over a period of time, you need to adjust the figures for inflation. The Bureau of Labor Statistics publishes the Consumer Price Index, which is used to deflate dollars. When you're working on national stories, you would

6.13 This dateline has two layers of information. One is that contained on each candidate's life. The other is comparing the candidates vertically.

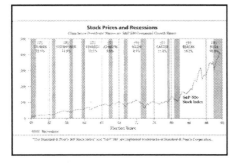

6.14 Despite its visual simplicity, there are several layers of information in this graphic. You can trace the S&P index, look at who was president and see which presidents presided over recessions and for how long.

use the national CPI. There are also urban and rural CPIs, and CPIs are available for specific product categories, such as meat, poultry and fish; household furnishings, shoes and medical care, to name just a few. The bureau also publishes CPIs for regions, and the figures are also available on a monthly basis. You can get the latest CPI by calling the Bureau of Labor Statistics in Washington, D.C., at (202) 523-9658 or by calling a BLS regional office. Historical figures are contained in the Statistical Abstract of the United States.

Here's how to adjust for inflation. The urban CPI for all items in the major groups—energy, food, shelter, etc.—for 1980 is 82.4. The CPI for 1990 is 130.7. Let's assume that you want to deflate your 1990 city budget to 1980 dollars. Here's the formula:

(1980 National CPI ÷ 1990 National CPI) x 1990 City Budget = Inflation-Adjusted Figure

(82.4 ÷ 130.7) x $100,000 = 1990 budget in 1980 dollars

0.63 x $100,000 = $63,000

You would do the same for each year between 1980 and 1990 to chart the annual budget changes in real dollars.

Datelines

History tends to conceal relationships; datelines reveal them. When you create a dateline, you can see patterns or relationships among events. In the opening chapter to this book, you see a dateline identifying developments that have affected newspaper design. Those developments include many different factors: the development of type and typesetting, machinery, presses and photography, even the price of newsprint. The increase in transmission speeds of word and pictures. Creation of the Society of Newspaper Design. When these are arranged chronologically, you can begin to see how a development in press plates, for instance, affected the design of the times.

USA Today showed us how the lives of the three men running for president in 1992 intersected—or failed to intersect (Fig. 6.13). There are layers of information. George Bush had already been in battle in World War II when Bill Clinton was born. Ross Perot was making his first million shortly before Bush won his first elected office. In short, the stacked datelines reveal information not detectable by looking at each separately.

The dateline concept can be combined with line charts and bar charts (Fig. 6.14). Copy blocks can identify events that might have affected the numbers being graphed.

Seven kinds of maps

Maps, which put us in touch with our world, are being used more and more. The New York Times nearly doubled its cartographers, from seven to 13, between 1961 and 1993. At the Associated Press, 14 artists create 5,000 maps a year.

Mass media use several kinds of maps, and only two of them—the transportation map and locator map—are used to show location. Several other kinds of maps—data maps, distribution maps, geologic maps, topographic maps and land use maps—offer journalists formats with which to tell stories. Cartographers use even more formats, but the following list includes those readers can most easily understand.

LOCATOR MAPS

Every newspaper ought to have a file of base locator maps, outlines of political subdivisions such as the ward, city, county or parish, state and nation. With base maps, you can quickly add the type needed to locate action in an accompanying story (Fig. 6.15).

All of us grew up with transportation or road maps. We learned the coding: the larger the type, the larger the city; different icons and colors to identify interstate highways, state highways and county roads. These codes are useful when making maps because your readers also know these codes. However, it is a mistake to adhere to them when you are not creating a transportation map. For instance, you may be creating a map to locate a disaster in a rural area several miles from the city in which you publish. Transportation map coding would require you to put the name of your city in large type and the location of the disaster in small type. That would defeat your purpose, which is to focus on the disaster area.

There are several things to remember when making locator maps (Fig. 6.16):

1. Identify north.
2. Include a mileage scale.
3. Create a type hierarchy that focuses the reader on the important location rather than the cities around it, even if they have larger populations.
4. Include enough of the surrounding territory to identify the location.
5. Eliminate unnecessary detail, including cities and streets that aren't needed to locate the place featured.
6. Include a small secondary map window to locate the exploded area within a larger division.
7. Keep map symbols to a minimum.
8. Curve the type along curved features, such as rivers.

DATA MAPS

Besides showing location, maps can show the geographical spread of data. The geographical distribution of data reveals what numbers

Base map

6.15 Base maps, such as this one showing the counties of Missouri, are invaluable time savers.

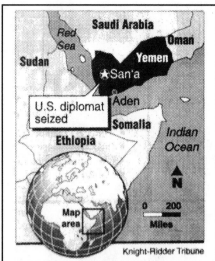

6.16 Locator maps don't need to take much space, but they should show the location, some context and have a directional indicator.

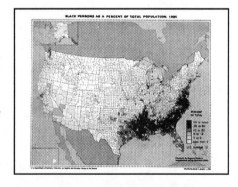

6.17 This data map, prepared by the Department of Commerce, shows the numbers of blacks and where they are living.

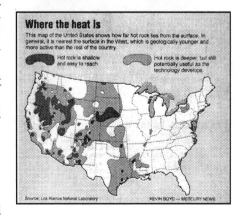

6.18 A distribution map shows the location and depth of hot rocks.

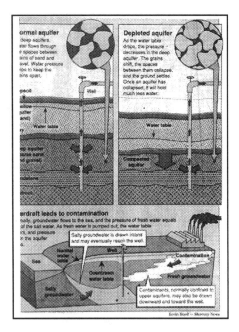

6.19 Geologic maps show what's under the ground.

The disappearing rain forest

Only about one-sixteenth of the world's land is tropical rain forest, places that get more than 100 inches of rain a year. It is being destroyed at the rate of 50 to 100 acres a minute. Trees are key in recycling water, removing heat-trapping carbon dioxide from the atmosphere and preventing soil erosion.

▨ Original tropical rain forests   ■ Remaining tropical rain forests

REUBEN STERN / Staff

6.20 Topographic maps show what's above ground.

City will not rezone ward

Land zoned for commercial use in the third ward is the dominant type of zoning. The Planning and Zoning Commission said it will not recomend any changes to this area of the city in its Land Use Plan update.

23rd Street

Jones Street

Broadway

Agricultural use

Multi-family use

Residential use

Commercial use

Industrial use

Rural use

N

6.21 A map showing the zoning for any political division would be an example of a land use map.

alone can't. Data maps show patterns and trends. Are citizens in some parts of the country more likely to have cancer, on a per capita basis, than those in others? Do some states or regions have higher divorce rates than others? What is a bank's real estate loan pattern throughout a city (Fig. 6.17)?

DISTRIBUTION MAPS

The first cousin of the data map is the distribution map. Instead of showing the distribution of numbers, it shows the distribution of items, such as natural resources (Fig. 6.18).

GEOLOGIC MAPS

Geologic maps show the area underneath the ground—layers of soil, rock formations, even underground streams (Fig. 6.19).

TOPOGRAPHIC MAPS

Topographic maps show land formations above the surface and usually include elevation information (Fig. 6.20).

LAND USE MAPS

Land use maps show how a given area is being used. It can show by zoning designations or by actual use within the zoning classification (Fig. 6.21).

WEATHER MAPS

Few newspapers prepare a full-scale weather map locally. Most use a map from the Associated Press or buy one from a service. However, even when the map is obtained from another source, many newspapers fail to include the key. Even though they have seen them for years in newspapers and on television, many readers cannot identify the map symbols that identify cold, warm and stationary fronts (Fig. 6.22).

Diagrams

Diagrams can take many forms; like pictures, they can be worth a thousand words. Some of them use thousands of words. They also use artwork and photographs. They may even incorporate some charts. Diagrams often use several formats to tell a story, ranging from the simple to the complex. All take time—time to gather the information and time to create the graphic.

You can explain in a story how hockey is played or you can draw and explain it (Fig. 6.23). You can describe a chase scene, accident or race routes, but you might be able to communicate more effectively by drawing them. Because few photographs were available during the Gulf War, newspapers use hundreds of maps and diagrams to explain what was happening (Fig. 6.24).

Like charts, diagrams should have headlines. Some graphic journalists, in fact, write the headlines before they start work. This forces them to focus on the main idea in the diagram. Whether there needs to be a copy block depends on the diagram. Some don't need it because there are text blocks throughout the diagram. Ironically, the danger in these large-scale projects is that the information becomes too complex. The goal, as always, is to make complex things simple.

Minorities in graphics

Graphic journalists have an obligation to see that people who appear in charts and illustrations reflect the multicultural community the newspaper serves. Sadly, many don't. A study of 50 lifestyle sections entered in the Penney-Missouri lifestyle section contest in 1990 turned up 194 illustrations with 381 people depicted. Of those, only 5 percent were identifiable as minorities. Of the 22 people shown in charts, none were identifiable as minorities.

Some newspapers aggressively try to reflect their communities in their photos and graphics. At the Nashville Tennessean, artists are encouraged to reflect the racial makeup of the community in all graphics and illustrations. To ensure representation in photographs and drawings, editors must indicate in their budgets whether the story or illustrations include minorities. A newsroom committee reviews the papers

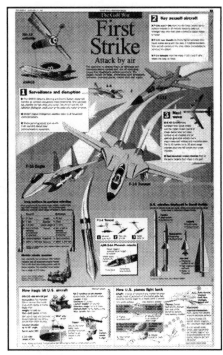

6.22 The weather map is one of the most common seen in newspapers, but despite its wide usage, journalists should remember to include the key on the map.

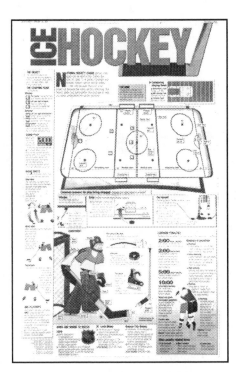

6.23 The illustration is a hybrid between art and text story. It's another story-telling device in the arsenal.

6.24 Newspapers depended heavily on illustrations and other graphics to tell the story of the Gulf War because photographers were restricted from the war zone.

each month and reports on how well they have done mainstreaming minorities into the coverage.

Every graphics department would do well to make a conscious effort to mainstream minorities into daily illustrations.

Graphics desk books

The staff at the Chicago Tribune has compiled a list of books that they think are necessary for daily use at a graphics desk. Among them are the following:

Air Force Magazine. Monthly. Air Force Association.
All the World's Aircraft. Jane's Publishing Co.
All the World's Fighting Ships. Jane's Publishing Co.
Almanac of Seapower. Navy League of the United States.
American Demographics. Monthly. Dow Jones.
Annual Energy Review by the U.S. Department of Energy. U.S.
    Government Printing Office.
The Arab-Israeli Conflict. Martin Gilbert.
Barnes & Noble Thesaurus of Chemistry.
Barnes & Noble Thesaurus of Geology.
Barnes & Noble Thesaurus of Science.
Commercial Atlas and Marketing Guide. Rand McNally.
Complete Book of Sports Facts. ABC News.
Congressional Quarterly Federal Regulatory Directory. Annually. U.S.
Government Printing Office.
County and City Data Book. A statistical abstract supplement. U.S.
Government Printing Office.
Current World Leaders. Eight times a year. International Academy,
    Santa Barbara.
Economic Committee by the Council of Economic Advisers. Annually.
U.S. Government Printing Office.
The Economist. Weekly. Greenwood Reprint Corp.
Europa Year Book. Annually. International Publications Service.
Illustrated Science and Invention Encyclopedia. Stuttman.
Information Please Almanac. Annually. S & S Press.
Jewish History Atlas. Martin Gilbert.
McGraw-Hill Encyclopedia of Energy.
Military Balance. Annually. International Institute for Strategic
    Studies, London.
National Directory of Addresses and Telephone Numbers. Annually.
Concord Reference Books.
Pan Am's World Guide. McGraw-Hill.
Peoples and Places of the Past. National Geographic Society.
Road Atlas. Annually. Rand McNally.
Rule Book. St. Martin's.
Social Security Bulletin Annual Statistical Supplement. Annually. U.S.
    Government Printing Office.
Statesman's Year-Book. Annually. St. Martin's.
The Statistical Abstract of the United States. Annually. Department of
    Commerce.
Strategic Survey. Annually. International Institute for Strategic

Studies, London.

Time-Life Book of the Family Car.

Times Atlas of World History. Times Books.

U.S. Geological Survey Yearbook. Annually. U.S. Government Printing Office.

U.S. Industrial Outlook. Annually. U.S. Government Printing Office.

Webster's New Geographical Dictionary. Merriam-Webster, Inc.

White Book of Ski Areas. Inter-Ski.

World Almanac and Book of Facts. Annually. Newspaper Enterprise Association.

World Book Encyclopedia. World Book.

World Fact Book. Annually. Central Intelligence Agency.

Graphical excellence is that which gives to the viewer the greatest number of ideas in the shortest time with the least ink in the smallest space...and graphical excellence requires telling the truth about data.

Edward R. Tufte
AUTHOR

7. CREATING ACCURATE INFORMATION GRAPHICS

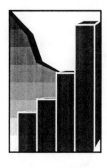

Information graphics create even stranger bedfellows than politics. The creators combine journalism (story), mathematics (numbers) and art (form). In academic circles, both journalists and artists are often known as "math avoiders." Too many journalists and artists fear numbers; they think figuring simple percentages is advanced algebra and deflating dollars is harder than getting to the moon. The results are evident daily in both stories and graphics in the mass media. These examples are all real:

—numbers that show the dramatic increase in city spending during the last 15 years but do not account for either inflation or population increases

—numbers that compare violent deaths in the United States with several other countries but do not account for population differences

—numbers that compare the percentage of Americans in various age groups over the years but do not account for the changing base on which those percentages were figured

Fortunately, most chart errors are unintentional and can be corrected with a little education. A few of the errors may be intentional, in the same way that a few journalists commit plagiarism, make up quotes or ignore information that doesn't fit a story. Those are exceptions. To correct the unintentional errors, we must pay more attention to the numbers. We must recognize the causes of distortion and de-

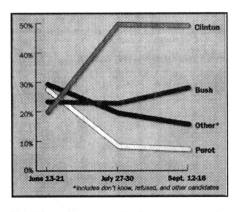

7.1 Line charts aren't always appropri-ate. This line chart appears to chart public opinion over three months; in fact, it only has figures for three dates within those three months.

Clinton takes a clear lead

Bill Clinton has taken a commanding lead in the news' public opinion poll. Results are based on a random selection of 500 voters. Other includes I don't know, refused to be polled and other candidates.

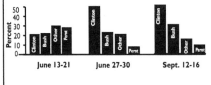

7.2 A bar chart, which freezes the numbers, would be a better format to show the changes in public opinion on the three dates polled.

Moms in the workplace

Today is Working Mother's Day. More women than ever are working or seeking work within a year of giving birth.

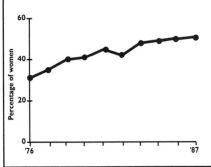

7.3 This chart purports to show the number of working moms between 1976 and 1987. However, count the tick marks on the X axis, and you will dis-cover two years of data are missing.

Moms in the workplace

Today is Working Mother's Day. More women than ever are working or seeking work within a year of giving birth.

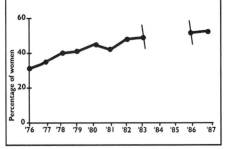

7.4 If you have missing data, let read-ers know. In this case, break the line to indicate which years are missing.

ception. We must make our graphics meet and surpass the same standards of honesty and completeness that we impose on stories. The first step is to recog-nize the problem. There are seven common charting errors:

1. Using the wrong chart form
2. Using uneven intervals along the x or y axes
3. Distorting the chart format
4. Using wrong or incomplete numbers
5. Comparing charts with dif-ferent y value intervals
6. Creating a visual inaccura-cy
7. Starting at other than zero base in column charts

Using the wrong chart form

Line charts connect data be-tween time intervals with a straight line. When the data is compiled yearly (crop production, automobile fatalities), the straight line is fine. However, some types of data are so volatile that the straight line may distort the trend. Sometimes you don't want to break down the time intervals because it would take too much space or because you don't have the data for the time between in-tervals. The solution is to use a column chart. For instance, vot-ers are notoriously fickle in their preferences for candidates during a campaign. In Figure 7.1, not only do the straight lines purport to show something that isn't known, the time intervals are not equal. It appears that Clinton en-joyed a steep, and continuous, rise in voter preference between June and July. He may have, but the newspaper doesn't know be-cause there were no polls between those two dates. The solution is to use column graphs to show the

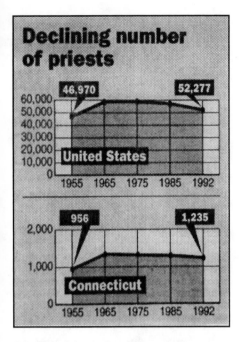

7.5 The tick marks on line charts should represent equal time intervals. This one shows intervals of ten years but finishes with seven. When the interval varies, it should be pointed out to the reader in the graph.

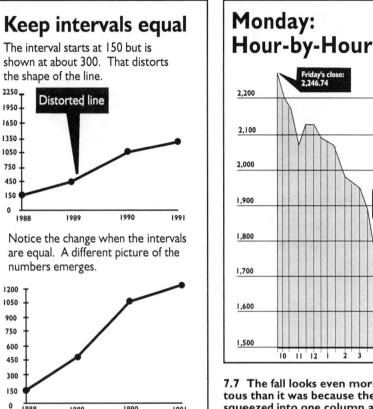

7.6 When the interval values along the y axis vary, the visual picture is distorted.

7.7 The fall looks even more precipitous than it was because the chart is squeezed into one column and the y axis is cropped below 1700.

polling results (Fig. 7.2).

Unless the missing data are clearly indicated, line charts that intend to show trends are inappropriate. In Figure 7.3, two years are missing on the x axis. Because the tick marks were not identified by years in the original, this error may have been intentional to obscure the missing years. The solution is not to hide the missing data; the solution is to use a column chart or to break the lines on the line chart (Fig. 7.4). Use the copy block to explain the missing data.

Comparing uneven intervals

Readers who will examine a chart closely enough to detect data charted during unequal time periods or to detect tick marks unevenly spaced are rare. When the time periods are unequal, quite often it is because the data are not available or not obtainable on deadline. Informing readers of the discrepancy will work if it could be assumed that the uneven time period does not change the visual picture. If there is doubt, a column chart should be used. An accurate line chart requires equal time periods. In Figure 7.5, the line chart has four intervals of 10 years and one of seven. The discrepancy is not called to the readers' attention.

Even more serious is when chart makers try to accommodate a wide range of data along the y axis by changing the interval values (Fig. 7.6). This distorts the visual picture for the casual reader.

Monday's Dow fell 508 points closing at 1738.74

A gently sloping line is produced by Y-axis amputation at 1700 and choice of a wide-shallow shape.

7.8 Here, the data are plotted horizontally and offer a different visual message.

3-D effect causes distortion in charts

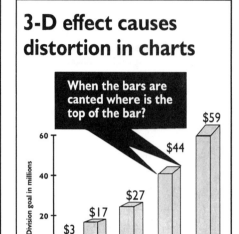

When the bars are canted where is the top of the bar?

$3
$17
$27
$44
$59

Library   Student fellowships   Faculty   Facilities   Programs

Division goal in millions

7.9 When you cant or choose to add dimension to graphics, it distorts the statistical message.

Graduation rates
In percent-1980-91

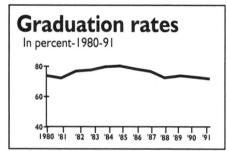

7.10 A single set of figures offers information but not knowledge. The numbers don't mean anything until they are compared to something else.

Distorting chart shapes

Whenever a line chart has one axis longer than the other, the picture created will be misleading. In newspapers and magazines, this occurs frequently because of the restrictions of column widths. If a chart maker tries to squeeze a chart into one column, the data often are distorted. The y axis ends up longer than the x axis, and the data are shown to rise or fall more steeply than deserved. In Figure 7.7, the 508-point decline in the stock market is graphed in one column. The y axis is about 2.25 times the length of the x axis, creating an image of disaster. The decline was significant enough without help from the chart format. When the format is corrected, the picture changes from disaster to steep decline (Fig. 7.8). The shorter the period charted, the more distorted the information will become.

An even more common form of distortion occurs when chart makers cant, or turn, the graphic. The intent—to create a more aesthetic graphic—is benign, but the result is a visual inaccuracy. Column, bar and pie charts that are canted to create a three-dimensional effect distort the information. In pies, the pieces of the

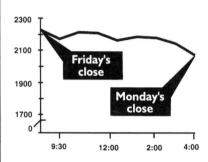

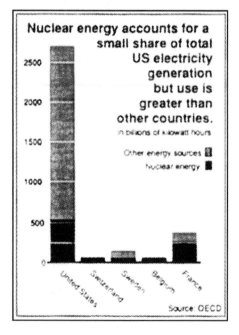

7.11 The words say that we are looking at the percentage of electricity generated by nuclear energy. Percentages cannot be compared unless they are figured on the same base. The visual message is that France uses about eight times more nuclear energy that the United States, which is incorrect.

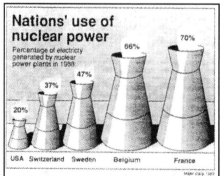

7.12 When you chart actual usage, we see that the United States uses much more nuclear energy than any other country.

More adolescent parents

The number of girls 17 and younger who give birth in Pinellas County each year has been increasing steadily.

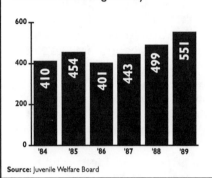

Source: Juvenile Welfare Board

7.13 If you chart just the number of girls 17 and younger who give birth, it appears that the problem is getting worse...

But rate is declining

The population is growing at a faster rate than the number of adolescent births in Pinellas County. Thus, the problem as a percentage basis is less severe than the raw numbers indicate.

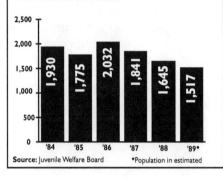

Source: Juvenile Welfare Board   *Population in estimated

7.14 ...However, when you use birth rates, it shows the problem is declining even as the gross numbers increase. By using rates, you can see whether the problem is worsening or it is getting worse as a function of increasing population.

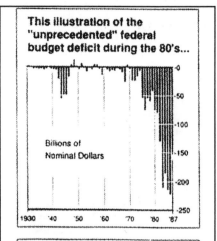

This illustration of the "unprecedented" federal budget deficit during the 80's...

Billions of Nominal Dollars

Fails to account for the dramatic effect of inflation during the 70's and 80's...

Dollars needed to buy one dollar's worth of 1929 goods and services

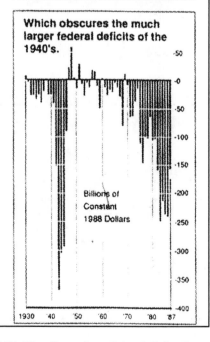

Which obscures the much larger federal deficits of the 1940's.

Billions of Constant 1988 Dollars

7.15 The discussion of the deficit often fails to account for inflation. This graph shows that the deficit in constant dollars was the worst in the last years of World War II.

pie are distorted because the area is expanded or compressed by the angle. To check the distortion on a canted pie chart, use a protractor. Because there are 360 degrees in a circle, each percentage point represents 3.6 degrees. Multiply each figure in your chart by 3.6 and compare with the percentage to assess the distortion. When column and bar charts are canted, readers don't know whether to read the back or front of the bar. Even if the bar is labeled with the exact value, the visual message remains distorted (Fig. 7.9).

Using wrong or incomplete numbers

When wrong numbers are used, it usually reveals a lack of understanding of how to tell stories with numbers. If journalists remember to ask themselves "compared with what?" they will begin to help readers understand the numbers. A single number, or a series of single numbers reporting the same phenomenon, is the most complicated number or series in the world. Numbers beg for context. Context converts data into understanding. Telling readers that General Motors has lost $17 billion on its North American operations in the last 10 years is meaningless until you add other things about the company, such as its annual revenues, its total profit or loss during the same period, its net operating revenue or Ford's performance during the same period.

Using numbers without comparing them to anything is an error of omission. When graduation rates were charted for the state of Missouri, real understanding was the victim (Fig. 7.10). The reader is shown only the internal comparison—the rates for one state over 11 years. Understanding results from comparison of those numbers with others: the rates for the nation, the rates for comparable states, the rates for Midwestern states. Understanding also results from listening to the experts describe the causes: increasing juvenile crime rates, less spending per pupil (on an inflation-adjusted basis), higher student-teacher ratios, etc.

When percentages figured on a changing base are charted, we are comparing apples and oranges. Consultant Loren Needles demonstrated the effect of using the wrong numbers in a graph on the international use of nuclear energy (Fig. 7.11). The chart purports to compare nuclear power usage among five countries. The casual reader could easily interpret the chart to mean that the United States uses significantly less nuclear power than the other countries. In fact, as Needles shows in the series of three corrective charts, the United States uses more than five times as much nuclear energy as France, the next highest. Even the gross numbers are inappropriate in this comparison. The U.S. population is much larger than that of any of the other countries. The appropriate numbers to chart represent per capita usage (Fig. 7.12).

Percentages work if the base on which the percentage is figured remains constant. That's why pie charts, which show a portion of one number, can use percentages. Column and bar charts can also show percentages with a constant base. The base, however, should be revealed in the copy block.

Per capita figures also come into play with a simple presentation of birth rates (Fig. 7.13). The graph using the actual numbers shows a steady increase between 1986 and 1989. Population increases during the same period put the numbers in context (Fig. 7.14).

Population and dollars change with time, and both should be factored into a study of those changes. Inflation changes the value of money. Nominal dollars should be converted to real or inflation-adjusted dollars (see Chapter 6 for the conversion formula). Again, Needles demonstrates the effect on charts about the federal deficit (Fig. 7.15). In nominal dollars, the deficit hits new highs almost yearly. But when

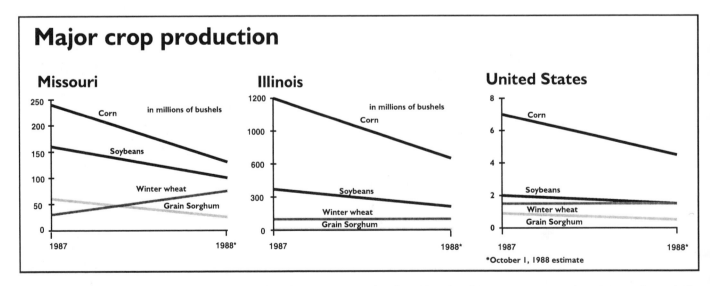

7.16 When you run graphs with different y axis values next to each other, the visual message may not be what you intended. Only a careful reader would realize that the y values are different on each of the three graphs.

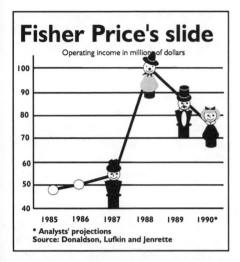

Fisher Price's slide

Operating income in millions of dollars

* Analysts' projections
Source: Donaldson, Lufkin and Jenrette

7.17 The drawings attract attention, but where, precisely, are the date marks?

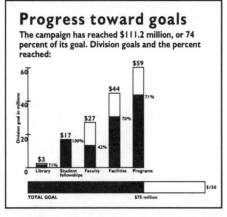

Progress toward goals

The campaign has reached $111.2 million, or 74 percent of its goal. Division goals and the percent reached:

7.18 By charting percentages, the actual amount raised and the comparison to the other divisions is distorted. Student fellowships, for instance, is completed, but at 17.2 million, it is only a third of the program activities' goal.

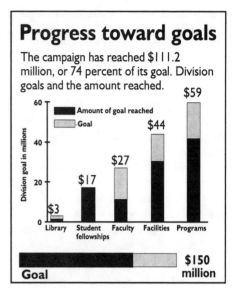

Progress toward goals

The campaign has reached $111.2 million, or 74 percent of its goal. Division goals and the amount reached.

7.19 By using a layered chart, you can accurately show visually both the goals and the portion raised.

the deficit is adjusted for inflation, it is then possible to see that the deficit is a "record" only in raw, not real numbers. The frequent debate about the minimum wage should be put in the same context. In 1938 the minimum wage was created at 25 cents. If it had kept pace with inflation, it would have been $6.34 in 1968. Yet the debate was whether to raise it to "record" levels of $4.25 in 1991.

Comparing charts with different y interval values

Charts that are accurate by themselves take on a different meaning when placed next to others to compare the data. If comparisons are to be made, the y axes must have the same value line. When they don't, casual readers—and sometimes even careful readers—will get the wrong message. In Figure 7.16, the y axis values top off at 250 million in the Missouri chart, 1,400 million in the Illinois chart and 8 billion in the U.S. chart. Each chart is accurate by itself, but stacked next to each other, the visual message is that Missouri produced more corn than Illinois in 1987. In fact, Illinois produced nearly five times as much. It also appears that the United States produced only slightly more corn than Illinois. The Missouri and Illinois charts could be adjacent if the y values were the same. The national chart needs to be separated.

Creating a visual distortion

Author Edward Tufte calls graphics overwhelmed by decoration "ducks," after a building constructed in the shape of a duck. "Chartjunk" reverses the process of decorating a building to building a decoration (Tufte 1983). The artwork incorporated into the Fisher-Price line chart in Figure 7.17 makes it impossible for the reader to determine how much was earned. Chart journalists should move the art off the data. Art, in the form of an icon, can be used to create the environment for the chart without overwhelming the message.

The problem is compounded when the art itself is substituted for

How to distort

The non-zero baseline exaggerates the apparent ratio of heights. The true ratio is 1.5 to 1 but a baseline of 50 makes the ratio look like 4 to 1.

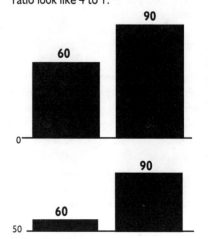

7.20

■■■■■■"■■■■■■

Now I find it very difficult to lead other people to do the sort of work I was doing. If somebody does what I consider a cute little drawing around a set of statistics, I'm going to judge that more harshly than if I had done it myself. I find myself here at Time stopping people from doing such things and arguing that I can't see the information. I wonder, if somebody had been that tough with me, whether I would have done what I did in the first place. When I was first here, there was nobody above me—I was brought in as the new look in statistics. I look back now and shudder at some of the work I did then. I should have been edited a lot more than I was. Although I was trying to make things understandable, sometimes I wasn't successful. I'm much tougher on my staff here than anyone was on me. After a while I started to listen to what I was saying—"You're here to be an information artist, not an illustrator."

So, I'm changing my tune. Even as I talk to you, I find it odd that I'm saying this. Maybe I'm growing up and listening to myself and to others arguing, "Readers are intelligent and can pick out meaning from statistics if you give it to them. They will take the time to do it and don't need a picture." That's quite a change from what I'd been advocating before. This doesn't mean that if someone comes up with a brilliant visual metaphor, that I will not run it. If a graphic does those three things—tells people what it's about, gives them the information, and explains the information—you've got a winner. However, doing those three things is harder and happens successfully less often than I thought.

There is considerable value in a picture, as opposed to a daunting set of statistics. I purposely avoid the word "boring." Statistics are not boring—they are daunting. People are scared of statistical displays, they don't have the time to study them and don't think they will understand them. So, a picture may help. I don't think that's patronizing. The value of the picture, as opposed to decoration, is to help people understand. But, if the picture takes over and obscures the information, then it would be better not to have it at all even if you risk losing the reader.

Nigel Holmes
Time

bars. Art expands proportionally. The surface area expands geometrically while the height grows mathematically. Look back at Figure 7.11 for an example. Needles points out that although 70 percent is 3.5 times larger than 20 percent, the surface area of the French cooling tower is about eight times larger.

Visual distortion also occurs when the art is used improperly to represent the numbers. In Figure 7.18, the numbers atop each column are not the same, even though the columns are the same height. The filled area represents the percentage of the goal attained. It could be a mistake or it could be a deception to deflect attention away from the fact that the goals for the various divisions are unequal. The correction shows the proper relationships (Fig. 7.19).

Changing the zero base

On column charts, the base must start at zero. When it doesn't, the space between the top of the bars inaccurately reflects the proportion. In Figure 7.20, the zero baseline shows one relationship; the non-zero baseline makes the difference look almost three times as large. A non-zero baseline works on line charts because the visual message is in the line or between the lines, not between the x axis and the line.

Mapping errors

Large maps have built-in inaccuracies that smaller ones don't have. Drawing the world on a flat surface is like trying to flatten an eggshell without breaking it. You can't portray three-dimensional objects in two dimensions. If the shapes of oceans and land masses are correct, the area is incorrect. If the area is correct, the shapes are incorrect. Mapmakers can't solve this problem, but they should recognize it. One solution is to omit the scale bar or label it for use only along the equator.

Another problem with large-area maps is showing routes. Take a look in the back of an airline magazine the next time you fly. Air routes are represented as ellipses rather than straight lines. Planes may be taking the shortest route, but because of the earth's curved surface, the route is curved. To produce more accurate large-scale maps, it is advisable to have access to an electronic mapping syndicate service.

Letters are to be read, not to be used as practice models for designers or to be molded by caprice or ignorance into fantastic forms of uncertain meaning. They are not shapes made to display the skill of their designers; they are forms fashioned solely to help the reader.

Frederic Goudy
TYPE DESIGNER

8. UNDERSTANDING TYPE

Type is to the graphic designer what the bat is to the baseball player. When a batter hits a home run, the fans appreciate the feat; they don't ask what kind of bat was used. When a graphic designer successfully completes a publication, readers appreciate the pleasing presentation and the ease of reading; they don't ask the name of the typeface or the mechanics of reproducing it.

Because approximately 80 percent of the printing area in a newspaper consists of type, its selection and use is critical to successful communication. Yet, perhaps because it is so pervasive, type is often overlooked for the flashier tools of the designer: illustration, white space and color. The headline face, the text type and the design of the advertisements, which are primarily type, give each publication a personality. The classic look of the Frankfurter Allgemeine is constructed on type and white space (Fig. 8.1). Despite the importance of type, there are few typographers in newspapers or magazines. Consultants and designers may perform this function on a hit-or-miss basis, but often the day-to-day use of type is left to personnel with inadequate training. Even so, given the proper type and instructions on how to use it, local staff members should be able to produce a daily or weekly product that is fundamentally sound typographically. Professionals who handle type every day should understand the basics of its use. This chapter, the first of three on typography, discusses the design, language, grouping and identification of type. Chapter 9 reviews legibility considerations, and Chapter

8.1 This paper from Germany uses typography in the classic sense. Leading, inter-letter spacing and white space are tightly controlled to enhance the type.

10 shows how to use type.

Type design

Although the Chinese and Koreans first invented movable type, Johann Gutenberg was the first Western printer to use it. Furthermore, Gutenberg solved the problem created by the different widths of letters. Understandably, his first typeface was a modified reproduction of the handwriting used to produce sacred works such as the Bible. From that point, printers modified type to reflect their tastes and cultures.

Although type was the first mass-produced item in history, nearly four centuries passed after Gutenberg produced his type before a typecasting machine was invented, and it was not until the end of the 19th century that the entire process became automated. By then, many of the great typefaces still commonly used today had already been designed.

William Caslon, for instance, was an English typographer who lived from 1692 to 1766. The rugged but dignified Caslon typeface has staying power. It was used in the American Declaration of Independence and the Constitution. More than 100 years after it was cut, it became popular again following its use in the first issue of Vogue magazine. In 1978, designer Peter Palazzo brought it back once more in modified form when he redesigned the Chicago Daily News. In 1750, another Englishman, John Baskerville, designed a face known by his name and still commonly used today. Giambattista Bodoni, an Italian printer, developed a face in 1760 that was the standard headline in American newspapers from the post–World War II era through the 1970s. In 1896, another Englishman, William Morris, reacting to the conformity brought about by the Industrial Revolution, produced The Works of Geoffrey Chaucer. The Chaucer type he designed, combined with specialized initial letters and artistry in design and printing, reawakened an interest in printing as an art form. Because his typefaces are highly stylized and personal, they are not used today for mass-circulation publications, but his work influenced more than a generation of designers.

One of the people Morris influenced was Frederic Goudy, the first great American type designer. Goudy, founder of the Village Press, cut 125 faces, many of which are still used today. Goudy lived until 1946. At one time, the types he designed, including the one carrying his name, dominated the American press. They fell out of favor after World War II, but when the 1980s brought a revival of the classic faces, Goudy was dusted off.

The 1900s brought a host of typefaces. Some were new; others were modifications of classic faces. Century Expanded was cut in 1900, Cheltenham in 1902, Cloister Old Style in 1913, Baskerville Roman in 1915 and Garamond in 1918. The interval between the wars produced two startling new faces. Paul Renner designed Futura in 1927. Stanley Morrison produced Times New Roman for the Times of London in 1932. In 1972 the Times switched to Times Europa because it printed better on the newsprint it was using. Because of offset printing and improvements in the typeface from digital typesetting, the newspaper switched back to Times New Roman in the mid-1980s. In 1991, the Times changed once again, this time to Times Millennium. Futura, a geometric sans serif face that is monotone in cut, ushered in an era of sans serif faces that brought us the popular Univers and Helvetica in the mid-1950s. Hermann Zapf is our most successful contemporary designer. In the 1950s, he designed both Optima and Palatino, the face used in the classic redesign of the New York Herald Tribune.

Most typefaces commonly used by newspapers and magazines today were designed before World War II. Tastes in type run in cycles, and some faces that are more than 200 years old are brought back periodically and modified to take advantage of technological innovations and modern tastes. The "modern faces," such as Helvetica, Univers and Optima, already are more than 40 years old, but they are mere infants in the life span of a typeface. The newspapers that rushed to embrace the modern look of Helvetica in the 1970s found themselves slightly out of step with fashion in the 1980s when the country began to turn back to traditional values. If the ubiquitous Helvetica is put on the shelf, it will be dusted off again later—maybe in 20 years, maybe in 50—just as the Caslons, Goudys and Bodonis keep reappearing.

The introduction of photocomposition essentially stopped the design of new typefaces for use in general-circulation publications. Foundries were busy converting their libraries to negatives for the new photocomposition machines. Most of the work involved modifying existing faces to take advantage of the new technology but still adhere to copyright laws. Some of the alterations have distorted the type and lowered the quality. Digital typesetting ushered in the present era. Now that the old faces have been digitized, new ones are coming out in waves. Software programs allow even amateurs to design typefaces or create hybrids out of existing faces. As could be expected, when ama-

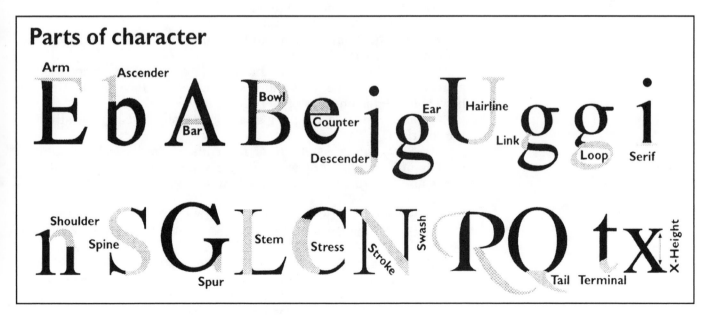

8.2 The screened portion of the letter is the area identified. Designers should acquire a vocabulary of typography the same way that copy editors acquire a vocabulary of grammar.

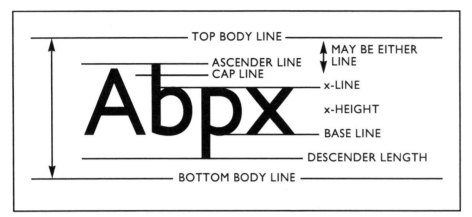

TOP BODY LINE
ASCENDER LINE
CAP LINE
MAY BE EITHER LINE
x-LINE
x-HEIGHT
BASE LINE
DESCENDER LENGTH
BOTTOM BODY LINE

8.3

teurs gain access to the technology, the results are inconsistent at best, horrible at worst.

If you're going to be a writer or editor, you must learn grammar. If you're going to be a designer, you must learn typography. This chapter is a start.

Parts of letters

The basic unit of all type designs is the individual letter. Just as we classify trees by the bark, leaves or needles, and shape, we classify type by its individual parts. Figure 8.2 provides a detailed examination of a piece of type. You need to acquire a working knowledge of most of these terms. Here is the basic vocabulary.

1. X-line: literally, the top of the lowercase x or any other lowercase letter before the ascender (Fig. 8.3).

2. Base line: the bottom of the lowercase x or of any lowercase letter without its descender.

3. X-height: the size of the lowercase x. X-height is the type's optical size; point size is its mechanical size. Types that are the same size look larger or smaller because the extenders are longer or shorter.

4. Ascender: that portion of the lowercase letter extending above the x-line. Capital letters are all the same and do not have ascenders or descenders.

5. Descender: that portion of the lowercase letter extending below the base line, or bottom, of the letter x.

6. Extenders: ascenders and descenders.

7. Bar: a horizontal or slanted line connected at both ends, such as is found in the letters e and H.

8. Bowl: the curved stroke that creates a hollow space enclosed by a stroke. The letters o, e, R and B, among others, have bowls. How the bowl is formed is one way of identifying a typeface.

9. Ear: on most faces, the g and r have a small distinctive stroke at the top right.

10. Serif: the cross-stroke at the ends of the basic letter form. A serif is ornamental, but when properly done it enhances legibility. Serifs are the principal means of giving a typeface a distinct personality.

11. Stroke: the primary part of the letter.

12. Stress: the thickness of a curved stroke, the shading of the letter.

13. Loop: a mark of distinction. The letters o, c and e, particularly, may slant off center. Sometimes the bottom of the g is left open.

14. Terminal: the distinctive finish to the stroke on sans serif (without serifs) type. It may be straight, concave or convex.

With these terms in mind, let's look at Bodoni Bold (Fig. 8.4). Bodoni is most easily recognized by the distinctive tail of the Q, which drops from the center and slopes to the right. The serifs join on the diagonal stroke of the W. The T has drooping serifs. The O,

Bodoni is a modern

8.4 Bodoni, a beautiful typeface, has a weaknesses as a headline face because of its hairlines.

U and C are symmetrical; there is no distinctive loop. The strokes are composed of consistent thick and thin lines to give each letter a precise, balanced quality. The stress of such letters as O, G and P is vertical rather than rounded. The serifs attach to the strokes at right angles. Because of its classic and elegant feel, Bodoni appears often as the display type in fashion stories and advertisements.

The language of type

The basic vocabulary of type doesn't end with the individual letters. You'll also need to be familiar with the following terms:

Uppercase: CAPITAL LETTERS. In metal type days when type was kept in cases, the capitals were kept in the top or upper case. Most type appears in "U&Lc," or upper and lowercase.

Small caps: small capital letters, usually about 75 percent of normal.

Text type: type below 14 points.

Display type: type 14 points and larger.

Leading: the horizontal space between the lines.

Letter spacing: the space between letters.

Word spacing: the space between words.

Mechanical spacing: equal spacing between letters based on the farthest right hand part of the letter to the farthest left hand part of the next letter (Fig. 8.5).

Optical spacing: setting the distance between letters so they look evenly spaced.

Kerning: selective reduction of white space between irregularly shaped letters to create even optical spacing (Fig. 8.6).

Inter-letter spacing: applying principles of kerning to display type. Tracking: fixing the spacing between letters in a block of type to achieve a certain color or density. Kerning applies to pairs of letters or a character and punctuation; tracking applies to a block of text.

Ligature: two or more characters designed as a single unit. Common ligatures include the combinations of ff, ffi, fi, ffl and fl. A ligature has to be created by design, not by kerning.

Color: the density of type in blocks of copy. Type with monotone strokes will have a darker color than type with thicks and thins, which look grayer in large amounts of text type.

Lowercase alphabet length (LCA): measurement of the width of a font. The length of an entire lowercase alphabet of a single type size is called the lowercase alphabet length. The width of a type is important when considering legibility and the amount of type that will fit on a line. The LCA is figured on a character per pica (CPP) basis and computed by counting the average number of letters that will fit in a given

Normal kerning

Moderate kerning

Tight kerning

8.5 Mechanical spacing leaves too much space between some letter combinations, such as "Wa."

Most-common kerning pairs

Yo We To Tr Ta Wo Tu Tw Ya
Te P. Ty Wa yo we T. Y. TA
PA WA

8.6 These letter combinations always need to be kerned.

horizontal space and dividing by the number of picas. Thus, if the average number of characters that will fit on a 10-pica line is 32, the CPP is 3.2. If the average is 32.45, retain the fraction. Unfortunately, even though the method of computing the alphabet lengths and CPP is standard, the results are not because of the way type producers have altered the face and spacing between letters. The CPP for Baskerville with italic when manufactured by Linotype in 10 point is 2.68; manufactured by Intertype, 2.35; and manufactured by Monotype, 2.48. When comparing the CPP counts of typefaces, it is critical for the designer to know the type manufacturer.

Font width: To describe variations of the width of a font, typographers use the terms ranging from condensed to expanded. In this computer age, the terms narrow, thin and wide are sometimes applied. In some software programs, you apply the squeeze command. However, this does not condense type so much as it squishes it. Each font, whether condensed or expanded, roman or italic, has its own proportions. When a software program is asked to condense or expand or to create an italic out of a sans serif, it simply squishes, stretches or pushes the type forward. None of the proportions or niceties of the typeface are preserved. It is preferable to buy the members of the family to ensure good typography.

Roman: letters straight up and down.

Italic: letters slanted right.

Oblique: sans serif type slanted like italic but without redrawing it.

Weight: the degree of thickness of the letter strokes. Weights range from light to bold, although popular types will offer several weight choices. Book weight is so-named because that is the weight the designer intends for mass use in text sizes.

Type grouping

To enable typographers to communicate about type and ensure harmonious use, type has been organized into races, families and fonts.

RACES

The race is the broadest system of categorization. Unfortunately, typographers dont' agree precisely on the number of categories. Having too many leaves typographers splitting hairlines, but having too few forces them to lump dissimilar type into the same race. The discussion in this book follows the guidelines of the authoritative Composition Manual, published by the Printing Industry of America. The six races are roman, square serif, sans serif, text letter, cursive and ornamental.

ROMAN

The term roman has been used to refer to the straight up-and-down design of the type as opposed to the italic or slanted-right version. Originally, that was an incorrect use of the term, but it has became so common that it is now widely accepted. For the purpose of identifying races, roman is also a classification of type that has serifs and thick-and-thin curved strokes, which distinguish it from another serif race, the square serifs. Some typographers believe roman is too general a designation and refer instead to five categories within the race: old style, modern, transitional, clarendon and glyphic. Each will be considered under the broad umbrella of roman.

Old style looks more informal because the letters are asymmetrical. The horizontal and upward strokes are light and downward strokes are heavy, but the differences between the strokes are minimal. The serifs appear to be molded or bracketed onto the stems. Garamond, for instance, is an old style typeface that bespeaks tradition and dignity (Fig. 8.7). Other well-known old style faces include Times Roman, Caslon and Janson.

Modern typefaces were introduced by Bodoni in 1760. His type was symmetrical and therefore had a more formal look. It also showed the influence of geometric forms. It is more precise than old style and has greater degrees of difference between the thick and thin strokes. The serifs were thin, straight lines (Fig. 8.8). As other faces were designed, the bowls became rounded, and the serif brackets were sharpened. Moderns have a vertical weight stress.

As a category, transitional was created when succeeding generations of designers produced type that took characteristics from both old style and modern. Baskerville and Caledonia are generally classified as transitional

Garamond is an old style

8.7

Bodoni is a modern

8.8

Baskerville is transitional

8.9

New Century Schoolbook

8.10

Optima is a glyphic

8.11

Lapland is a square serif

8.12

(Fig. 8.9). The weight contrast is more than old styles but less than moderns. They all have attributes of both old style and modern.

Clarendons have big, solid serifs. The strokes are full. Bookman and New Century Schoolbook are Clarendons (Fig. 8.10), as is the typeface called Clarendon.

Glyphic refers to a group of type that often is mistaken for sans serif. They are classified under roman because the terminals are flared or triangular shaped. They have a lapidary feel. Friz Quadrata and Optima are glyphics (Fig. 8.11).

SQUARE SERIF

On square serif type, the strokes are nearly monotone in weight, and as the name suggests, the serifs are rectangles. Many of the square serifs have Egyptian-sounding names, such as Karnak (Fig. 8.12). Square serifs were first designed about 1815 to be used in advertising. They preceded sans serif by about 30 years.

SANS SERIF

Befitting the mood of the day, the 1850s brought sans serif type. Sans is the French word for "without," and the type is without serifs. The type is easily identified not only by the lack of serifs but also by the uniformity in the strokes (Fig. 8.13). Sans serif type became popular in the 1920s. The purpose of the design was to eliminate all flourishes, including serifs, and produce a type that served the function of communicating without any of the aesthetic benefits that serifs offer. In the United States the sans serif race was also referred to as gothic. The most popular sans serifs are Helvetica, Futura, Univers and Franklin Gothic.

TEXT LETTER

This race, also called black letter, has type that is medieval in appearance. It is the style that Gutenberg used to print the Bible. Its designers were influenced by Gothic architecture, which was popular at the time. Cloister Black, Old English and Goudy Text are examples of this race (Fig. 8.14).

CURSIVE OR SCRIPT

This race is also self-descriptive. The type is a stylized reproduction of formal handwriting (Fig. 8.15) and is most often found in formal announcements of events such as weddings and anniversaries.

ORNAMENTAL OR NOVELTY

This race is a catchall for type that has been designed to portray a particular mood or emotion (Fig. 8.16) and is so unusual it cannot be used for other messages. The type is most frequently used in posters, movie advertising, cartoons and display advertising. Newspapers occasionally use a novelty type on features to reflect the content.

FAMILIES

Like all families, type families share the same last name. Although they share genetic similarities, each family member also has unique characteristics. The differences are based on width, weight and form. Some families have several members (Fig. 8.17); Caslon has at least 15, Cheltenham at least 18, and Univers nearly 30. The widths range from condensed to expanded; the weights from light to black. Most types have two different forms—roman and italic. When the type is available in special form, such as an outline or shadow version, it generally is classified under the novelty race.

FONTS

A font is a complete set of one member of a family. Nearly all families have fonts that include uppercase and lowercase type, punctuation and symbols; some include an alphabet of small caps. Some also have ligatures, such as

8.13

8.14

8.15

8.16

8.17 Helvetica, like nearly all typefaces, has a variety of weights and forms. These are just a few.

8.18 A font is all the letters, numbers and characters of a given typeface.

ITC Weidemann Medium

abcdefghijklmnopqrstuvwxyz
ABCDEFGHIJKLMNOPQRSTUVWXYZ 1234567890
ABCDEFGHIJKLMNOPQRSTUVWXYZ1234567890

Excellence in typography is the result of nothing more than an attitude. Its appeal comes from the understanding used in its plannin g; the designer must care. In contemporary advertising the perfect integration of design elements often demands unorthodox typog raphy. It may require the use of compact spacing, minus leading, unusual sizes and weights; whatever is needed to improve appeara nce and impact. Stating specific principles or guides on the subject of typography is difficult because the principle applying to one jo 6 b may not fit the next. No two jobs are identical even though the same point sizes and typefaces are used. It is worthwhile to empha

Alphabet Length 68

abcdefghijklmnopqrstuvwxyz
ABCDEFGHIJKLMNOPQRSTUVWXYZ 1234567890
ABCDEFGHIJKLMNOPQRSTUVWXYZ1234567890

Excellence in typography is the result of nothing more than an attitude. Its appeal comes from the understanding used in its planning; the designer must care. In contemporary advertising the perfect integration of design eleme nts often demands unorthodox typography. It may require the use of compact spacing, minus leading, unusual si zes and weights; whatever is needed to improve appearance and impact. Stating specific principles or guides on 7 the subject of typography is difficult because the principle applying to one job may not fit the next. No two jobs a   79

abcdefghijklmnopqrstuvwxyz
ABCDEFGHIJKLMNOPQRSTUVWXYZ 1234567890
ABCDEFGHIJKLMNOPQRSTUVWXYZ1234567890

Excellence in typography is the result of nothing more than an attitude. Its appeal comes from the understanding used in its planning; the designer must care. In contemporary advertising the perfe ct integration of design elements often demands unorthodox typography. It may require the use of compact spacing, minus leading, unusual sizes and weights; whatever is needed to improve appear 8 ance and impact. Stating specific principles or guides on the subject of typography is difficult becau   90

abcdefghijklmnopqrstuvwxyz
ABCDEFGHIJKLMNOPQRSTUVWXYZ 1234567890
ABCDEFGHIJKLMNOPQRSTUVWXYZ1234567890

Excellence in typography is the result of nothing more than an attitude. Its appeal come s from the understanding used in its planning; the designer must care. In contemporary advertising the perfect integration of design elements often demands unorthodox typo graphy. It may require the use of compact spacing, minus leading, unusual sizes and wei 9 ghts; whatever is needed to improve appearance and impact. Stating specific principles   102

abcdefghijklmnopqrstuvwxyz
ABCDEFGHIJKLMNOPQRSTUVWXYZ 1234567890
ABCDEFGHIJKLMNOPQRSTUVWXYZ1234567890

Excellence in typography is the result of nothing more than an attitude. Its app eal comes from the understanding used in its planning; the designer must care In contemporary advertising the perfect integration of design elements often d emands unorthodox typography. It may require the use of compact spacing, mi 10 nus leading, unusual sizes and weights; whatever is needed to improve appear   114

abcdefghijklmnopqrstuvwxyz
ABCDEFGHIJKLMNOPQRSTUVWXYZ 1234567890
ABCDEFGHIJKLMNOPQRSTUVWXYZ1234567890

Excellence in typography is the result of nothing more than an attitude I ts appeal comes from the understanding used in its planning; the desig ner must care. In contemporary advertising the perfect integration of d esign elements often demands unorthodox typography. It may require t 11 he use of compact spacing, minus leading, unusual sizes and weights; w   124

abcdefghijklmnopqrstuvwxyz
ABCDEFGHIJKLMNOPQRSTUVWXYZ 1234567890
ABCDEFGHIJKLMNOPQRSTUVWXYZ1234567890

Excellence in typography is the result of nothing more than an att itude. Its appeal comes from the understanding used in its planni ng; the designer must care. In contemporary advertising the perfe ct integration of design elements often demands unorthodox typ 12 ography. It may require the use of compact spacing, minus leadin   136

8.19 ITC's Weidemann was designed with a large x-height but also a high count of characters per line to make it an efficient text choice.

ff, ffi, fi, ffl, and fl. Others have special symbols (Fig. 8.18).

Application

How this knowledge of type classifications, vocabulary and history are applied is illustrated in the International Typeface Corp. (ITC) discussion of Weidemann (Fig. 8.19). Noting that the typeface was commissioned in Germany by the German Bible Society, ITC reported in its publication (U&lc 1983) that one of the primary goals was to make a space-efficient type without sacrificing legibility. Thus, "Weidemann was created with relatively narrow character proportions, a larger than average x-height, distinct character design traits, and optically even stroke thickness." ITC reported that compared with Times Roman, Weidemann can be read more rapidly. The designer, Kurt Weidemann, echoed old style roman design characteristics. His reasons, according to ITC, were:

1. The bracketed serifs of old style faces help to retain baseline definition (Fig. 8.20).

2. The relatively even strokes in old style roman letter forms ensure a uniform typographic color, which results in less show-through on lightweight paper stock.

3. An old style face permits more distinctive shapes of individual letters than many other serif types.

Identifying type

The Printing Industry of America has compiled the following list of 10 ways to identify typefaces:

1. Serifs. All type immediately

8.20 Note the different ways that the serifs can be bracketed to the stem.

breaks down into serif or sans serif, but the differences between types with serifs can be startling.

2. Terminations on top of the strokes of E, F, or T.

3. Weight of strokes. Are they thick or thin, and how much contrast is there?

4. Shape of the rounded characters BCGOPQbcgopq. Are the bowls symmetrical or balanced diagonally? How is the weight distributed (Fig. 8.21)?

5. Length of descenders.

6. Formation of terminals on J and F. The curves or angles are good clues to the identity of the letter.

7. Formation of the ears of the letters. Look particularly at the r.

8. The shapes of key letters of the font. Look at a, e, g, r, m and H (Fig. 8.22).

9. General proportions of the letter. Is the bar of the H located above, below or at center? Are the letters equally proportioned or do they tend to be condensed or extended?

10. Overall appearance on the page when the type is massed. What is its personality?

Bog

Garamond

Bog

Times New Roman

Bog

Palatino

Bog

Bookman

8.21 All these typefaces are from the Roman race, but notice the difference in the shapes of the rounded characters.

Bodoni

Bookman

Garamond

Lubalin Graph Book

8.22 "R's," like any letter, come in many different styles. Each offers a different personality and level of legibility.

Most graphics editors and designers have a working knowledge of six to 12 typefaces. For additional faces, they consult a type book. It is not necessary to memorize large numbers of typefaces, but you should become acquainted with those most commonly used in newspapers and, especially, the publications you read regularly. The popular sans serif Helios, for instance, is identifiable by its uniform but dignified cut. It has short extenders, a square dot on the lowercase i and j, a distinctive capital G and a straight tail on the capital Q, which is slanted and starts on the inside of the bowl. The stem of the a curves

ABCDEFGHIJKLMNOPQRSTUVWXYZ
abcdefghijklmnopqrstuvwxyz–Gill Sans

ABCDEFGHIJKLMNOPQRSTUVWXYZ
abcdefghijklmnopqrstuvwxyz– Helvetica

8.23 Look closely, and you will find differences between these two sans serif faces. Gill sans is more rounded. Check the uppercase "G." Gills sans is used in cutlines throughout this book.

at the baseline.

Compare Triumvirate, another name for Helios, with another popular sans serif face, Univers (Fig. 8.23). Univers also has a uniform cut, square dots over the i and j and short extenders. However, Univers has a sloped bracket at the cross-stroke of the t, does not have the finial or line extending downward from the G, and the tail of the Q does not start within the bowl and is lower on the letter. The stem of the a finishes at the baseline.

Unfortunately, type identification is becoming increasingly difficult because of the barely distinguishable alterations performed for computer fonts. There is no effective protection for new typeface designs in the United States. The popular Helvetica, for instance, is produced with little or no variation under the names of Vega, Boston, Claro, Corvus, Galaxy, Geneva, Triumvirate, Helios, Swiss, American Gothic, Ag Book, Newton and Megaron. Optima is marketed by different manufacturers under the name of Chelmsford, Oracle, Orleans, Musica, Orsa and Zenith. Palatino also has several imitators, including Palateno, Elegante, Patina, Andover, Palladium, Pontiac, Michelangelo and Sistina. By whatever name they are known, however, they are still Helvetica, Optima and Palatino.

Reading is the most important part of the whole design. If you limit this—if you slow down the speed of reading—I think it is wrong.

Hermann Zapf
TYPE DESIGNER

9. LEGIBILITY OF TYPE

For more than 70 years, researchers have been studying the variables that affect legibility. The findings have been enlarged significantly since Miles Tinker's pioneering studies in the 1920s. His work in later years, notably with D. G. Paterson, added significantly to the body of knowledge about legibility. The Merganthaler Linotype Co. published The Legibility of Type in 1936 and a similar volume in 1947 in an attempt to distribute the research findings from the ivory tower to the grass-roots level. G. W. Ovink published "Legibility, Atmosphere-Value and Forms of Printing Types" in 1938. Sir Cyril Burt published the landmark "Psychological Study of Typography" in 1959. Tinker's 1963 "Legibility of Print" pulled together hundreds of studies that he and others had conducted. Bror Zachrisson and his colleagues at the Graphic Institute in Stockholm spent 10 years researching legibility variables and published the results in "Studies in the Legibility of Printed Text" in 1965. Rolfe Rehe compiled the results of hundreds of tests in his 1979 book "Typography: How to Make It Most Legible." The studies continue, but dissemination of the results to the people working with type daily in American newspapers still lags far behind the research.

For too long, knowledge of legibility has been buried in academic journals or limited to the province of professional consultants. The men and women who work on newspapers every day must have the opportunity to learn and understand the factors that affect legibility. The daily examples of type printed over an illustration, reversed, or set

In typography, function is of major importance, form is secondary, and fashion almost meaningless.

Aaron Burns
TYPOGRAPHER

too small, too narrow or too wide indicate that many editors have still not awakened to the need to remove typographic barriers between the reporter and reader.

Perhaps the reason that many editors are just beginning to inquire about the proper use of type is that for the first time they have more control over typesetting and the flexibility to be creative. Designers can directly control everything from letterspacing to line spacing, from weight and width choices to line length. Designers can wrap copy in any shape imaginable. This control is both liberating and daunting. It's liberating in that designs are exploding off the page with vigor. It's daunting in that designers must remember that their goal is to communicate, not decorate. If readers can't follow the type or if the design slows reading appreciably, the designer has failed. Unread type is expensive. A new era has begun, and editors are asking the right questions. The new graphics design editors will need to have the answers. This chapter distills the results of hundreds of legibility research projects, but it is not a substitute for reading the original research. Several studies and books referred to in this chapter are listed in the bibliographic sections at the end of the book.

Legibility considerations

Legibility and readability are often confused. Legibility is the measurement of the speed and accuracy with which type can be read and understood. Readability is a measure of the difficulty of the content. Legibility research has been conducted by typographers, educators, journalists, printers and ophthalmologists, all of whom have a stake in the printed word.

Some research methods are more useful for testing legibility factors than others. Visibility measurements, for example, test reading speed by controlling the amount of light. This is useful for measuring the effect of contrast. Another method resembles the familiar eye test and measures what can be read at various distances. This test is most useful for work with large advertisements such as posters and billboards. Many other testing methods have been used through the years, but the most effective has been to measure reading speed while controlling all but one variable, such as line length.

Researchers have also been able to track eye movement by using still cameras, video cameras and various electrical devices. The results show that we read in saccadic jumps, the movements from fixed point to fixed point. For a split second when the reader pauses, reading occurs. The reader scans shapes, not individual letters, and fills in the context. The right half and upper portion of the letters are most helpful in character recognition. To illustrate how readers fill in the forms, one researcher gave this *xa*ple of * se*te*ce *it* mi*si*g l*tt*rs.

The results of all these tests are not uniform. Some of the discrepancies are attributable to incomplete control of the variables, others to the different measuring methods used. The measurement of legibility is an inexact science, but there are some general principles that can be extracted from the great body of research.

Legibility is determined by at least nine factors: (1) the reader's interest in the text, (2) type design, (3) type size, (4) line width, (5) word spacing and letterspacing, (6) leading, or line spacing, (7) form, (8) contrast, and (9) reproduction quality.

In testing, reader interest is controlled by comparing results against a control group. However, the editor who is publishing a daily or weekly product is interested in the level of reader interest because it is critical not only to legibility but also to sales and customer satisfaction. By the same token, the quality of reproduction, which depends on the paper and printing process, is important. In tests, researchers can control reproduction quality carefully. Editors, unfortunately, can't. The newspaper is printed on an off-white, flimsy paper called newsprint. The texture is disagreeable, and the resulting contrast between the black type and the background is not as good as that found in magazines using coated paper. However, other variables that contribute to legibility can be manipulated with little or no expense to the newspaper. The most important factor to remember is that no one variable can be taken by itself. For instance, leading requirements change as the type and line width change; if the type size is changed, several other variables must be altered also.

TYPE DESIGN

For textual material, the basic type choice is serif or sans serif. A study conducted in 1974 for the American Newspaper Publishers Association by Hvistendahl and Kahl (1975) found that roman type was read seven to 10 words a minute faster than sans serif type. The roman (serif) body typefaces that were used included Imperial, Royal and variations of Corona; the sans serif faces were Helvetica, Futura, Sans Heavy and News Sans. The researchers found that the subjects in the study read the roman text faster, and two-thirds said they preferred it. This study confirmed the earlier work by Tinker and Paterson (1929), who found that a sans serif face was read 2.2 percent more slowly than a roman face (Dowding 1957). Robinson et al. (1971) found it took 7.5 percent more time to read sans serif than roman type. Serifs help identify small letters.

This limited research does not mean that newspapers should never use sans serif in text. The Star Tribune in Minneapolis uses sans serif throughout. It does mean, however, that editors might want to consider restricting its use to special sections or features. For instance, some newspapers that use a roman text type use sans serif in the personality, people or newsmaker features. It is also used successfully in cutlines.

Weight should be medium or slightly heavier. Readers do notice the difference. The St. Louis Post-Dispatch's ombudsman wrote, "Probably the most frequently heard request is for darker print. Many of you tell me you have to carry the paper into brighter light—maybe to a window—in order to read the text of news stories. The printing is so light as to be hard on the eyes, I keep hearing, even to the point of threats of cancellation, sometimes" (Fiquette, p. 2).

Mass circulation publications use only a handful of the roman text faces. Corona, Ionic No. 5, Imperial, Times Roman and Excelsior have proved themselves on newsprint. The Los Angeles Times chose an extended version of Paragon when it redesigned in 1980. Bookman is a

American newspaper designers produce excellent pages, using technology and color and graphics to improve a paper's appearance and appeal. Where the Americans fall short is with typography. There are few American newspapers with truly strong typography.

Rolfe Rehe
DESIGNER

distinguished text type, but some typographers shy away from it because it takes more space than most of the other commonly used faces. Other text possibilities include Cheltenham, Newton, Plantin and Century.

Like all type, these text faces have been marketed by different companies under different names. To guide your type search, here (according to Monotype) are some of the common synonyms (key to typeface manufacturers: Autologic, AI; Compugraphic, CG; Harris, HI; Itek, IT; Monotype, MO; Linotype, LI):

—Ionic No. 5 (LI), News No. 9 and No. 10 (CG), Regal (HI) and IC (IT).

—Times New Roman (MO), Times 2 New Roman (AI), English Times (CG), Times Roman (HI and LI) and TR (IT).

—Excelsior, Paragon and Opticon (LI), News No. 14 (CG), Regal (HI) and EX (IT).

—Corona and Aurora (LI), Crown and Nimbus (AI), News No. 2, No. 3, No. 5 and No. 6 (CG), Royal (HI) and CR (IT).

—Imperial (HI), Bedford and New Bedford (AI), News No. 4 (CG) and Gazette (LI).

TYPE SIZE

The proper size of type is closely related to the line width and subject matter. Tinker (1963) found that moderate type sizes (9 to 12 points) are the easiest to read. A discussion of type sizes in points, however, can be misleading. The x-height is a more accurate measurement of the actual size of the type (Fig. 9.1). When testing legibility, Poulton (1955) had to use 9.5-point Univers and 12-point Bembo to equalize the x-heights. Another researcher found that 60-point Univers Bold, 72-point Caslon Bold and 85-point Bodoni Bold were needed to get an x-height of 12.6 mm. The x-height of Linotron's 9-point Helvetica is 4.8 points, but its Caledonia is 3.8. The difference is in the length of the extenders. If there are long extenders, the distance between the base line and x-line is smaller; if there are short extenders, the size of the bowl is larger and the type appears larger. X-height, then, is the critical determinant of type size.

A smaller type size can be used for reference material such as sports scores, box summaries or classified ads because readers don't read large amounts of it. When the columns are wider, as for editorials, a larger type size may be appropriate. Depending on the x-height, 11- or 12-point type is appropriate for material set wider than 18 picas. A rule of thumb is that type can be used twice the width of its size.

Of the 314 American and Canadian newspapers that responded to a National Readership Council request for text type samples in 1980, 103 indicated their body type was less than 9 points. Many of these, however, were using Corona, which has a large x-height, or a modification manufactured under another name. Even though there have been improvements in the size of type in newspapers, more needs to be done. Editors reluctant to lose space to larger type are ignoring a significant portion of the potential audience. Poindexter (1978) found that

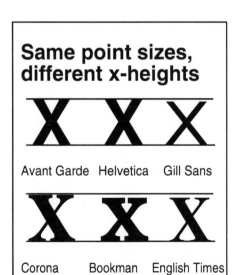

9.1 The point size is the same, but the x-height is different. The x-height creates the optical size, which is more important than the mechanical size.

8.5 percent of the nonreaders did not read newspapers because of poor eyesight. A Gannett researcher found that 16 percent of the subscribers wanted larger type and that the percentage was even higher among people over 50, who are among the most loyal newspaper readers. Another newspaper found that one-third of its readers wanted larger type (Curley, J. 1979). Newspapers, which use column widths ranging from 11 to 15 picas, should use type between 9 and 10 points with a good x-height.

One of the most popular text faces is Times, also known as English Times, Times Roman or Times New Roman. It is popular because it often is included in pagination software packages. Times has a modest x-height but an excellent lowercase alphabet length. It uses space economically. It is a good compromise between x-height and character width. However, Times is more legible at 10 points than 9. By contrast, Corona, Olympia, Nimrod and Ionic have larger x-heights and are adequate at 9 points.

LINE WIDTH

In newspapers, column widths range from slightly less than 9 picas to 15 picas, but all run bastard settings even wider. Some newspapers do not have a standard setting for pages with no ads. The St. Petersburg Times permits settings between 11 and 22.6 picas for its 9-point Century Schoolbook.

Newspaper column widths have historically been shaped by advertising rather than by legibility considerations. Advertising is sold by the column inch, and eight columns produce more column inches than five or six columns, even though the total space on the page doesn't change. Consequently, newspapers were loath to change to a six-column format even when it became commonly known that it produced a more legible line length. Such a change also required a sizable increase in advertising rates on a column-inch basis to maintain the same income per page. As a result, some newspapers converted to a nine-column advertising format and a six-column news format.

The six-column format was an improvement over the eight-column format because the line widths are between 12 and 14 picas for most newspapers. Tinker and Paterson (1929) found that a line width of 18 to 24 picas provides the easiest reading when 10-point type is used. This width provides 10 to 12 words per line, which they found to be the optimal number. Because most newspapers use type of about 9 points, the 12- to 14-pica range produces nearly the same number of words per line. Hvistendahl and Kahl (1975) found that the highest reading speed was obtained when they set roman type in 14-pica columns.

In the 1980s advertising again forced a change in column widths. In its first-ever attempt to standardize columns to attract national advertisers, the industry settled on a format that reduced column widths to about 12.2 picas in the six-column format. That width is nearly the same as it was when newspapers had eight columns but wider pages. All newspapers use bastard settings. Any setting is legible in small amounts, but when stories go beyond approximately 10 inches, then the designer should consider changing the size and leading to accom-

Regular spacing

The spacing between letters also affects the speed of reading. By tightening letterspacing, more words can be printed in the same amount of space. With proper handling, this can increase reading speed. Condensed type in particular, whether text or display, should not have a large amount of letterspacing.

Set too tight

Up to the point that the letters lose their shape, the closer the letters are, the faster we will read them because we will take in more of them during eye pause. However, every letter needs some space around it, or it loses recognizable form.

9.2 When you don't allow enough space between letters, the eye cannot quickly recognize the shapes the words. That slows reading speed.

modate a setting wider than 18 to 20 picas.

WORD SPACING AND LETTERSPACING

We read by perceiving shapes and groups of words. If words are widely spaced like this, it slows reading speed considerably. More stops are necessary, and words must be read as individual units rather than as parts of phrases. For newspaper purposes, type is read most comfortably when word spacing is between 3 to the em and 4 to the em. An em is the square space of the letter m in the type size being used. The term 3 to the em means one-third of an em spacing. Word spacing should not be greater than the leading.

The spacing between letters also affects reading speed. Tightened letterspacing allows more words to be printed in the same amount of space. With proper handling, this can increase reading speed. Condensed type in particular, whether text or display, should not have a large amount of letterspacing.

Up to the point that the letters lose their shape, the closer the letters, the faster we will read them because we will take in more of them during each eye pause. However, every letter needs some space around it, or it loses it recognizable form (Fig. 9.2).

9 pt. with no leading

The amount of leading required depends upon the width of the line, x-height and design of the type. For newspaper purposes, 9-pt. type set at 12 to 14 picas should have about I pt. of leading.

The amount of leading required depends upon the width of the line, x-height and design of the type. For newspaper purposes, 9-pt. type set at 12 to 14 picas should have about 1 pt. of leading.

9 pt. with I pt. leading

The amount of leading required depends upon the width of the line, x-height and design of the type. For newspaper purposes, 9-pt. type set at 12 to 14 picas should have about I pt. of leading.

The amount of leading required depends upon the width of the line, x-height and design of the type. For newspaper purposes, 9-pt. type set at 12 to 14 picas should have about 1 pt. of leading.

9 pt. with 3 pt. leading

The amount of leading required depends upon the width of the line, x-height and design of the type. For newspaper purposes, 9-pt. type set at 12 to 14 picas should have about I pt. of leading.

The amount of leading required depends upon the width of the line, x-height and design of the type. For newspaper purposes, 9-pt. type set at 12 to 14 picas should have about 1 pt. of leading.

9.3 Observe the difference the varying amounts of leading create for the sans serif and the serif type samples. In this example, the sans serif type has a relatively small x-height, the serif type, a large x-height. X-height is a key factor in correct leading.

LEADING

The correct amount of leading depends on the width of the line and the size and design of the type. Unleaded material generally slows reading speed (Becker et al. 1970), but too much leading can have the same effect. For newspapers that have columns in the 12- to 15-pica range and use 9-point type, Tinker (1963) found that 1-point leading is desirable. He also found that 10-point type set solid (no leading) was read faster and was more pleasing to readers than 8-point type with 2-point leading (Fig. 9.3). However, newspapers can easily use a half point of leading, which saves space without reducing legibility. Less leading, however, does change the color or airiness of the page.

There are some situations in which the designer will have to apply common sense because research does not answer all the questions. For instance:

1. Type with a large x-height

generally needs more leading than type with a small x-height. The large x-height has shorter descenders and gives the impression of less space between lines.

2. Sans serif type generally needs more leading than serif type because sans serif has a strong vertical flow, and leading will counteract this. Serif type with a strong vertical stress, such as Bodoni, also needs more leading.

3. Leading for headlines can be much tighter than for body copy because the type is large and consists of only a few words. In fact, some newspapers have gone to minus leading in headlines. For instance, try setting 24- and 30-point headlines at minus 2-point leading; type above 36 points can be set at minus 4-point leading.

FORM

The design of the type and how it is used affects legibility. For newspapers and magazine purposes, editors are primarily concerned with the legibility of text type between 9 and 12 points. Readers prefer moderate designs—neither too condensed nor too extended—for textual material. The shape of the bowls and, for roman type, the design of the serifs are also factors. The space within the bowls determines legibility (Roethlein 1912), which is why boldface is slower to read in large quantities. Boldface type has heavier lines and less white space within the letters (Fig. 9.4). If you compare a typewritten page from a typewriter that has not been cleaned against one that has, you'll see that it's far more difficult to read a page when the letters are filled in. If the serifs are too fine, they may not reproduce well on newsprint in small sizes. That's why some modern roman types such as Bodoni, with its thin serifs, are not used as text type. Among the sans serif types, the differentiation among letters is even more important than it is for roman faces. News Gothic has been successful in this regard (Poulton 1955).

Once the typeface is selected, the editor must decide how emphasis will be added. Boldface in small amounts is a good method. Italic type is another. But both of these forms are harder to read in volume. Tinker (1963) concluded that "the use of italics should be restricted to those rare occasions when added emphasis is needed." In display use, however, bold and italic forms do not affect legibility because of the size and number of words involved.

Text or headlines in all-capital letters should be avoided, except as special treatment, because it slows reading and displeases readers. Because readers perceive shapes, IT IS MORE DIFFICULT TO READ ALL-CAP MATERIAL. THE SHAPES BECOME UNIFORM, AND THE READER IS FORCED TO LOOK AT INDIVIDUAL LETTERS RATHER THAN WORDS AND PHRASES. A headline style that requires capitalization of the first letter of the first word and proper nouns only is more legible than one that requires capitalization of all words. In addition, the more capitals used, the more space required. All-cap style in text headlines is not economical. An occasional headline or title in all caps, however, has no effect on legibility.

Another aspect of form that is increasingly coming into question is whether to justify the copy to produce an even right margin or run it

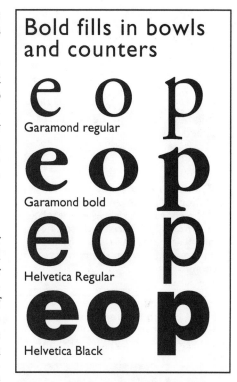

Bold fills in bowls and counters

Garamond regular

Garamond bold

Helvetica Regular

Helvetica Black

9.4 The bolder the type, the less space there is inside the bowls and counters. That means bold type is read slower than regular weight in text. In display type, the difference is negligible.

Type set justified

Type set justifed looks more formal. It is more appropriate to news content. Type set ragged right is more relaxed. It is more appropriate for soft news and features. There is no significant difference between the two in reading speed.

Type set justifed looks more formal. It is more appropriate to news content. Type set ragged right is more relaxed. It is more appropriate for soft news and features. There is no significant difference between the two in reading speed.

Type set ragged right

Type set justifed looks more formal. It is more appropriate to news content. Type set ragged right is more relaxed. It is more appropriate for soft news and features. There is no significant difference between the two in reading speed.

Type set justifed looks more formal. It is more appropriate to news content. Type set ragged right is more relaxed. It is more appropriate for soft news and features. There is no significant difference between the two in reading speed.

9.5 The choice between justified and ragged right boils down to the atmosphere you are trying to create on the page or publication. There is no difference in reading speed or the amount of space taken.

Reverse type slows reading

Type reversed slows reading speed 15 to 20 percent. The contrast is the same, so why the difference? It's because we read by shapes, not the individual letters. We don't recognize the shapes of type when it is reversed, so we have to slow down and look at the words and letters. Reverse type offers some dramatic possibilities for the designer, however. The fact that it is slower to read this copy doesn't mean you should never use it.

This paragraph is set in 11 pt. New Times Roman. You can compensate for most legibility problems by changin other variables. Even though this line length is a bit short for 11 pt. type, you can see that the copy is easier to rea. That's because the type is larger. If you want to reverse type, do it in small amounts and increase the type size. Consider running 12-24 pt. type as a teaser.

9.6 Reverse type slows reading speed dramatically, but used in larger sizes and small amounts, reverse type is fine.

unjustified (ragged right). The research to date suggests that there is no significant difference in reading speed between justified and ragged right copy (Fabrizio et al. 1967). Hartley and Barnhill (1971) found no significant differences in reading speed when the line length was determined by grammatical constraints and hyphenation was avoided whenever possible, when about 33 percent of the lines were hyphenated, or when type was set ragged right over double column formats of varying widths.

Although there may be no difference in reading speed between justified and unjustified lines, there certainly is a difference in appearance (Fig. 9.5). Justified type in narrow newspaper columns requires a great deal of hyphenation and causes variation in the space between words. Unjustified type permits the editor to standardize the word spacing and avoid illogical breaks in words. When type was hand set, unjustified type was much faster to produce, but now that a computer justifies the lines, that advantage no longer exists. The choice of justified or ragged right type is reduced to a question of personality. The Hartford Courant claims it was the first American newspaper to use ragged right throughout the newspaper.

Justified type is formal, and the orderliness of the margins gives a feeling of precision and control, factors that may enhance a news product. Ragged right type is informal, more relaxed, less precise. Consequently, it may be more appropriate for feature sections. If ragged right is chosen, it is preferable to use a modified ragged right type, which permits hyphenation whenever a line is less than an established minimum length, such as 50 percent of the potential line. This eliminates unusually short lines, which are noticed for their contrast rather than their message.

Ragged left type should be avoided except in small amounts. If the reader doesn't have a fixed left hand margin, reading speed is seriously impaired. Ragged left should never be used in textual material of any significant length.

CONTRAST

The contrast in color between the type and its background is another important factor in legibility. Black on white offers great contrast and therefore is legible. (Black on yellow is even more legible, but who wants to re-create yellow journalism?) The reverse, however, is not true. White print on a black background slows reading speed significantly (Holmes 1931). The dramatic effect that can be achieved by reversing type must be balanced against the loss of legibility. Reversed type should be used only in small quantities, such as a paragraph or two, and in larger-than-normal text type, such as at least 14 points. When it is not, the copy often becomes unreadable (Fig. 9.6).

Be careful when color tints are used over text type. Screen it back to 5 or 10 percent. If the story goes longer than 10 inches, consider increasing the type size. Black print on yellow paper and red print on white paper have scored well in legibility tests (Tinker 1963).

Newspapers are fighting an increasingly difficult battle to produce a legible product. As newsprint prices have increased, paper quality has decreased. In the mid-1970s, in an attempt to restrain increasing costs, newsprint mills dropped the basis weight of newsprint from 32 to 30. The lighter paper is easier and cheaper to make but, according to an analysis by the Knight-Ridder group, has caused expensive web breaks and reduced printing quality. Now some newspapers are using even thinner paper. Unless new inks are developed, the result for newspapers will be more show-through of ink from one side of the page to the other. This in turn will decrease legibility.

REPRODUCTION QUALITY

If the quality of newsprint continues to decrease, it will become even more difficult to control other variables, such as camera and press work, which affect the reproduction quality. Offset presses need good-quality paper. As the basis weight for newsprint decreases, the pressroom operators have to work even harder to control the amount of ink. Unfortunately, there is a limit to how much the operators can do to prevent show-through with lighter weight paper.

Although the texture of the paper does not directly affect legibility, it does affect the reader's attitude toward the product. It is almost impossible to read a newspaper these days without getting ink all over your hands and clothes. NBC television correspondent Irving R. Levine always wears gloves when he reads a newspaper, a practice that invites curious glances and comments.

9.7 Of these faces commonly used as text type, Olympian, Corona, Nimrod and Ionic have the largest x-heights. Times New Roman, Imperial and Jubilee have the best lowercase alphabet lengths.

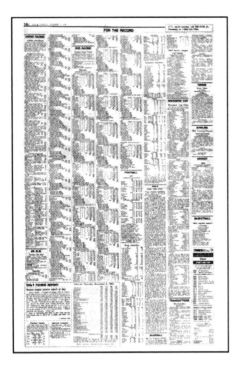

9.8 A narrower column actually increases the legibility of smaller type and makes more efficient use of the space, especially in sports agate.

Selecting text type

Although x-height, set width and color are important in selecting a display typeface, many editors put a premium on aesthetics and trends. Text type, however, is less susceptible to trends. It is the workhorse of the newspaper—not much appreciated, but if readers start to notice it, the publication is in trouble.

Earlier in this chapter, we cited several text typefaces that will work well. All of them meet the basic criteria: uniform or nearly uniform stroke widths, good x-height and shorter-than-average set width. In addition, whichever typeface is selected, editors ought to use medium weight or slightly bolder than medium weight.

Of the typefaces shown in Figure 9.7, Olympian and Corona have the best x-heights; Nimrod and Ionic are right behind them. The typefaces with the shortest lowercase alphabets are Times New Roman, Imperial and Jubilee.

The problem for newspapers is that the faces with the best x-height usually have the widest set width or longest lowercase alphabet. To alleviate this problem, many newspapers are altering the set width of the text type. That way the large x-height can be preserved while increasing the number of characters per line. Newspapers must be careful, though, not to tighten set width so much that legibility suffers.

Editors must avoid the temptation to change the size of type without considering the line width, leading and type design. Editors must eschew the dramatic at times to produce the legible. Nevertheless, every factor discussed here can be violated to a minimal extent. Type can be reversed if it is done in small quantities and in larger type. Screening type decreases contrast and thus legibility, but as a labeling device it can be effective. A 5 or 10 percent screen over type should be used only on short stories. If the story is longer and a screen is used, increase the type size. There is no doubt that all-caps type is more difficult to read than lowercase, but a two- or three-word headline in all caps is not going to affect reading speed. All these factors should be considered in relation to one another.

One application of these factors is in sports agate. (Agate is a metal-type term meaning 5 1/2 points; these days, agate simply refers to the small type used to list sports standings and results.) Most newspapers run the sports standings in 7 or 8 points. Much of the material is in tables—league standings, batting averages, etc. You can use the space more efficiently by going to a seven- or eight-column grid (Fig. 9.8). Readers who look at sports agate don't read it as they do text. They scan and select. That's why smaller type is acceptable, although it does rule out perhaps 10 percent of the readership. Beyond that, you can get more type in the same amount of space because the narrower column results in less space between tabular columns. Sans serif is the popular choice because the smaller the type, the less likely the serifs will reproduce well.

A message that we hear is soon forgotten, but the one that we see and read is more permanent because it penetrates memory on more than one level and can be referred to over and over again. This explains the growing significance of typography as a world-wide communication tool—a tool that we must improve steadily by studying it as we use it.

Will Burton
TYPOGRAPHER

10. USING TYPE

Just as the clothes we wear reveal our personality, the type used to dress our newspaper says a great deal about the publication. Type is an essential part of a newspaper's personality. Imagine reader reaction if the New York Times nameplate was set in Helvetica or the Wall Street Journal in Garamond (Fig. 10.1). Those type choices would be as inappropriate as wearing a T-shirt to a formal dinner party. Researchers have shown that laypeople are able to attribute characteristics to type similar to those used by professionals (Tannenbaum et al. 1964) and that the selection of a correct typeface appears to make more difference with some types of content than others (Haskins 1958). Benton (1979) found that the sans serif face Helvetica was not perceived as differing significantly from serif faces Garamond, Bodoni, Palatino and Times Roman, except that it was considered more modern. For years, many newspapers used a lighter type in the women's section than elsewhere. Haskins and Flynne (1974) found that even though readers ascribed feminine characteristics to certain typefaces, the use of those faces in the section did not affect readership. Not enough research has been done to determine whether readership is enhanced by appropriate typefaces, but it is generally conceded that type does have a connotative effect. That is, type communicates an emotion, a feeling. The successful designer uses type with the understanding that the form is part of the message and not merely a decoration.

This chapter will look at display type selection and use.

111

10.1 Type creates a personality for a publication. Changing that typeface changes the personality.

Headline type choices

Headlines are the bridge between the reader and the story. Readers scan 70 to 80 percent of the headlines and decks and choose which they wish to cross. Considering that readers look at about 25 percent of the stories, it is obvious that headlines play an important role in attracting readership. That's why designers should be concerned not only with the selection of the display faces but also with the formats and wording of headlines.

The selection of a proper headline typeface rests on legibility considerations, the image the editors wish to project, the tradition that needs to be preserved and the mood and lifestyle of the community. After World War II, Americans were hungry to improve their lives. A home, two cars and vacations became possible for millions. Americans trashed the old and devoured the new. During a period like that, modern-looking typefaces such as Helvetica and Univers had a strong appeal. Moods change, however.

When the oil embargo overturned the world economy in the late 1970s, Americans first elected a president who preached self-denial and then one who advocated a return to traditional values. Throughout the country, there was a strong yearning from the "good old days," and political conservatism enjoyed a revival.

The theme of the administration that took office in 1981 was "A New Beginning," but it was based on a return to classic American values. At that time, many American newspapers going through redesigns selected classic typefaces instead of the more modern ones. The Dallas Times Herald and the Los Angeles Times adopted Times New Roman. The Kansas City Star chose Goudy Bold. The Milwaukee Journal adopted Baker Argentine. All these are serif typefaces. Times change; tastes change. There is no "right" display face. Type should be chosen on the basis of its legibility, its connotative image, its credibility and the mood of the community in which the paper is published.

Type is a large part of the newspaper's personality. To check the personality of your paper, draw up a list of opposite characteristics (traditional/modern, credible/not credible, old/young, aggressive/passive, cold/warm) and put them on a scale of 1 to 7. Compare the staff's perception with that of an audience sample. This kind of measurement is also a good way to field test a proposed type change.

Assuring contrast

Once editors have decided on the image they want, they have four ways to provide contrast with the display face:

1. Choose one weight of one typeface and use size differentiation only.
2. Choose one typeface with two or more weights.
3. Choose one typeface and use italic or oblique of the same face.
4. Choose different but complementary typefaces.

A fifth option, which is not desirable, is the use of any typeface from condensed to extended. The extended styles should be avoided for the main display face because they draw attention to themselves rather than the words, and the headline count is inadequate. Some typefaces offer a beautiful condensed font that is legible. Naturally, all condensed fonts offer better headline counts. Most width variations work better as departmental identifiers and column logos than as the workhorse headlines.

SIZE DIFFERENTIATION

Traditionally, newspapers have relied on more than one size of type to relieve the dullness inherent in the use of a single weight of type. Size differentiation not only breaks the page monotony but also communicates to readers your news judgment. The more important the story, the larger the headline. The Wall Street Journal has no type hierarchy on its front page, but nearly every other newspaper in the United States does. The size of headlines depends on the newspaper's personality, whether it is a street edition or home delivery and the weight of the font. Some newspapers use 100-point type or larger for street editions; others never exceed 48-point for a lead story. Newspapers such as the St. Petersburg Times, which uses Univers Bold for its basic face, do not need as much size to carry a page. As a result, the range of type sizes used is much smaller. A typical Times front page (Fig. 10.2), for example, ranges between 30- and 60-point type. Most headlines are 36 or 42 points. However, metropolitan papers that use a medium weight could range above 80 points, and 48-, 60-, and 72-point type is seen frequently. The Baltimore Sun uses

10.2 The Times uses a bold typeface, which permits it to use smaller headlines without losing impact.

10.3 The lighter Bookman gives the Sun a lighter appearance.

10.4 Not as black as the St. Petersburg paper, not as light as the Baltimore paper, the Des Moines Register uses a bold head that creates a pleasing contrast on the page.

10.5 The weight differences between main head and deck provide a pleasing contrast on every page. Ft. Lauderdale Sun Sentinel.

10.6 Des Moines offers a contrast of both weight and form.

I - Combine at will 2 - Not a conservative choice 3 - Think again **Text**	Displays	Avant Garde Gothic	Bauhaus	Bembo	Bodoni	Bookman	Caslon	Century	Cheltenham	Franklin Gothic	Futura	Garamond	Gill Sans	Helvetica	Kabel	Korinna	Optima	Palatino	Quorum	Souvenir	Times Roman	Univers	Zapf Book
Avant Garde Gothic	1	1	1	1	1	1	1	1	1	3	1	1	2	3	1	1	1	2	1	1	1	3	1
Bauhaus	3	1	1	1	1	1	1	1	1	2	2	1	2	2	2	1	2	1	2	1	1	3	1
Bembo	1	1	3	1	1	2	2	1	1	2	2	2	1	1	2	1	1	2	1	2	1	1	1
Bodoni	1	1	1	1	1	2	2	1	1	1	1	1	1	2	3	2	1	1	1	1	1	1	3
Bookman	1	1	1	1	1	1	2	2	1	1	1	1	1	2	2	1	1	2	1	1	1	2
Caslon	1	2	2	2	1	1	2	2	1	2	2	1	1	3	2	1	2	1	2	1	1	2
Century	1	2	2	2	2	1	1	1	1	2	2	1	1	3	2	1	2	1	3	1	2
Cheltenham	1	1	1	2	2	1	1	1	1	2	1	1	1	2	1	2	2	1	1	2
Franklin Gothic	3	1	1	1	1	1	1	1	1	2	3	1	1	1	1	1	3	1
Futura	3	3	1	1	1	1	1	2	1	3	3	2	1	3	1	2	1	1	3	1
Garamond	1	2	3	1	1	2	2	2	1	2	1	1	1	2	2	1	2	2	2	1	1
Gill Sans	2	2	1	1	1	1	1	2	1	1	1	2	1	1	2	2	1	1	3	1
Helvetica	3	1	1	1	1	1	1	3	1	1	2	1	1	1	1	1	1	3	1
Kabel	2	3	1	1	1	1	1	1	1	3	3	1	3	3	2	1	2	1	2	1	1	3
Korinna	1	1	1	2	2	1	1	3	1	1	1	1	1	1	2	1	2	1	1	2
Optima	2	1	1	1	1	1	1	1	1	2	1	1	1	1	1	1	1	1	2
Palatino	1	2	3	1	1	2	2	2	1	3	2	1	1	2	2	1	1	2	2	1
Quorum	2	2	1	1	1	1	1	1	1	1	3	1	1	1	1	2	1	1	2
Souvenir	1	1	1	1	1	2	1	1	2	1	2	1	1	1	1	1	1	1	1	2
Times Roman	1	2	2	2	1	2	3	1	1	2	2	2	1	2	2	1	2	1	1	1
Univers	3	3	1	1	1	1	1	1	3	3	1	3	3	3	1	2	1	2	1	1	1
Zapf Book	1	1	1	3	2	2	2	2	1	1	1	1	1	1	2	1	2	1	2	2	1

10.7 ITC offers this chart for mixing typefaces, but it must be applied carefully in newspapers, where several typefaces sit on the same page. In a magazine or brochure, where there would be few display heads on the page, some mixtures are more acceptable.

Bookman in two weights (Fig. 10.3), both light compared with the bolder look of the St. Paul Pioneer Press (Fig. 10.4).

WEIGHT DIFFERENTIATION

If designers select a single display typeface for editorial content, contrast can be achieved from weight differentiation. One face helps to ensure the designer of concord, the blending of typographic elements to give a uniform impression. When all the type is the same weight, however, the uniformity produces dullness. The bold-light interplay offers contrast. A designer should work with at least two or three weights. The basic headline face is usually in the medium-to-bold range. Different weights are used most effectively in subordinate type—the decks, readouts and blurbs. As an alternative, some newspapers alternate bold and light or medium weights in main heads throughout the page. This approach is more suited to a paper with a vertical format. The two weights help to solve the problem of tombstoning. However, for most papers in a horizontal format, the interplay between the bold and light in the same headline shows off the contrast to better advantage (Fig. 10.5).

CONTRAST BY FORM

Some designers prefer to achieve contrast by using the italic or oblique fonts of the main headline. Normally, designers combine form and weight contrast. For instance, by using a bold main head and a medium-weight italic for the deck, the Des Moines Register offers a contrast of weight and form (Fig. 10.6).

CONTRAST BY RACE

Newspapers are starting to use typefaces from different races in their basic formats, and most are better for it. But if the proper types are not matched, the effect will be the same kind of clash that results from mixing a striped shirt with plaid slacks. The International Typeface Corp. has published a chart with suggestions for type interplay (Fig. 10.7). They are bold enough to suggest even mixing typefaces within the same race. Be careful, though. There is a difference between type use in an advertisement or a magazine spread and selecting typefaces for something as repetitive as newspaper headline formats.

To be effective in headlines, the contrast must be sharp. Timidity in type choice produces conflict. That is, typographers normally would not mix two types from the same race, such as Helvetica and Futura. The Kansas City Star uses the serif English Times in its main heads but the sans serif Franklin Gothic in its conversational decks. The mix works (Fig. 10.8).

Not all serif faces complement all sans serif faces. Look for contrasting characteristics when seeking a match. For instance, Helvetica, Univers and Franklin Gothic all have similar characteristics: the strokes are uniform and functional, the color is strong and the x-height is large. Now look in the serif race for types with contrasting characteristics. In faces such as Century, Janson and Caslon, we find classic form with enough contrast in stroke widths but not so much as to lose the thin serifs in printing. If we were to look for a matching face for the sans serif Futura, which is less bold than Helvetica, Univers and Franklin Gothic and has a smaller x-height and slightly longer extenders, we might see a match in a serif typeface such as Bookman, which has nearly uniform strokes and a solid color (Fig. 10.9).

You sometimes have occasion in feature packages to go outside your headline fonts. When you are matching text letter, cursive or ornamental, you are almost always forced to use sans serif or square serif as the complementary face. A cursive type would clash with an italic serif; they look similar enough to appear to be a mismatch. Most novelties are so stylized that a sans or square serif is needed as a calming match. Some sans serifs can be used with some square serifs also.

10.8 The Star expertly mixes type from two races. One reason it works is that the paper uses the combination consistently and does not rotate them.

Helvetica bold
English Times Italic

Bookman Bold CF
Helvetica Regular

New Baskerville
Gill Sans Bold

10.9 Look for like characteristics in typefaces from different races when you are looking for a match.

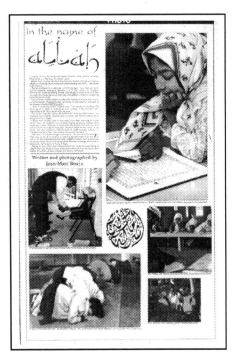

in the name of
aLLaH

Written and photographed by
Jean-Marc Bouju

10.10 The display typeface is an appropriate match with the story subject.

SPECIAL OCCASIONS

It is often difficult to decide when to deviate from the newspaper's basic face and use a type that reflects the content of a specific story. A newspaper page has several elements on it; the use of special typefaces for one or more of them invites discord. Even the magazine news weeklies stick to their basic face or faces. Like newspapers, their element count is high. Other magazines, though, have fewer stories, and their openings are often separated by several pages. Consequently, the use of type appropriate to the content of each story does not cause disharmony because each spread is a separate unit of the magazine, and the type from one story is not adjacent to the type of another.

Still, newspapers are increasingly using typefaces that match content on feature, photo pages, one-topic sections and reprints. Judicious use of special type, often a novelty face, for a story heading (Fig. 10.10) can be fun.

Working with display type

Once you have selected the headline type, turn your attention to the content. Content depends directly on the format. Headlines inform and entertain. They make history, incite emotion and cause people to laugh or cry. In most cases, however, they are dull.

Newspaper headline writers have been straitjacketed into some unusual formats. Once, it was fashionable to write headlines that exactly filled each line. At another time, headlines had one to two counts less in each succeeding line—the stepped-down format. Narrow columns and capitalization requirements further restricted the ability of headline writers to tell and sell stories. Developments in newspaper design that accompanied the introduction of cold type eased some of the restrictions but also took away an essential element of the headline—the deck. Functionalism was incorrectly interpreted to mean that decks were superfluous. The fact that decks allow headline writers to tell the story more accurately and fully was overlooked. The elimination of decks for design purposes was a case of form over content. Both form and content are served by the increased use of well-designed display type. Regardless of size, headlines contain five to seven words. That's not much space to tell and sell the story. Bring on the subordinate type.

For the most part, the decks that are reappearing are decks only in the sense that they are subordinate to the main head. Traditionally, decks were one column wide and three or more lines deep and had to be written to fit a tyrannical count system. Now, type that is subordinate to the main head appears in a variety of formats: traditional decks, conversational decks, pullout blurbs, quotes and summary boxes. The traditional deck still must be written to fit, although the format no longer is always vertical. Easier-to-write, horizontal decks are becoming common. Some of the subordinate head styles avoid the restrictions of count.

The Tampa Tribune may have been the first newspaper in the United States to use conversational decks, and now, many papers are using them. In the early 1980s, the Tribune introduced what it called nutgraphs. By whatever name—they are also known as summary decks and WHATTAA graphs (What's This All About?)—-they are an effective way of getting more display type into a small amount of space. Like the main head, traditional decks also have five to seven words. The conversational deck, usually written in 14- to 16-point type, can offer 10 to 20 words in less space. Many newspapers write them in complete sentences, not headlinese. Some introduce them with a word or two, usually in boldface:

> County ponders real estate transfer tax revenue:
> The county needs to fill a $2 million deficit,
> and to tax is being ruled out.

Some papers use bold on the first couple of words without the label introduction. Bold is used initially to draw more attention to the deck. Unlike traditional decks, which are ordered by lines with specific counts for each line, editors write conversational decks without regard for count and often without regard for the number of lines. A designer can accommodate a difference of one or two lines in 16-point type. The format has three strengths. First, it offer scanners more information than the traditional deck format. That means we ought to be able to entice more people to read the story. Second, even if scanners read the headline and deck and still choose not to read the story, they have more information than they would with the traditional format. Third, the format is space-efficient.

Many editors will tell you that the primary source of complaints from readers is headlines that are misleading, incomplete or unfair. The conversational deck allows the editor to do a better job of telling controversial stories in display type.

Blurbs, quotes and summary or highlight boxes serve a function similar to decks. Sometimes they appear along with decks; sometimes they appear in lieu of them. They represent layers of information: One layer for the hurried or less-interested reader; another layer for the reader with more interest. Look at the layered page from the Portland Oregonian (Fig. 10.11). The Tukufu story has a conversational deck, pullquote and summary box. All the other stories also have conversational decks, and the homeless story has a service-journalism feature: a "How To Help" pullout. Some newspapers call summary boxes Fast Fax, some call them At a Glance. By whatever name, they use display type to attract readership.

Summary boxes are especially useful when reporting on meetings at which several issues are discussed. The story lead will contain the issue judged by the reporter to affect the most readers. Even if the reporter is right, the most readers will still be a minority of readers. Because the headline reflects the lead, readers who are not affected by that particular issue may ignore the entire story. Readers are self-centered; they look for information that helps them. A summary box allows the designer to let more people know that the story contains information of interest to them.

Blurbs and pullquotes also entice the scanner to pause. These terms refer to the use of type (usually in the 14- to 18-point range) to highlight a quote, relate an anecdote or set the stage for confrontation.

10.11 The Oregonian aggressively layers the page so readers who are in a hurry can get something from the paper and readers who have more time can get even more.

10.12 The Morning News broke the display into small bites. The presentation is designed to serve both scanners and readers.

10.13 Type has a connotative message. That is, the design of the type comments on the message.

10.14 Have fun with word pairs. It's a good way to learn how to use type.

The Dallas Morning News used pullquotes, pictures and biographies of Dallas police chiefs and a box of the new chief's comments on several issues as pullouts (Fig. 10.12). It's a presentation that dares the reader to ignore it, even though it's on an inside page. Quotes and blurbs are good; a picture with them is even stronger.

The average reader spends about 15 to 20 minutes with the daily newspaper. Even if scanners are not enticed to read the whole story, and some will be, they should be given as much usable information as possible. Readers who find their newspapers useful are likely to continue subscribing.

Type can talk

Hear what the type is saying in Figure 10.13? The connotative message embedded in the type design adds a layer of meaning to the words. And when the message is an antonym, it snaps your head back.

Picking a typeface that matches the subject matter is tricky business. Others may not see what you see. That's because your experiences and your culture determine what you see in the typeface design. The examples in Figure 10.12 are easy ones, yet not everyone will agree on them. What if the subject were hunting, sewing, vegetables or sexual abuse? Not every subject has a typeface suited especially to it. Some subjects work with three or four choices. Don't overreach. If it isn't obvious, not only to you but to others, use your regular typeface. But if others can see what you see, have fun.

One way to test your perception is to have fun with word pairs (Fig. 10.14). Have contests with others at the design desk. See who comes up with the best solutions. When you have found the typeface you want, start working with the arrangement of the words. That's how you REALLY make type talk.

Type can scream and whisper. You can add inflection to type by using capitalization, changing the size or weight of type or varying the form from regular to italics. Most of the time, type only carries words. Once you have determined what you want to say, it's time to arrange the type. It's easier to stack type in vertical spaces. Type run horizontally echoes the news presentation. Vertical space allows you to look for alignment, tighten the fit. Start with the title. Then look for repetition of letters. Remember that uppercase eliminates the extenders and allows you to set the words tight. A combination of uppercase and lowercase allows you to connect the letters or tuck smaller lines into bigger words (Fig. 10.15).

Used to its potential, type attracts attention, tells what the story is about, converts scanners to readers, creates a focal point, adds inflection, entertains and pleases with its aesthetics. An excellent example of this is international designer Herb Lubalin's "Families" and "Marriage" (Fig. 10.16). He took something complex and made it simple. The TRUTHRUMOR pun in Figure 10.17 works because of its simplicity. It doesn't take a genius to improve the use of type in newspapers, but it does take a knowledge of the alternatives and the willingness to try.

10.15 After you've chosen the typeface, work in vertical spaces and add inflection to the type by varying the size, weight or form.

10.16 By manipulating the letters, the designer is communicating on two levels.

10.17 Type can talk in exciting ways.

Newspapers ought to distinguish themselves not just by how well they produce color, not just by how much color, but also by what the color says.

N. Christian Anderson
Orange County Register

11. COMMUNICATING WITH COLOR

 One of the enduring myths of color is that bulls get mad when they see red. In truth, bulls can't see color. They're attracted to the motion of the cape. Another myth is that lots of color attracts readers. Readers aren't attracted to color; they're attracted to color used well. Roy Peter Clark, synthesizing the Poynter Institute for Media Studies research, wrote: "It appears that color is just one of many tools that editors can use to present the news to readers in powerful ways. Color seems not to work independently, but synergistically" (Garcia and Stark 1991, p. vii).

Clearly, color sells. Media General researchers placed newspapers in boxes at seven locations. In one version, a photograph in the upper right hand corner was black and white. In the other, the photo was in color, and two blue lines ran across the page above the photo. The rest of the paper was identical. Color outsold the black-and-white version four to one (Mauro 1986). In a similar study reported by the Orange County Register, the color version outsold the black-and-white version two to one. The Poynter Institute color study found that readers like color even when it doesn't always translate into higher readership. But there were some caveats: "Color can guide the reader's eye from top to bottom on the page.... Readers prefer color over black and white when presented with a choice.... Color tints over text do make the information stand out more prominently.... The size and placement of a photograph appear to have greater importance than the question of color versus black and white" (Garcia and Stark 1991, p. 2).

11.1 When a firefighter retreated from a wildfire flung himself over a fence, a Spokane photographer captured the action in color. The newspaper, which recognized that the picture told the story, appropriately devoted most of the front page to it.

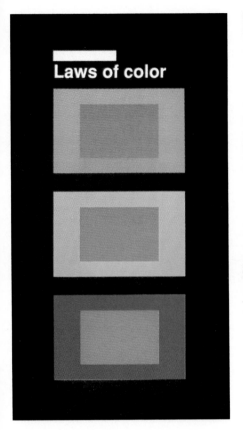

Laws of color

11.2 The red makes the orange appear more yellow and the red more blue; yellow-green appears to be green against red; but red and green, as complements, do not change each other's characteristics.

11.3 This picture is produced by the four-color process. The scanner produces the four separations in Figures 11.4-11.7.

11.4 The yellow separation.

11.5 The magenta or red separation.

11.6 The cyan or blue separation.

11.7 The black separation.

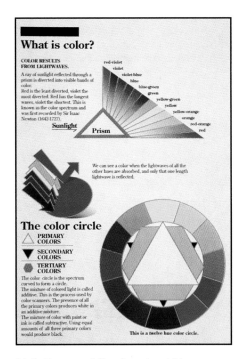

11.8 Every publication should have a color circle available to help designers choose colors.

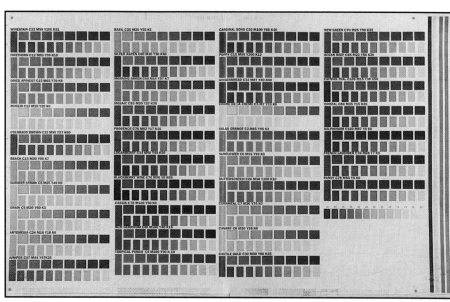

11.9 Every newspaper should produce color chart to show exactly what colors are produced on its press at specified percentages. The colors will vary from press to press and depend on the newsprint, brand of inks and the water.

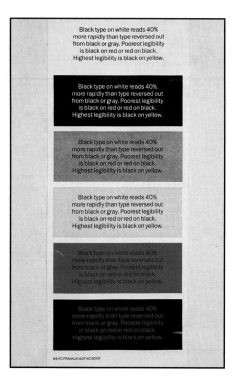

11.10 Legibility is determined, in part, by contrast. Different color combination enhance or destroy legibility. Black on yellow, for instance, is easy to read. Red on black isn't.

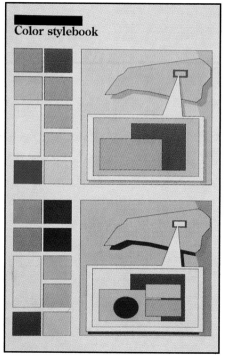

11.11 This sample stylebook shows two palettes from which to construct maps. Every newspaper should consider creating a color stylebook to achieve consistent color usage.

> *By always using the same tint of blue for the sea and the same tint of green for the land, the reader of the maps will soon accept this as the norm and go immediately to the important information.*
>
> **Peter Sullivan**
> **AUTHOR**

11.12 In a flock of sparrows, the red birds stands out. The corollary is also true. In a flock of red birds, the sparrow stands out. Good color used well makes your pages stand out.

Color in newspaper advertising gets results at a higher rate than black-and-white advertising. The results vary, but all the tests show at least a 30 percent increase in readership. Even the New York Times introduced color advertising in its advance sections in 1993. Most other newspapers had been offering it for years. The St. Petersburg Times has long been printing excellent color. The Orange County Register invested millions in 1980 and began producing high-quality color. When it began in 1982, USA Today demonstrated to publishers across the country that good color can be produced on a short deadline in multiple pressrooms. The rush to color had begun.

Color not only sells papers and affects how readers investigate a page, it also can help journalists communicate information better. Some pictures are seen more easily in color; some graphs are more understandable with color used to distinguish the lines or bars; some relationships can be established more clearly with color. Color has become a design basic, and it is up to the generation now entering the profession to learn how to use it to communicate effectively (Fig. 11.1).

Seeing color

When we see color, our brain adds the complement to create a neutral gray. Equal parts of the three primary colors create a neutral gray. The way our eye sees color and the way our brain creates the neutral gray lead to three general principles in presenting color (Fig. 11.2):

1. Color put against another color seems to absorb the complementary value of the background color.

2. A color looks lighter against a darker color and vice versa.

3. Complementary colors seem to emphasize each other when placed next to each other. They will not change each other's hue.

Vocabulary of color

Before discussing how to use color, we must first know the vocabulary.

1. Four-color process printing: color reproduction achieved by separating each color on individual pieces of film and burning them on separate printing plates. The process colors are cyan (process blue), magenta (process red), yellow and black. They are known by the abbreviations C, M, Y and K. Black is K so that it doesn't get confused with B for blue.

2. Color separation: the product of a method of separating a color print or transparency by camera, scanner or computer into its three primary colors and black.

3. Duotone: one color plus black, achieved by shooting two halftone negatives of a picture and producing two plates for the page. A duotone look can be produced by using a color screen tint behind the black halftone. This merely tints the reproduction.

4. Transparency: a positive photographic image produced on slide film. A transparency is viewed by passing light through it.

5. Color print: a color photograph produced from negative film and

commonly referred to as reflection copy because it is viewed by reflected light.

6. Spot color: a single color other than black on paper.

7. Key plate: the printing plate that prints the most detail. All of the other plates must be in register with the key plate to prevent printing what looks like two or more images.

8. Scanner: electronic device that transfers visuals into impulses. Scanners separate the four process colors of a photograph or illustration and transfer the image to a negative called a separation. Scanners are either electronic or laser.

9. Hues: a specific color. Red hues include burgundy and crimson.

10. Tints: white with a hue.

11. Shades: black with a hue.

12. Tones: white and black with a hue.

13. Value: the degree of lightness or darkness of a color.

14. Chroma: the strength of a color as compared with how close it seems to gray. Also called intensity or saturation.

15. Secondary colors: mixture of two primary colors.

16. Tertiary colors: mixture of one primary and one secondary color.

17. Cool colors: all of the hues except yellow on the left side of the color wheel.

18. Warm colors: all the hues except violet on the right side of the color wheel.

19. Analogous colors: colors adjacent to each other on the color wheel; from the same color family.

20. Complementary color: colors opposite each other on the color wheel.

Producing color

Before May 1980, the Detroit Free Press had never published color photography in its news section. Since then, the newspaper has published it nearly every day. Like the Free Press, Long Island's Newsday didn't run color until 1980. The Chicago Tribune ran spot color often, but it wasn't until the 1980s when it built a new printing plant that it started reporting the news in color. At the Tribune, the installation of offset presses preceded the frequent use of color photographs. The industry's gradual acceptance of color photography was due less to a lack of enthusiasm than to the mechanical requirements needed to produce it.

The Tribune, for instance, invested several million dollars in a new plant with new presses and new prepress systems to print color. To introduce color, the New York Times spent $450 million on a new printing plant in Edison, N.J. It began operating in 1993.

Smaller newspapers began printing color earlier than most metros. That's because most of them were already offset. When scanners became affordable for small papers and when desktop publishing systems allowed them to make separations from a computer, color became common in newspapers.

Rapidly developing technology has cut the time needed to produce color, and that is a critical reason why more newspapers are running color photography on page 1. The same technology is also allowing

Because human memory does not possess exact color recall, we are forced to distinguish between close colors by using side-by-side comparisons.
Steven J. Abramson
TRUMATCH INC.

color, and that is a critical reason why more newspapers are running color photography on page 1. The same technology is also allowing newspapers to produce good-quality color. That technology begins with the film and extends through the presses.

The print or transparency goes to the camera room or the scanner to be separated into the primary colors and black. Separations can be made by using filters on the process camera. However, the procedure takes longer, the operator has no way of correcting color, and the separations produced are susceptible to uneven shrinkage. If they shrink unevenly, it becomes impossible for the press to print the colors in register. That's when the photograph looks like three or four photos slightly off kilter.

Scanners can produce the four separations in 15 minutes to an hour, depending on the model of scanner and the size of the image. Scanners and desktop publishing systems have cut the time required to make separations and increased their quality.

After the photograph is separated into the four versions of the same picture, each representing a process color and black (Figs. 11.4 through 11.7), a plate is made to place on the press. A plate must be made for each process color and black. That's why printing color requires so much press capacity. Instead of the entire page requiring one plate position on the press, a page with process color requires four plate positions.

Producing quality color on newsprint requires the combined talents of everyone from the photographer to the people operating the press. Many newspapers expect the printers to make up for any inadequacies in preparation, but papers with the most experience in producing color place the least amount of responsibility in the pressroom. Of all the people involved in color production, the press operators are the least able to adjust for poor-quality transparencies or separations or to compensate for plates that are not in register. Color can be adjusted on the press, but any adjustment affects the entire picture or page, not just an area of the picture. Press operators should be primarily concerned about getting the press in register once the color is adjusted.

At the St. Petersburg Times, the responsibility starts with the photographers. Because they use transparencies, photographers know they must fill in shadow areas, which usually means using flash and flash fill. Times staff photographer Ricardo Ferro says that the original quality of the photograph is the most important determinant: "If you start your color reproduction with an inferior product...and process it through the world's best production system, the end result will be a perfectly reproduced poor-quality photo." The scanner operators there know that the press gains, or produces a darker color, on blue and loses on red, and they make the separations accordingly. The platemakers must reproduce the separations dot for dot and place the material in exactly the right position on the plate to reduce registration problems.

Qualities of color

Scientists at the Institute of Biosocial Research in Tacoma, Wash., found that pink reduces anger, aggression and physical strength. As a supposed to make you hungry. Red is also associated with anger and love. Even without research, we know instinctively that we associate certain colors with certain emotions. Research shows us that many of us react to colors in the same ways. Researcher Bernard Aaronson asked 33 women and 33 men to rate certain hues and black and white according to a list of adjectives. Both red and orange were rated as assertive; yellow was active but did not draw a negative response; yellow-green was regarded as aggressive; blue-green was adventurous but calm; blue was the calmest; purple was regarded as antisocial; white was associated with obedience, gray with depression and black with official or somber moods (Aaronson 1970).

Red is hot; blue is not. Yellow is active; tan is passive. Designers must think of the effect of the package, not just one element. A reader looking at a page full of active colors would be bouncing all over. Every color would be screaming for attention. Yellow is so active that a small patch of it could detract from a large picture or the headline on the lead story. Red and orange are also aggressive. Green is a calming influence on yellow; yellow-green and green tend to sit on the page. Green is static. Blue is calm because it has a tendency to recede. Blue-green attracts you. Gray is neutral, a rest stop. It is a good buffer between other colors or between colors and the white of the newsprint. Black is the farthest away. Designers should try to match these qualities with the content of the article.

Using color

Of the many theories of color harmony, the two most applicable to the journalist are analogous and complementary harmonies.

Analogous colors are next to each other on the color wheel (Fig. 11.9). The wheel shows that yellow-orange and yellow-green would go with yellow; that red-violet or blue-violet would go with violet; that is, the colors on either side of a color match each other. Working with that philosophy, a designer who had a color picture with a dominant color of blue could pick blue-violet or blue-green as a color for a title or other accessories in the package. One advantage of adjacent colors, Birren (1961) points out, is that they define a precise mood—"active where the arrangement is warm, passive where it is cool."

However, the harmony of complementary colors is based on contrasting colors. Such harmony is perhaps more popular with artists and should be more popular with journalists. As we see on the color wheel, red and green complement each other. So do red-orange and blue-green, orange and blue, yellow-orange and blue-violet, yellow and violet, and yellow-green and red-violet. Designers who are choosing colors should remember not only the emotional values of colors but also the mix on the page. Birren (1961) recommends using warm colors as the feature color because they are aggressive. Cool hues are useful as background colors because they are passive. Tints, shades and tones are also retiring. The stronger the color, the less is needed. With active colors, the designer can use neutrals, such as tan, peach or gray. The Orange County Register has used peach so effectively as a buffer that it has become known informally in the industry as "Orange County peach." The Register uses a peach of 10 percent magenta and

10 percent yellow. That would be shown as 10R, 10Y. That means the color is produced by using a 10 percent screen of each color, the same effect you get by calling for a 10 percent gray screen. Another way of saying this is that you want 90 percent of the color withheld. Thus, a 10 percent gray screen means you block 90 percent of the black. A 100 percent gray screen, if there were such a thing, would produce white. Each newspaper that runs color regularly should have a color chart showing exactly what the color combinations will look like on your press (Fig. 11.9). Newspapers trying to duplicate the Register's peach probably would have a slightly different percentage of red and magenta because it is being produced on a different scanner, different presses and different paper.

If the designer is making an effort to harmonize colors, it's important to be able to get as close as possible to the actual color that will be produced. To give you some idea of the complexity of trying to specify colors, consider this: Your color monitor can create 16.7 million combinations. Fewer than 5,000 of them can be produced on newsprint, and most of us can't distinguish among many of them.

Creating a color stylebook

Color is just as important in creating a personality for a newspaper as typography. The philosophy that guides color usage should be well thought out in each market. Assuming that you can produce good-quality color, what remains primarily are decisions about whether to use color screens on type and specifications for a color palette.

Color screens influence a reader's perception of the publication. USA Today uses color tints to create an active publication. The tints are consistent with its short stories, graphics and bold typography. Many other newspapers use color screens in all sections. Some restrict them to feature sections, and some outlaw them altogether. Screens apparently do attract attention to the stories, but they don't necessarily translate into readership at any greater rates than unscreened stories (Garcia and Stark 1991). They can also cause legibility problems if the color is too dark and the type is too small (Fig. 11.10). Multiple color screens on the same page can create aesthetic problems.

Color choices create a personality for the publication. Those newspapers that do not operate off a palette—and that includes most—risk creating a different and unintended personality each day. Given that many of the people making the day-to-day decisions have had little or no color training, a newspaper without a color stylebook is risking coloring the news.

To achieve consistency, a color stylebook might prescribe one or more palettes for such standing elements as graphics and teasers (Plate 11.12). It might specify how to pick up a color from a photograph to use with a related story by matching or using a complementary color. It might specify the color mix of screens over copy. It might specify how to create the memory colors, the hues of familiar objects such as water, trees and fire trucks. The Chicago Tribune, for example, specifies that water is 15 cyan and 3 magenta. A second water tone would be 15 cyan. The Tribune's color philosophy can be summed up in these six directives from its stylebook:

1. Avoid straight process colors.
2. Use warm colors to highlight areas.
3. Use cool colors for backgrounds.
4. Use memory colors in graphics.
5. Use color sparingly.
6. Avoid color rules around photographs.

Other newspapers have different philosophies, but the important thing is to adopt one and be consistent.

One thing that all newspapers should have in common is the idea that color is used to communicate, not decorate. This means not simply applying a paint brush to a page but building color into the page. Elements such as teasers and graphics are natural locations for color. Colors matched to the subject can create an environment in which to reach the subject. Color can help define the beginning and end of a package and help show relationships among related items. One researcher found that given a mixed set of triangles, circles and squares, most people will arrange them by shape. That is, they will put all the triangles together. However, if you color one triangle, one circle and one square the same color, most people will arrange them by color. Designers should use that knowledge in using colors to show relationships on the page.

On the other hand, color that is added to make pages livelier is often counterproductive. Color around color photos, for instance, changes the look of the color in the photos. Color randomly placed on headlines may emphasize something that shouldn't be emphasized. Inappropriate color choices, such as a diagram of an accident in hot colors, may make readers think you are sensationalizing tragic news. There is another good reason for specifying color use: Some of the people who decide which colors to use are color blind. Eight percent of North American white males are color blind compared with only 1 percent of North American white females. The inability to distinguish between red and green is even more prevalent among men; some estimates are as high as 25 percent. Color blindness shows up in about 4 percent of black males and in only 2 percent of Hispanic males. Few females in any category are color blind (Sharpe 1974). These statistics lead to the first rule of newspaper color usage: Test for color blindness those staff members who are handling color decisions.

Newspapers would do well to remember what a circulation director of a Dallas paper said when asked about the value of color. We should consider, he suggested, which attracts more attention, the red bird or the sparrow. The corollary is also true: In a flock of red birds, the sparrow stands out.

III.

The Team Effort

12. MANAGEMENT BY DESIGN

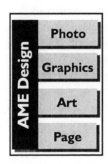

When Henry Ford introduced the assembly line to produce his automobiles quickly and cheaply, he started a revolution in mass production. He proved he could manufacture a car in 93 minutes; others adapted the technique to include manufacturing everything from cans to toothpaste.

As Ford was tinkering in Detroit with his new concept, newsrooms were already operating on the assembly line principle: reporters reported, writers rewrote, copy editors edited and wrote headlines and layout editors placed it all in the paper. As the copy moved along the symbolic conveyor belt from reporter to layout editor, each desk applied its expertise. Journalists seldom talked to one another.

Now fast-forward to the 1990s. At the modern newspaper, an editor calls a "huddle"—a brief gathering of a reporter, city editor and photographer—to discuss how they are going to report a story. At another newspaper, a maestro, or team coordinator, calls a meeting of a section editor, reporter, photographer, copy editor, graphic artist and designer. They are brainstorming an idea. The maestro listens to the reporter's idea. "Why should I care?" she asks. "So what?" someone else asks. As the meeting continues, the questions change. "What else does the reader need to know?" "What's the best way to tell that part of the story?" This is a team, and it will carry this story through to production.

At the Hartford Courant and hundreds of other newspapers, staff members talked about how they would cover the Gulf War. The

135

12.1 Planning permitted newspapers to react quickly when the United States bombed Iraq, even when there were few pictures available during the first news cycles. Many of the graphics had been prepared ahead of time.

Associated Press prepared graphics; many newspapers prepared dozens of pages of background information. Everyone knew for a couple of months at the end of 1991 that a war was possible. But no one knew that when it broke out, there would be no pictures for the first edition. That's when designers turned to the best way available to tell the story: maps and diagrams. The Courant, like many other newspapers, used a graphic and type as the dominant display element (Fig. 12.1). Planning couldn't prepare them for everything, but it prepared them to make good decisions against deadline.

Variations of alternatives to the assembly line process are sprouting up in newsrooms everywhere. These variations appear under such names as "maestro," "newsroom without walls," "News 2000" and "clusters." All of them are designed to produce a newspaper that is more useful to readers.

These innovations haven't reached every newsroom, nor will they ever. Most newspapers still operate under the traditional hierarchical system. We'll look at that system and then look more closely at how newspapers are reorganizing.

Traditional organization

Newspapers today carry more pictures and information graphics and many use color, but their format is not unlike that in Ford's day. This is not surprising because newsroom organization hasn't changed substantially in most newspapers since that time.

However, readers and the ways they spend their working and leisure time have changed. Radio, television, special-interest magazines and electronic delivery systems have captured some of the readers' time and interest. Although technological developments permit newspapers to publish a better product faster with fewer people, the organization of most newsrooms tends to fragment the work of highly trained, highly specialized journalists.

Traditional newsroom organization is a barrier to successful communication with the reader. Ever since photography became a part of the newspaper, the disadvantages of the assembly line process have outweighed the advantages, but few editors recognize the problem. The result is a product that fails to convert data to understanding for the reader. Too often, the system fails to take advantage of the synergy of the reporters, editors, photographers, artists and designers.

The traditional newsroom is organized vertically to move the raw materials horizontally. As Figure 12.2 illustrates, the decision-making authority flows downward from the editor to the departments. Each department produces its own product: stories from the city desk, photographs from the photography department, graphics from the art department, headlines from the copy desk and layouts from the news or design desk. This structure creates unnecessary barriers. Reporters often are not consulted about editing changes, and photographers are seldom asked about selection, cropping or display. Artists too often are told to produce illustrations, charts and maps on short notice and with incomplete information. Furthermore, the designer who puts all these efforts together often doesn't know what is coming until it arrives. The managing editor often specifies what should be on page 1 with little regard for the effect on photo size, white space or the number of jumps.

It doesn't have to be this way, even in the traditional newsroom structure, and at some newspapers, it isn't. Copy desks consult with reporters; reporters suggest headlines; a photo editor trained in photography works at the copy desk; planning sessions are held in anticipation of big projects or disasters; the person who writes the cutline is the same person who has edited the story and written the headline. Good people can and do make any system work. But it can work better and more easily if we tap the creative power of minds working together.

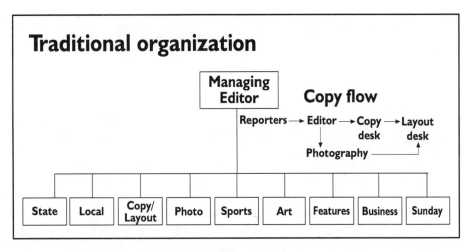

12.2 In the traditional organization, authority flows downward, and the newspaper production process is organized much like an assembly line.

Newsroom specialization is the classic good-news/bad-news joke. It's good news when reporters know more about a particular field, such as medicine or the environment, or photographers know how to operate a variety of equipment, gather facts on film, crop for maximum effect and display to attract attention. But it's bad news when the division of labor inside the newsroom becomes so severe that journalists don't talk to each other.

In the 1970s, some farsighted publishers, such as those in St. Petersburg, Fla., and Allentown, Pa., began to tinker with newsroom organization because of their growing awareness of the newspaper as a visual medium. Oddly enough, at most newspapers it wasn't the management experts who started this newsroom evolution but first the photographers, then the designers.

Photographers argued loudly and often eloquently that the photo department needed to be more than a service agency that took orders but had no say about the assignment or display. These photographers saw themselves as photojournalists who were able to report with a camera, often more dramatically than reporters. They needed a voice in the planning and execution of the product.

It was only natural that journalists trained to deal with words were reluctant to invite photographers, much less designers, into the councils where news judgments were being made. There was, and still is, little appreciation for the total product in those councils. The efforts of professors Cliff Edom and Angus MacDougall, through the University of Missouri Pictures-of-the-Year competition, had a profound effect on the industry. Their students argued forcefully for the merits of photojournalism.

At many newspapers, photographers still have little voice in planning. A University of Georgia Journalism School survey in 1983 found that only 17 percent of photographers are usually involved in the early planning, 24 percent were involved midway in the project, 39 percent after planning is complete and 20 percent after the story is done.

> *We're anticipating the creation of news teams of editors, designers, picture editors—people who normally work away from each other but will now work side by side. So when we put together pages, we'll have input from people who have a reason to be on that particular page, and have their own area of expertise.*
>
> **Ed Kohorst**
> **EDITORIAL ART DIRECTOR**
> **Dallas Morning News**

Photography is gradually moving from a service department to equal footing with other departments.

Now art departments need to travel the same route. Designers, who put the package together, started showing how their involvement could attract attention and explain the content. As early as 1960, the St. Petersburg Times recognized that the presentation of information was part of the message. In the 1970s at the Allentown (Pa.) Morning Call, art director Robert Lockwood and executive editor Edward Miller revolutionized the newsroom process. The design director became an equal to the assistant managing editor in making news judgments and coordinating the paper's content. Miller and Lockwood also experimented with "villages," teams that worked together and included everyone from reporters and photographers to paste-up employees. In each case, the newsroom organization was changed to make the newspaper a better product for readers and advertisers.

Reorganizing the newsroom

Any reorganization of the newsroom must be based on the goal of the organization. The most successful publications are those that recognize they are selling understanding, not just newspapers.

Newsrooms are not organized to produce stories, type, charts and photographs that work together. Many stories have no pictures or graphs, and the traditional system facilitates the need to meet daily deadlines. If stories do or should have pictures, maps or graphs, the system depends on the whims of a reporter and city editor, who may or may not think of photos and graphics early in the process. There are plenty of disaster stories.

At one newspaper, a five-member reporting and photography team worked for three weeks on a special fashion section. The two employees responsible for laying out the section found only the pictures and cutlines when they came to work on a holiday. They put together the entire section without any of the stories. The layout editors weren't involved in the planning, and the section was a disaster.

At another newspaper, a reporter worked for days on an exclusive story about a local judge who was a client of the prostitutes who were being brought before him in court. The story contained a vivid description of the judge meeting the pimp in a seedy bar, walking across the dark street to a three-story house and going up the carpeted stairs to the third floor to visit a prostitute. Although nearly two pages were devoted to the story, it didn't have a single picture or illustration. Why not? The reporter and his city editor failed to tell other departments they were working on the story until it was too late to make photographs or illustrations without delaying the publication date. The story was written, passed on for editing and a headline, and placed in the paper in classic assembly line fashion.

Those examples both involved enterprise stories, but it also could have happened with spot news. Contrary to what most journalists believe, little news is unexpected. A fire breaks out. Someone is shot. Two cars collide. You never know when these things are going to happen. Still, most of the stories in the news section can be anticipated. A study of three large dailies for three days revealed that 75 to 85 percent of the stories in the news section can be anticipated (Moen 1992). In the sports section, this percentage is even higher. You know when the high school basketball team will play. You can plan your coverage. You know when the city council and school board will meet and what is on the agenda. You can plan your coverage. You know ahead of time candidates' schedule and, often, what they are going to say. You can plan your coverage. You know the court docket. You can plan your coverage. Add your enterprise stories, and you have accounted for more than three out of four news and sports stories.

A newsroom that treats each day as a surprise is a newsroom that is always two cycles behind the readers. Fortunately, this sort of thing is happening less frequently. That's because two changes are occurring: Design editors, who have an interdisciplinary concept of how stories can be told, are being integrated into the management structure; and teams, including the people who traditionally originate stories and those who traditionally present stories, are working together. Some papers tap the expertise scattered throughout the newsroom only in the planning of major stories and projects. Others are building it into the daily process.

A key player is the graphics or design editor, a relatively new position. So new, in fact, that Hilliard (1990) found substantial confusion among executive and managing editors about the role of the design editor. Of 67 large-circulation newspapers responding to his survey, 35 senior editors compared the position of design editor to that of a city editor, 29 compared it to the features editor and 14 compared it to an assistant managing editor. (They could select more than one.) The survey showed that design editors are being integrated into the newsroom management structure slowly but surely. At 30 percent of the respondents, the decision on how to tell the story was shared by the graphics and news editors; at 26 percent, it was shared by the graphics and city editors; at 16 percent, the managing editor decided; and at 10 percent, the news editor decided.

Figure 12.3 shows that a new position has appeared on the newsroom chart: Assistant Managing Editor—Design. This position is at the hub of the newspaper. The design editor or a designee must be involved in both the daily production cycle and special projects and also have the authority to make news judgments in consultation with others.

Design editors, whether they are called art directors, graphics editors or assistant managing editors, come from a variety of backgrounds. They may have been photographers, designers, artists or former copy editors who did

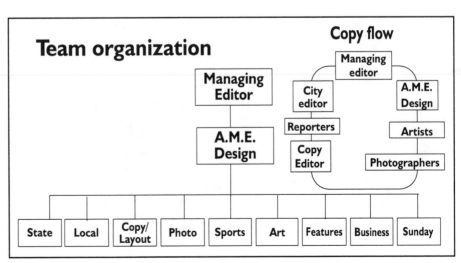

12.3 When the newsroom is organized in teams, many ideas flow from the bottom up, and everyone responsible for any part of production is involved from the beginning.

Qualities of designers

1. They must be journalists. Design editors must understand news values, know how news and features are gathered and be aware of readers' expectations.

2. They must be photo editors, though not necessarily photographers. They must be able to differentiate between situations that have potential for pictures and those that do not. In addition, they must know how to select, crop, group and display pictures.

3. They must be artistic, though not necessarily artists.

4. They must be typographers, knowing how to work with type and use type legibly.

5. They must know publication reproduction processes. Design editors need to know everything from programming the computer for proper type spacing to color production methods.

6. They must be able to work with others. Design editors must be able to persuade others by earning their respect. In turn, they must respect others.

7. They must have the vision to think the unthinkable, the courage to experiment and the wisdom to remember always that the reader must be served.

12.4

layout. Because of the standards being established by these pioneers, those who follow will need to be even better qualified. For the design editors of the future, there are at least seven requisites (Fig. 12.4).

It is not necessary for the design editor to have firsthand knowledge of all the functions of the job. The designer needs to know the best spacing between letters in headlines and text, but a computer programmer can achieve the desired results. The designer needs to know how to use photographs, but a photo editor can make most of the day-to-day decisions. The designer needs to understand how color is reproduced, but the artist can make overlays.

Ironically, the smaller the publication, the more important it is for the design editor to have a broad base because it is less likely there will be computer programmers, photo editors, artists or lab technicians to do the actual work.

Because of the nature of the job specifications, photo journalists who have backgrounds in typography are likely candidates for design editor positions. In fact, more than half of the first design editors were former photographers (Gentry and Zang 1988). Regardless of whether the design editor is a former photographer, the photography and art departments must be elevated from service agencies (as shown in Fig. 12.2) to departments on equal footing with other newsroom divisions (as shown in Fig. 12.3). This will allow the photo editor to initiate assignments, make suggestions on photo orders from other departments and even reject inappropriate requests. Such an action would be subject to an override only by the design editor or managing editor.

It is essential that the authority of the design editor, photo editor and chief artist be built into the newsroom structure. If it is left to the preferences of the editor or managing editor, it can change overnight as editors move from one position to another. If authority rests on the shoulders of only one person, it also leaves with that one person. This is particularly true at small and medium-sized newspapers that, like a campfire, glow brightly with the work of a single person but die quickly when the editor leaves.

Once the structure exists, management must provide the means for the appropriate departments to work together. The assembly line system requires cooperation but doesn't provide for the interchange of ideas or offer the benefits of collaborative efforts. The team system does.

Newsrooms are being restructured to bring specialists onto a team. When it works, no managing editor or design director has to issue decrees. The team will have made the decisions as the story progresses. More importantly, the right questions will have been asked early enough in the process for answers to be found. The readers' questions will be answered in a story format that makes sense. Text, pictures, illustrations and a range of information graphics will be used to tell appropriate parts of the story.

The team system

The team approach, which involves more people earlier in the process, ensures adequate planning. One version of the team approach is the maestro concept, popularized by Leland Ryan of Northwestern

University. The approach requires one person to orchestrate brainstorming story sessions. If the reporter can justify the story from the readers' standpoint, then the group turns its attention to defining the best ways to tell the story. Main story? Sidebar? Pictures? Graphics? Illustrations? How much space? What's the headline? What will it look like on the page? The maestro leads the team to the crescendo.

At other newspapers, the composition of the team is determined by the project. If it is a sports feature, the sports editor, reporter and design editor are included. At the initial conference, which may take only a few minutes for some stories, the team determines the subject, focus and deadline. The design editor might have suggestions about angles or tie-ins with other departments and may also assign a photographer to work with the reporter from the beginning. The reporter-photographer team might make decisions in the field that will change the focus. Even so, the words and visuals will still work together because of the team effort.

Planning sessions for other projects may need to include more people and be more formal. For instance, an investigative project might include the reporters and their project editor, design editor, copy editor, photo editor, artist and managing editor or assistant managing editor. The wide variety of perspectives strengthens the fact-gathering process. By involving all the people who will be working on the package at some stage, management is making the most use of available talent, ego and pride. Because everyone is involved and has a stake in the success of the project, they will work harder and understand what they are doing. Participating in idea and planning sessions is always stimulating to creative people. Ideas subjected to challenge and scrutiny become more clearly focused. The process is enriching for the participants, fruitful for the newspaper and beneficial to the readers.

Teams offer many advantages. The copy editor who is reading the daily memos along with the project editor is less likely to edit out essential information, edit in errors or write a bad headline. Involving the design editor at the beginning of the project ensures that the photographers will have access to the reporters, people, places and events as well as sufficient time to complete their work. Planning also permits artists and photographers to go into the field with the reporters, not two weeks later when conditions have changed. In addition, the design editor can have a series logo prepared ahead of time rather than one hour before deadline. Finally, the package can be designed for maximum effect in the appropriate space.

Some newspapers have a backout schedule, which shows every deadline until publication. It indicates deadlines for reporters, photographers and artists, and it also shows when the copy and management editors must complete their work. Such a schedule helps organize the team members and assigns responsibility to each.

Expecting the unexpected

Every newspaper that has survived a major disaster—a hurricane, earthquake, major fire—becomes a convert to planning. One of those newspapers is the Charlotte Observer, where Dick Van Halsma and his colleagues put together a list of recommendations after they survived

One reason we're successful is that the art department has always been a part of the editorial process. We're only eleven years old, so we were able to be integral from the beginning.
Joe Scopin
AME-DESIGN
Washington Times

Hurricane Hugo. Here's what they suggest for the photo department:

1. Keep the photographers' communication network—scanners, radios, cellular phones—working.

2. Photographers should have a set of maps in their cars.

3. Keep at least a week of lab supplies on hand. In a disaster, there won't be any deliveries.

4. Make sure local police, firefighters and paramedics recognize you. In a disaster, it might be the difference between access and no access.

5. Know your legal rights.

6. Carry protective gear in your cars.

7. Develop access to the local ham radio system.

8. Establish charge accounts with helicopter and airplane rental companies.

And for the graphics department:

1. Back up files on disks weekly.

2. Be sure your map files are organized and accessible, even after a crash.

3. Keep an additional master file of regional cities.

4. Keep a comprehensive set of street maps on hand.

5. Keep your newspaper's headline and body copy fonts loaded on a PC. The mainframe may go down.

These lists are a start, but they illustrate the power of planning. When Hurricane Andrew devastated South Florida, the Miami Herald took a hard shot, but it was ready because it had planned. Its prize-winning coverage helped the region recover (Figs. 12.4 through 12.7). Just ask any newspaper the value of planning when the power goes out for extended periods. That's when you wish someone had thought of having a backup generator.

12.5 In the aftermath of Hurricane Andrew, The Miami Herald's efforts were concentrated not only on telling the story but also on helping readers cope.

12.6 Photography reported what words couldn't.

12.7 Much of the Herald's efforts were directed toward getting people who needed help in touch with those offering help.

12.8 One reason the Herald was able to react so well to Hurricane Andrew is that the newspaper has a disaster plan. Management and staff members knew what they were supposed to do.

No matter how great the author's wisdom or how vital the message or how remarkable the printer's skill, unread print is merely a lot of paper and a little ink. The true economics of printing must be measured by how much is read and understood and not by how much is produced.

Herbert Spencer
PHILOSOPHER

13. WORDS AND VISUALS IN TANDEM

Advertising agencies form creative teams to work on a client's campaign. The team is composed of specialists who work together with other team members. Their product is the best that the team can produce. Most newsrooms operate, for the most part, on the Lone Ranger principle, which holds that each individual applies his or her expertise to the problem then passes it on to the next person. The product is the best that a group of individuals working alone can produce.

But this product isn't as good as can be. In Chapter 12, we discussed the advantages of the team approach. When it comes to integrating the words and visuals in the display, newsrooms either have to adopt a team approach to the design, make certain someone coordinates the work or provide for one person to cross the specialty lines. Fragmented work produces fragmented or redundant information.

This chapter supposes that the package that moves to the copy or design desk has been conceived and produced by a team. Now it remains for the designer to make the words and visuals supplement each other. Elements that work in tandem show a dependence on each other. Photographs, cutlines, headlines, decks, pullouts and graphics depend on each other to tell the story. Even thorough readers make decisions based on headlines, photographs and secondary display type. Each of these points is a visual stop sign for scanners. Only when scanners pause and read do designers have an opportunity to tell and sell. The goal, then, is to get people to stop and listen to the

13.1 The words tie the lead picture and story together and set a fun tone for the package.

sales pitch. Each of the stops—the headline, photograph, cutline, decks and pullouts—should add new information to the sales pitch.

The picture and headline are the heavyweights; more than any other element, they attract attention. The picture should feed to the cutline, which should explain the photograph and foreshadow the story. The headline bridges what the reader sees in the photograph and will find in the story. The deck continues with enticing details. The pullouts and blurbs sell a quote or tidbit that piques interest. The charts tell part of the story. The chart copy block explains the graphics and, like the cutline, foreshadows the story.

Impossible? No. But not likely in most of today's newsrooms, at least on a consistent basis. Big news events and special reports are more likely to produce interdependent packages than the daily flow. That's because of fragmentation of efforts at the copy and design desks. A designer draws the page. A copy editor edits the story and writes the headline and decks, often without seeing the design. A photographer writes a cutline without seeing the story. A copy editor, sometimes not even the same one who edited the story, may rewrite the cutline. The chart arrives from the art department; someone has written the chart's headline and copy block without seeing the headline and story. Yet another person may pull a quote or blurb, and even if it's the same copy editor who has edited the story, the choice often is not made in the context of the total package.

Fortunately, it doesn't happen this way at every newspaper, but even a casual observer of today's newspapers can see that everyone involved in the package isn't working toward the same goal. As a test, let's check the execution for the straightforward package of two pictures and one story in Figure 13.1.

The first thing you notice is the wonderful headline that plays off the picture. It could not have been written if the copy editor had not been looking at the picture as well as reading the story. The title bridges the picture and the deck, which gives scanners enough additional information to understand the pun in the title. The deck also plays off the secondary photograph. So far, so good.

Now let's look at the cutline under the dominant picture: "Susan Currier of Columbia places head in hands and laughs as saxophone player Lloyd Shatto gives her an earful of music." This wouldn't be a good cutline even if it didn't repeat the information in the headline. As you know from Chapter 5, cutlines shouldn't state the obvious. We can see she has her head on her hand (not hands). The cutline identifies the people, but it doesn't tell us why Lloyd is blowing his horn at her or why they are outdoors. Are they both members of the band? Are they having fun during a break in practice? And what could be extracted from the story to entice us to read?

Now let's look at the second picture. We've been attracted to the package with a large picture of a close-up; now we're given a context shot. They complement one another. The cutline tells us, "John Rhein and Vivian Barner of Columbia cut loose at Katy Station to the music of the Storeyville Stompers before a Missouri home football game." This cutline does a better job of telling us what we can't see: the names of the people and the band, the location and the occasion. Like the first, though, it doesn't tease the reader into the story. Had the cutline writer been using the story better, he or she could have told us the connection between the band's name and its New Orleans origin. Or that the band makes the rounds of six restaurants before each home football game and the date of the next outing.

The DeBerg headline plays off the picture and the story (Fig. 13.2). The use of "exits" is rein-

13.2 The word "exits" ties the headline to the picture and story.

13.3 The cutline repeats the information in the headline instead of introducing a new element from the story.

forced by the picture, which shows DeBerg packing a car. The deck and cutline have an unfortunate redundancy. The deck: "The QB puts the best face on his release by the Bucs, celebrating 17 years and still feeling in demand." The cutline: "Steve DeBerg, waived by the Bucs on Tuesday, packs away the residue of a 17-year NFL career." The cutline's metaphorical reference to his luggage works well. By taking the 17-year reference out of the deck, the writers could have added another detail.

Redundancy also exists in the headline and cutline in the fair-lending package (Fig. 13.3). The cutline says, "Attorney General Janet Reno and HUD Secretary Henry G. Cisneros pledge tougher enforcement of fair-lending laws at a hearing Thursday. 'We are changing the way we do business,' Cisneros said." The first line repeats the headline. Based on the story, a better cutline might have been, "Attorney General Janet Reno and HUD Secretary Henry G. Cisneros pledged Thursday that the government will enforce the law that bars discrimination in the granting of mortgage and home-equity loans. Only one lender has been prosecuted since the law was passed in 1968."

Another headline bridges the picture and the story about activities at the Children's Museum. "Class molds young artists" sits under a picture of a couple working with clay (Fig. 13.4). The use of the word "molds" isn't an accident. The same theme extends into the deck with the use of "shape." The cutline introduces us to Sue Sumpter and her son. However, the story starts with another parent-child couple at work on a pottery sculpture. The desk did the best it could with what it had to work with, but what it had to work with was the output of a reporter and photographer who didn't work together. The story has been edited with the pullout in mind; the information is not repeated in the story.

The headline bridge is not as obvious in the story about the 11-year-old girl who is a star player in Pop Warner football (Fig. 13.5). The picture shows a girl; "The Girl" ties the picture to the story, which explains that is how she is known to opponents. Both cutlines draw information from the story that could entice a reader. The lead cutline reports, "Dana Galloway, captain of the Hanlon Park 49ers, has rushed for 1,000 yards in seven games and starts at middle linebacker." The secondary cutline offers a quote: "'It took them about four

13.4 The headline and deck uses "molds" and "shape" to tie the picture and story together, but the story focuses on a parent and child not pictured.

13.5 All the elements, the picture, headline, deck and cutlines, work in tandem to sell this package to the scanner.

13.6 The photographer captured the concept, and the words reinforce the visual image.

13.7 "Religion and Politics" plays nicely off the illustration, but the presentation lacks subordinate type to tell readers what angle this story takes.

13.8 The photographer or illustrator can work from a title; or the desk can write a title to reflect the illustration. This title immediately identifies for Chicago readers the visual pun. Jane Byrne is a former mayor.

games to accept me,' says Dana Galloway of her Hanlon Park teammates of three years ago." The elements in this package work in tandem.

So do the elements in "Still Growing." When packages are planned, the photographer knows the theme, and the journalist adding the words knows the intent of the photographer and provides the right words to make it work (Fig. 13.6). Packages in which the words and visuals work in tandem elicit an immediate reaction from even the most hurried of readers.

That's what the words and illustrations do in Figures 13.7, 13.8 and 13.9. Religion & Politics plays off the cross sitting atop a capitol dome; Jane Byrne in Exile plays off the artist's conception of the former mayor as Napoleon Bonaparte in exile; and the words reinforce the photo illustration of a dog dressed formally for dinner.

Such word and photo interplay can and should also be accomplished on deadline. The Detroit News did it when longtime Piston Bill Laimbeer retired during the season (Fig. 13.10). The headline immediately makes sense to Detroit sports fans, who had been hearing rumors of the impending retirement for days. The picture is not a file action shot; it is a picture of Laimbeer sitting on the bench at what turned out to be his last game. The designers across the street at the Detroit Free Press succeeded when Andre Agassi won Wimbledon. Bold photo cropping and display combine with a winning headline to create an arresting presentation (Fig. 13.11).

What all these examples have in common is teamwork. If the headline or title writer isn't look-

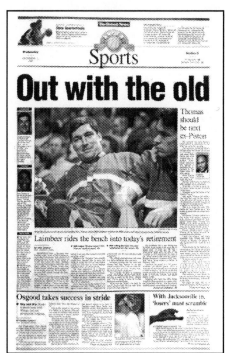

13.9 Give a photographer that title, and you are almost guaranteed a good illustration.

13.10 Most Detroit readers would immediately realize the meaning of the bold headline, but for those who don't, the headline under the picture explains.

13.11 Agassi won, but not before suffering some agony. An excellent picture crop and great words creates a stunning package.

ing at the story and photo or illustration, there's little chance the words will bridge the visual and verbal. Visuals, cutlines, headlines and pullouts have a symbiotic relationship. The sum is greater than the parts. A system that encourages communication among the people working on the packages gives them a chance to produce this kind of journalism. The people executing the package also have to know that the goal is to make the elements work together.

IV.

APPLYING THE LESSONS:
SPECIALIZED APPLICATIONS

14. DESIGNING FOR COLLEGE NEWSPAPERS

College papers are a breed apart, though you often wouldn't know it. For all the differences in audience, many college papers merely echo what they see in general-circulation daily newspapers. That's okay as a learning tool, of course, but it doesn't serve the market of the college paper. If 20-year-olds can create computer software and build solar cars that outdo those from General Motors, surely college designers can create pages that will attract college students.

That's not easy work, but who better to do it than fellow students? You know their interests (Fig. 14.1). You know how to reach them. And now you have the tools. Pagemaker and QuarkXpress put the tools of invention in the palm of your hand. If you're able to turn college students on to newspapers, the profession will be indebted to you.

The audience should define the content and design of college papers, and that audience is college students. Primarily 18 to 22-years old, primarily single. Interested in relationships, entertainment, and the price of tuition, books, room and board. Graduation requirements. Who the good profs are. Sports. Campus safety. Sure, they're also interested in history and physics, but they don't look to the newspaper for that. If you asked a random sample of college students to rank their interests and then compared it with the space devoted to those subjects in the campus newspapers, you might not find a good correlation.

Nor would you find a good correlation between the presentation of

14.1 Now that you've got their attention...

153

the information and graphic world this audience lives in. Look at the posters on their dorm and apartment walls. Look at Rolling Stone, The Village Voice and the alternative press. Then look at your newspaper. Chances are, your newspaper has much more in common with your local Hometown News than ray gun. Most of your audience sits somewhere between those extremes.

One-quarter of the college audience turns over annually. Change is a constant on campus. So it should be a constant in the newspaper. Redesigns should occur almost annually. New people have new ideas. Your Hometown News has essentially the same audience year after year. It has subscribers who are still mad about the last time the flag was changed. Most college students wouldn't even remember what the flag looked like last year. The professionals should be looking to you for ideas. Some are, and they're finding them. In these examples, you'll find the familiar and unfamiliar, the classic and the outlandish. All of them have lessons to offer. Probably the most important lesson, though, is to stretch. Do you have to break the rules to be innovative? The answer is summed up in this exchange quoted by Dale Peskin in the Society of Newspaper Design's magazine:

There was Bob Shema, the innovator from Dallas, touting the twisted typography of the avant-garde publication ray gun.

And there was Tony Sutton, the classicist from Toronto, stroking his beard trying to read the letterforms.

"We need to mimic this, to be inspired by this," Shema implored. "What do you think, Tony?"

"This sucks...BIG TIME," responded Sutton.

Shema wasn't necessarily advocating type chaos, and Sutton wasn't saying that all innovation is bad. Just as professionals are trying to find the limits, so should you. Here are some examples from college papers to guide your search.

14.2 The Herald offers excellent photos displayed well and pleasing contrast in the headline typography.

14.3 By creating the briefs across the bottom, the News Record was able to devote appropriate space to the big news.

14.4 The Sagamore features a magazine treatment of its lead story.

14.7 The cover illustration sets the tone for the story.

14.5 Lacking photographs, the Guardian uses typography, variable grid and white space to create an interesting page.

14.6 The Minnesota Daily did an entertaining take-off of a grocery-store tabloid.

14.8 Designers selected appropriate typography to match the illustration and the story.

14.9 The special-effects treatment of file photos appropriately communicates age.

14.10 Designers used the black background to create a striking cover with reverse type.

14.11 Ray gun typography reaches the campus.

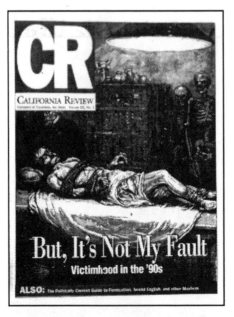

14.12 Color and black-and-white, illustration and words both are effective partners. In the original, "CR" is presented against a bright red background, the strip across the bottom is white type against red.

14.13 Designers show that science pages don't have to be dull.

14.14 Typography and white space are used expertly to create an inviting package. The icons help break up the type and organize the subject matter.

14.15 Classic design principles are applied to create a modern-looking page.

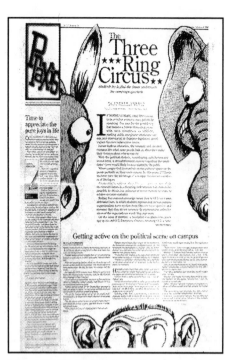

14.16 The cropping and placement of the illustrations direct the readers' eyes to the headlines and text.

14.17 The vertical column creates just enough contrast on the page to make it work.

14.18 The echo of ray gun typography and the pullout quote demand the readers' attention.

14.19 The controlled use of white space—from the leading to the space between elements—creates an appropriate personality consistent with the subject matter.

14.20 The subject is floppy clothes. The designer bends but does not break the rules of type and photo usage to create a presentation consistent with the content.

14.21 Within a formal balance presentation, the designer creates tension and a sense of playfulness sure to attract a scanner's attention.

14.22 It's not your usual New Year's presentation, and it shouldn't be. It's college students talking to college students.

14.23 The stylized illustration takes center stage. The illustration is a story in itself. The designer uses type contrast, stacking and tight letter spacing to create a compelling title.

14.24 There's an enormous amount of type on the page, but the designer uses white space and subheads to make it look like a series of short articles.

14.25 The type wraps around the top pullout to protect the readers' path. The bottom pullout also adds relief while adding another point of entry without interfering with the reader.

14.26 The gray of the text, screens and white space play off against contrasting shapes and sizes to make this page pleasing without calling attention to itself.

14.27 The designer uses type contrast in form and color to move the reader around the page.

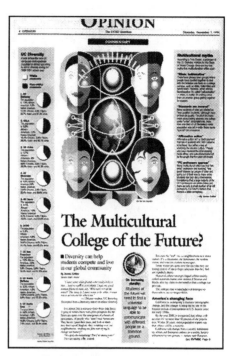

14.28 How do you tell the story? With text, information graphics, an illustration and a pullout. It's a well thought-out presentation.

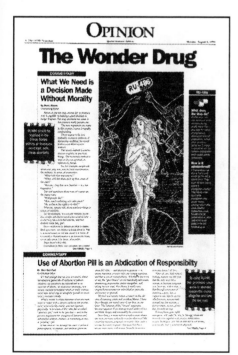
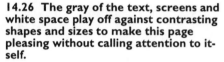

14.29 The designer echoes the tone in the illustration with the pullouts.

14.30 This is a typographic solution to a page with only minor illustrations. The white space and type contrast creates an inviting page.

14.31 The type and the illustration work together to create tension, which is appropriate to the story.

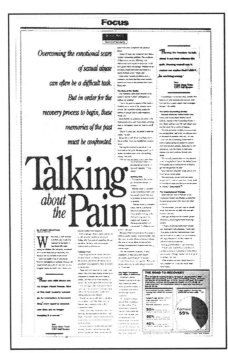

14.32 This is a tough design to do well. You must have control of the typographic elements. The type size and leading needs to be appropriate to the line length and type design.

14.33 Another designer creates a successful typographic solution to a page without illustrations or pictures.

14.34 The title and lead picture work together. The page offers a variety of shapes and sizes in the photos.

14.35 The fundamental guidelines for picture pages are illustrated here: select a dominant photo, maintain consistent interior margins and use a variety of shapes and sizes.

14.36 Good photography displayed well creates compelling pages. The only thing lacking is cutlines under each photo.

14.37 The vertical space devoted to the page label and promos sets up a page with a strong horizontal emphasis. The display type offers contrast in weight and form.

14.38 An essay is a collection of pictures that tells a story, as these do. The designer adheres to the basic guidelines of photo usage.

14.39 The designer created a grid instead of trying to fit the pictures to a standard grid. The title works off the signature or headline picture alongside it.

14.40 Dramatic cropping and the right words combine to create a display with impact.

14.41 Simplicity creates impact on deadline—even in a losing cause.

14.42 A beautiful page label gives the page a good start. The designer worked off the strong vertical element on the page. Many designers forget about the need for vertical elements.

14.43 Now you see where the design for the page label in Fig. 14.42 comes from.

14.44 Take away the type and illustrations and look at the contrasting shapes on the page. Then you begin to understand why it looks interesting and organized.

14.45 The professional-looking illustration, use of the vertical element and fine use of typography combine to make this page a winner.

15 DESIGNING FOR TABLOIDS AND SUNDAY MAGAZINES

The idea for an American tabloid newspaper came out of a visit between a son of a publisher of The Chicago Tribune and an English press baron. Joseph Medill Patterson told his cousin, Robert McCormick, of his meeting with Lord Northbrook, and in 1919 they started publishing the Illustrated Daily News in New York. They hoped to emulate Lord Northbrook's success with the tabloid Daily Mirror, which had a circulation of one million in England. Before achieving that kind of success, however, they had to slog through the yellow journalism sensationalism of the 1920s and 1930s and battle upstart competitors. The excesses committed in the name of circulation peaked in 1928 when the News brought in Tom Howard, a Chicago Tribune staff member, to surreptitiously take a picture of the execution of Ruth Synder, who had been convicted of murder. Public reaction to such sensationalism finally forced this type of newspaper to change or shut down. The News changed and went on to become the largest general circulation newspaper in the United States at one time. Unfortunately, the stigma associated with yellow journalism lingered long after the worst practices had been corrected, and it slowed the acceptance of tabloids. In 1940, Alicia Patterson, Joseph Patterson's daughter, started a tabloid on Long Island. Newsday has since become one of the most successful newspapers in America. Now owned by the Times Mirror Company, Newsday grew up with Long Island and, in content and looks, redefined the image of the tabloid. Newsday made the tabloid so respectable, in fact, that by 1979 even the conservative

163

Our Sunday Visitor, the largest Catholic weekly in the country, had changed from broadsheet to tabloid and reported that reader reaction to the restyled paper was "overwhelmingly positive." On the other hand, the Tempe (Ariz.) News switched to tabloid but returned to broadsheet two years later because of reader complaints. The Middletown (N.Y.) Daily Record went from tabloid to broadsheet and then back to tabloid.

These days, tradition and the fear that a smaller paper will bring less advertising revenue, not the negative image of tabloids, keeps publishers from switching to the smaller size, which is widely acknowledged to be more convenient for readers. In tabloids, advertisers can buy smaller ads, usually at higher rates, and still dominate the page. Even a full page in a tabloid is only a half page in a broadsheet. Most national advertising is designed for broadsheet newspapers; tabloids often must reduce the ads to make them fit. As a consequence, tabloids are seen most often where they have existed successfully for years. There are 33 daily tabloids in the United States, and four of the 20 largest-circulation papers published are tabloids. Hundreds more papers in the high school, college, weekly, city business, association, religious and ethnic press are tabloids. Some special-interest papers (Village Voice, Rolling Stone) are tabloids. The grocery-store papers (National Enquirer, National Star) are the last vestiges of yellow journalism. Many broadsheet newspapers use tabloids for special theme sections, which usually revolve around an advertising promotion. Many newspapers also have magazines that are usually tabloid or close to it. The growing number of Sunday newspapers and their corresponding Sunday magazines makes this type of tabloid an increasingly important product with a need for its own design philosophy.

Making the decision

Every successful business organization tries to maximize the strengths and minimize the weaknesses of its product. Publishers who are trying to decide whether to publish a broadsheet or tabloid must first know the advantages and disadvantages of each.

ADVANTAGES

1. Tabloids are more convenient for the reader to handle. At the breakfast table, the open broadsheet is big enough to cover three cereal bowls and the coffee; the tabloid is less intrusive. On the bus or subway, the tab does not have to be folded to be read.

2. Editors usually have more open pages. At Newsday, the first four pages are considered to be equivalent to the front page of a broadsheet. It is more economical for small papers with less advertising to set aside a full page for departments. An open page in a broadsheet represents twice the investment in the editorial product than the tabloid does.

3. Content, even within a section, is easier to divide in a tabloid than in a broadsheet where many stories on various subjects appear on a single page.

4. The tabloid size permits smaller papers to look and feel hefty with only half the content of the broadsheet. Falling advertising rev-

enue and increasing newsprint costs forced the Christian Science Monitor to switch to tabloid.

5. Tabloids offer publishers more flexibility in the number of pages that can be added or subtracted. Depending on the press, broadsheet must go up or down in increments of two, four, or eight pages. The number of pages in a tabloid can be changed in increments of four on most presses.

6. Because of the preponderance of broadsheets, the tabloid offers publishers an opportunity to differentiate their product from others in the market. This is particularly advantageous to new publications in competitive markets.

7. The advertiser benefits by spending less money to dominate a page.

DISADVANTAGES

1. What advertisers gain, publishers lose. Although large advertisers may buy multiple pages of advertising, smaller merchants often settle for less than they would in a broadsheet. Rates can be increased to make up some of the difference but only if the tab is operating in a noncompetitive market.

2. Advertising and circulation success breeds problems. Newsday and the Rocky Mountain News are often too bulky. Successful broadsheets have problems with heft on Sundays, but tabs often face this problem several days of the week.

3. A smaller front page limits the number of elements tabloid editors can use to attract the same variety of readers obtained by the broadsheet. And when the big news event occurs, the broadsheet can use multiple pictures and stories on the front page. The tabloid cannot do this without sacrificing impact.

4. The tabloid cannot be sectionalized as easily as a broadsheet. The tab has only one section even though it may have pullouts. The broadsheet, however, can be divided into numerous sections, depending on press facilities.

5. Tabloids still suffer from a lingering image problem. Present generations are not influenced by memories of yellow journalism, but some of them associate tabloids with sensational papers. Even people who buy those tabloids do not necessarily want their news presented in the same format. The four most successful daily tabloid newspapers, the Daily News, Newsday, Chicago Sun-Times and the Rocky Mountain News try to maximize the advantages of their size. All are published in communities where mass transportation is available, yet all sell thousands of copies to homes also. If mass transportation was better developed in other large cities, the tabloid might be more popular because of ease of reading while riding. San Francisco and, to a lesser degree, Washington, D.C., have decent mass transportation systems. In those two cities, the second newspapers, the Examiner and the Times, might be candidates for tabloids, but both are established as broadsheets, and the disadvantages of a change in size probably outweigh the advantages.

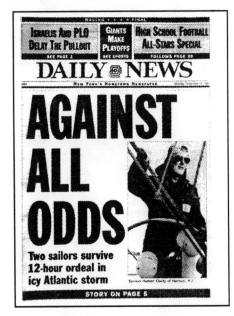

15.1 The Daily News often uses its cover as a billboard.

15.2 The Rocky Mountain News offers an active mini-newspaper.

15.3 The Leader, a Canadian paper, offers a quieter mini-newspaper.

15.4 The Atlanta Tribune uses a magazine-type cover.

15.5 The Voice uses a variety of approaches. This one shouts through a typographic megaphone.

15.6 The Riverfront Times, an alternative paper in St. Louis, has a magazine feel to it on the cover.

Differentiating the tabloid

Beyond recognizing the advantages and disadvantages, editors must also identify the unique problems and possibilities that a tabloid presents, or it will be treated merely as a small-sized newspaper. The tabloid is different from a broadsheet in six areas: Page 1 philosophy, sectionalizing, spreads, sizing, typography and jumps.

DEVELOPING A PAGE 1 PHILOSOPHY

Editors of broadsheets must decide whether they want a high or low story count, but tabloid editors must decide whether they want a low story count or no stories at all. On Page 1, tabloids have more in common with news magazines than with broadsheets. Both must concentrate on one or two elements because of size restrictions. Like the news weeklies, tabloids must retain immediacy while providing focus. That means stripping away the clutter. Some concentrate on type, some of pictures, some on art. Some look like a smaller version of a broadsheet. The papers in Figures 15.1-15.6 illustrate the range of covers. The Daily News is one of the last great metropolitan street-sales tabloids; its poster headlines smack readers across the forehead. The Rocky Mountain News runs teasers or synopsis of stories, but rarely runs the stories on Page 1. The Leader, a weekly paper in British Columbia, looks like a small broadsheet. The Atlanta Tribune fills the front with an illustration and a few type promos. The Village Voice offers its typical typographical cover. The Riverfront Times, a business paper, uses a combination of type and illustration for a magazine-like cover.

There are five ways to present the tabloid:

1. Use it as a poster to sell several stories inside. Both display

type and illustrations can be used, but even one decently sized illustration will substantially restrict the number or items that can be teased.

2. Use it as a small-newspaper page.

3. Emphasize illustrations. Instead of display type, use one, two, or even three photographs to sell the paper. The image would be more visual than that of a traditional newspaper.

4. Use a single-cover illustration in the tradition of the news magazines. Overprinting permits giving the illustration a title and promoting other stories inside.

5. All of the above. An editor may feel that the flexibility to choose any of the approaches on consecutive days is more important than being consistent. Any publication will discard a standard format to handle the big event; extraordinary news requires extraordinary handling.

It does not matter whether the cover contains news, display type or illustration because readers do not spend much time on Page 1 of a tabloid. That is why it is even more important for tabloid editors to lure the reader inside and provide a wealth of material there. Most of the successful tabloids open the first few pages to editorial content. Whatever items are located up front, the first few pages are essential for creating reader traffic throughout the publication. The Leader offers a second front on the important Page 3 position and follows with another open page (Figs. 15.7-15.8). Separate sections relieve broadsheet editors of some of that burden.

SECTIONALIZING

None of the successful tabs can adequately overcome the problem of size. Newsday publishes nearly 200 pages an issue. Some issues are as large as 250 pages.

To create internal departments, some large tabs start sectionalized interest areas on the right-hand page so that readers can pull out the entire section. Unfortunately, unless readers work from the middle out, they will probably pull out several other sections too. Newsday once developed a thumb index punch on the side of the paper to help readers find sections but dropped the idea. Many tabloids start the sports section on the back page and work in. Some run a broadsheet food section tucked sideways into the tab. That section, which takes advantage of the full-page grocery advertisements, can easily be pulled out. Some print business and sports in a section that can be pulled from the middle.

Design is an important element in identifying sections. The move from news to a section can be signaled not only by the traditional labeling but also by a different grid, different use of white space, altering the horizontal-vertical emphasis and typography. Because it is not easy to separate sections physically, it is more important that tabloid sections have different personalities. The Rocky Mountain News achieves a non-news look in its Money section (Fig. 15.9). The New York Daily News news pages (Fig. 15.10) looks distinctly different from its Now Health section (Fig. 15.11), primarily because of the way white space is used.

15.7 The Leader invites readers inside by presenting two pages full of interesting material.

15.8 Page 4 continues to get the reader into the habit of opening the paper from the front.

15.9 A lower element count and white space combine to give the Money section front a different feel from the news pages.

In the softer feature or lifestyle sections, ragged right type can be used to signify the less formal approach. In entertainment, it might be appropriate to use heavy rules freely, but in a fashion section, thin rules would give a more dignified aura. Headline formats, if not the typeface, can also be changed according to section. The news can be presented in traditional style, while features rely on titles, labels and readouts.

It is important to create different personalities for each section, but the publication should be unified. One say this is done is by standardizing section headers. Standardized identifiers can be designed by using the same headline face throughout, even if the format is different, using the same basic format for teasers on the section fronts throughout, or stipulating that all section fronts have summaries or standard indexes. The effort to unify the sections becomes more important as the differentiation between the sections increases. The points are not contradictory. Publications that do not choose to create separate personalities for sections have less need for standardized promotional approaches and indexes. On the other hand, publications that do create different personalities must show the reader that the sections are part of the same family even though they are different in content and approach.

Inside, the tabloid has an opportunity to adopt a newspaper or magazine format. A newspaper format has headlines running over all the legs of the story, and the heads usually are large. A magazine format is more vertical, has smaller heads, and wraps type out from beneath heads (Fig. 15.12).

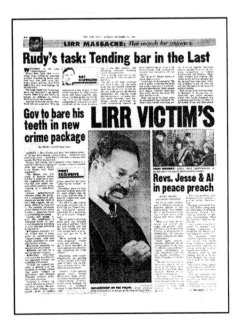

15.10 The Daily News' news pages are loud and brash.

15.11 But the News changes pace when it reaches the Health section. Designers use smaller type, fewer elements and more white space.

15.12 The magazine format features fewer elements and copy wrapping from under headlines.

SPREADS

The manageable size of an open tabloid permits the design editor to treat facing pages as a single unit. Even when stories or pictures do not use the gutter between facing pages, the designer should treat the pages or spread as one unit for purposes of balance and flow. In the tabloid, it is often possible to continue stories and pictures from the left-hand to the right-hand page, and even the gutter can be used on the spread in the middle of a section. Using the gutter elsewhere is always risky because a continuous sheet of paper is not always available, and headlines and photographs may not align properly.

When a double truck is done properly (Fig. 15.13), it takes advantage of the extra inch or so in the gutter and brings two vertical pages together into one horizontal unit. Notice that the copy and illustration flow across the gutter, and the space is not divided in halves.

15.13 The double truck uses the space in the margin between pages. The page is also properly divided one-third, two-thirds.

RELATIVE SIZING

The most important design principle for tabloid editors to remember is that sizing is relative to the dimension of the publication. A 1-column picture in a broadside newspaper would look large in Reader's Digest or TV Guide. A 3-column picture in a broadsheet would look large in a tabloid. The fact that National Geographic, with its 33 by 52 1/2-pica page size, has been able to establish itself as a quality photo graphic magazine is a testament
to the principle of proportion.

Certainly a tabloid can never match the broadsheet newspaper's ability to run a picture 78 picas wide on Page 1. A photograph run as wide as the tabloid page will look large in relation to the size of the newspaper. Consequently, it is important for editors to use photographs properly in tandem to emphasize large and small shapes.

TYPOGRAPHY

Display type selection is also different for tabloids because there are fewer headlines and choices of size. Consequently, weight becomes an effective way to show contrast. A headline schedule built around a bold or extrabold face would permit the editors to downsize heads, an appropriate measure for a tabloid. Smaller heads save space and preserve the proportions on a tab page. A lighter face should be available for decks and blurbs.

15.14 Art and white space give the Herald's business tabloid a distinctive look.

15.15 The tab looks and feels like a magazine within the newspaper.

15.16 In color, the "W" and the woman's blazer are the same shade of red; the "oman" and the title are the same yellow-gold. All the elements work together.

JUMPS

Jumps are a problem in any publication but, properly handled, are less so for tabloids than broadsheets. In a tabloid, however, the writing must be tighter to avoid the necessity of jumping a large number of stories. A medium-sized story in a broadsheet might jump past several pages and, in the process, lose the reader. The tabloid can capitalize on its magazine-like format and continue to the next page, which is less annoying to the reader and is a pattern familiar to magazine readers. When tabs jump stories several pages away, they lose their advantage over the broadsheets.

Tabloids can also jump from one page to a facing page without using continued lines if ads do not intervene. A blurb or pullout quotes would be a good devices to replace the jump head.

Tabloid inserts

Tabloid inserts devoted to subjects ranging from business to entertainment to senior citizens are among the most common uses of tabloids. Here designers apply the elements listed earlier in the chapter. Is the subject matter newsy? Features? Primarily listings? The Miami Herald's Business Monday section covers are built around type and illustration to give it a distinctive look (Figs. 15.14-15.15). When photos are used as a poster front, designers have to be careful to preserve the legibility of the type. Tabloid cover photographs should be shot with the understanding that type will be added. Designers should also be alert to the colors in the picture and the promo type (Fig. 15.16). Inside, the pages range from a compilation of quick and relaxed reads, and the designs should reflect it (Figs. 15.17-15.19).

15.17 The use of ragged right type gives the page a more relaxed look.

15.18 Generous use of white space gives the page a non-news feel.

15.19 The designer played with the typography to produce a page that has a featurish look.

Super tabs

Not all tabloids are the same size. Tabloids in Europe, for instance, are larger. The typical tabloid in the United States and Canada is about 62 X 90-picas. By contrast, the super tab is about 70 x 99-picas. The larger size offers readers the advantages of handling, but also gives the designer a slightly larger canvas and more options (Fig. 15.20). The tabloid created for the Olympics in Spain was the familiar European size (Fig. 15.21- 15.22). It's a size that deserves to get more attention and consideration in the United States.

Sunday magazines

Newspaper Sunday magazines often are similar in size to the tabloid format. Sometimes they are even printed on newsprint. Often, though, they are printed on better quality paper stock and have a personality distinct from the daily sections of the newspaper.

The principles of design are constant from format to format, but some general practices are common among Sunday magazines. Most of these practices are based on the belief that the magazine audience is more selective and will take time to read that section. The following principles should be kept in mind:

1. A good advertising arrangement and proper editorial space is essential to success. Ad sizes should be restricted to full, half and quarter pages (except perhaps in a special section for small advertisers) to create modular spaces for editorial copy. Try to dedicate at least one open spread (two facing pages) for the cover story or a right-hand lead page that opens to a spread.

2. The beginning of the editorial content should be clearly estab-

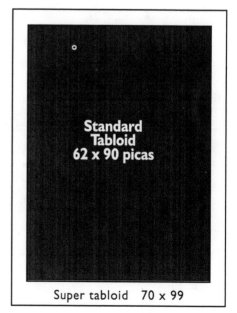

15.20 The standard tabloid would fit comfortably inside the super tab, which is eight picas wider and about nine picas longer than the standard broadsheet.

15.21 The super tab offers readers ease of handling and offers editors a bigger canvass than the standard tab.

15.22 The super tab page offers designers an opportunity to place more elements on the page without clutter than a standard-size tab.

15.23 The one-third, two-third division of space creates a pleasing contrast of sizes and shapes on the page.

lished. Some magazines are so crammed with advertising that the reader must turn several pages before finding editorial copy. Place some surefire reader interest material up front.

3. Begin each story with a strong focus. The reader should recognize immediately where each story starts. Use large type and photographs or illustrations for openers. The spread in the Ft. Lauderdale Sun-Sentinel's magazine uses the classic one-third, two-thirds division of space (Fig. 15.23).

4. Use plenty of white space in the magazine, especially around the title that starts the story. The magazine page is not be like the newspaper page, which is usually full from margin to margin. Put the title about 30 percent of the way down the opening page. White space in the margins is also important. The outer margin usually is larger than the interior, or interpage, margin. There should be more white space between the editorial copy and the advertising than there is between elements within the editorial spread.

5. Although the white space in the margins enhances the text that it surrounds, that margin area can also be used effectively for bleeds—pictures or illustrations that run to the edge of the page. Bleeds permit larger picture display and provide page contrast.

6. Design facing pages as one unit whenever possible. Create a strong horizontal left-to-right flow rather than a vertical flow.

7. Display typefaces appropriate to the content can be used on the larger stories without producing clutter. Newspapers with several different stories on each page usually cannot use different typefaces without producing a type specimen book. Once a typeface has been selected, it should be used throughout that particular story to provide a unity of design and ensure reader

recognition.

8. Use titles and labels rather than news heads. Within reason, the designer and staff should write the headlines and then determine the format rather than specifying a format into which the content must be squeezed. There is always room for compromise, but the magazine staff should take advantage of the use of fewer stories to tell and sell the way they want.

9. Avoid ending a story with a graphic explosion. In fact, it is usually better not to place art or photographs on the last page of a story because they may compete with the opening of the next spread.

10. Have a strong reader feature at the back of the magazine. A significant number of readers move from the back to the front. Do not let them sneak up on you. The nationally syndicated *Parade* puts its popular Personality Parade on Page 2. *USA Weekend* ends with a burst of short items (Fig. 15.24).

11. Try to build a rhythm into your magazine. Do not bunch all the long or short stories together; alternate. Work closely with the advertising department to be sure you get enough space to hook the reader before the story disappears into the columns of advertising.

12. Avoid jump lines when stories continue on consecutive pages. However, try to place a sales pitch, such as a blurb or quote pull-out, on each page. Each page represents an opportunity to get readers interested in the story.

13. Anchor your standing elements. Readers need to know where things are located.

14. Use the cover to advertise the magazine. It is just one of several sections available to Sunday newspaper customers and something must attract their attention to make them pick it up. Esquire says "read me" from the newsstand; the Sunday magazine says it from the coffee table.

15.24 The last inside page of USA Weekend offers readers plenty of snippets. Many readers start reading magazines and tabloids from the back to the front. Editors have started placing material at the back to entice them further.

> *In selecting and arranging elements, the advertising designer tries to achieve both order and beauty. The order which the designer creates out of a chaos of pictures, copy blocks, headlines, and white space makes it easy for the reader to read and understand the ad. The beauty makes the reader glad to be there.*
>
> **Roy Paul Nelson**
> **AUTHOR**

16. DESIGNING ADVERTISING

 Few newspaper managers look carefully at the newspaper as an integrated whole. The advertising and editorial departments are as separate as church and state. That's necessary to ensure editorial integrity, but editorial and advertising messages share space on most pages. They shouldn't both just show up there; the interplay between the two affects readership of both. The arrangement of the advertisements, the spacing and rules between editorial and advertising, the typography in the ads all contribute—or detract from—the overall presentation of the page and thus the readership. Conversely, editorial has understandably guarded traditional open pages on front, editorial, op-ed and section fronts. The concept of such open pages is more common in the United States than in other parts of the world. It is possible that at least some papers should examine the design relationships between editorial and advertising.

The symbiotic relationship

The arrangement of advertisements on the page is the major factor affecting presentation on inside pages. Perhaps one of the strongest myths in advertising is that readership of ads is increased if editorial copy touches the ad. That sales pitch, designed to counter competition from shoppers, which don't carry editorial, justifies advertising wells and pyramided stacks. Although few newspapers use the wells—with the ads stacking both right and left on a page—most use a pyramid stack either right or left. The alternative is a modular stack, in which

175

16.1 When the ads are squared off, the editorial copy is left with a modular space. The page is easier to design and offers much less clutter.

16.2 This Canadian paper runs an advertisement in the same space on Page 1 daily. Newspapers used to publish advertisements regularly on Page 1.

the ads are squared off. Editorial and advertising coexist more peacefully in modular stacks (Fig. 16.1). Researchers have found no significant difference in the readership of advertisements that don't touch editorial copy from those that do. In addition, readers said they found the pages with modular advertising stacks more attractive (Lewis 1989). Ironically, more than 70 percent of daily newspapers now also offer shoppers as part of a total market coverage strategy.

Modular ad stacks require that the newspaper restrict ad sizes to quarter, half and full pages and any ad that runs the width of the page. A compromise is to sell any size and square the ads off as much as possible. Three two-column by 5-inch ads, for instance, square off as a six-column by 5-inch ad. Regardless of the arrangement of the advertisements, newspapers should consider leaving at least 2 picas between advertising and editorial and specifying that all advertisements have a cutoff rule.

The typeface used in headlines should also be off-limits to the advertising departments. If English Times is used in headlines, it can be confusing to see it also as the lead headline in an advertisement. Although it is impossible to control the typography of agency ads, most newspaper ads are designed in-house. Such a rule would have a beneficial effect on the overall look of the page.

Similarly, editorial departments should re-examine the traditional open pages. Newspapers in many countries offer advertising on page 1 without confusing readers or unduly interfering with the news presentation. The Globe and Mail, a Toronto, Ontario, paper, runs a strip advertisement at the bottom of Page 1 (Fig. 16.2). Whether they appear on Page 1 or section fronts, such ads in dedicated spaces that span the width of the page can be accommodated into the design of a page and increase newspaper revenues. Section fronts usually are advance pages; that is, they are done a day or two before publication. To make this workable, the advertising department also has to have an early deadline or sell the space only on a long-term contract basis. If the dedicated space were 3 to 5 inches deep and six columns wide, the page designers would have no trouble accommodating them. USA Today has introduced an advertisement at the top of Page 1; the New York Times has run a quarter page on its op-ed page for years.

Another approach that has appeared in magazines is the flex form ad, which breaks out of the traditional rectangle or square. Such an ad may run not only across the bottom but also extend one or two columns wide the length of the page. Such approaches are guaranteed to attract readers' attention to the ad but are not calculated to create an integrated display of editorial and advertising.

Still, it's a subject worth researchers' time. Whether it's flex form ads or placement of ads less obtrusively on traditional open pages, newspapers should know not only how ads affects how the reader views the elements on the page but also how the reader perceives the newspaper.

Typography

Typography is to advertising what style is to an automobile. The type not only communicates what the advertiser wants said but carries the message in the proper body. The connotative messages of type—the message that derives from the design of the typeface—is part of the message. The designer selects the proper typefaces, some to communicate the feel or atmosphere or subject matter, and some to carry the load of communicating the details. The different atmospheres typefaces can create are illustrated in two advertisements commemorating Martin Luther King Day (Figs. 16.3 and 16.4). The typeface in Figure 16.3 reflects children's handwriting; the typeface in Figure 16.4 reflects chiseled Greek inscriptions. One is playful; one is formal. Look again at the company signatures. Pepsi is young, modern, forward looking. Nordstrom, a top-of-the-line department store, is quiet and dignified. The typefaces reflect the messages and the advertisers.

16.3 The typography on the blackboard reinforces the art work and the theme of the advertisement.

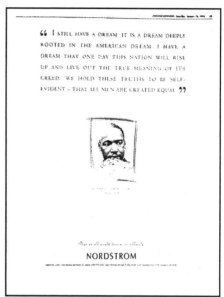

16.4 The typography establishes a different mood from that shown in Fig. 16.3.

Typeface weights and forms offer the designer opportunities to use contrast to avoid typographic monotony and to emphasize some parts of the message. The principles explained in Chapters 8 through 10 apply here. Designers use bold to speak loudly, light to speak softly; they use large type to yell, small type to tell. When you walk down a carnival midway, everyone is yelling at you. Most of the messages are lost. But if you spot one barker nodding, speaking softly, you would be attracted. We pick out a whisper in a cacophony of voices, a shout among whispers. Contrast is a powerful typographic tool. The designer uses large sizes and bold weights to emphasize, smaller sizes and medium weights to provide details.

The designer protects the legibility of type by making certain that if type is reversed, it's run large; if a gray screen or color tint is used, the type size is increased to compensate. Stylized typefaces that are fine for signatures and large headlines may not be for advertising text.

Working with visuals

Designers work with photographs and illustrations. With the availability of software that manipulates photographs, it's easier and less expensive to create photographs designed to sell products. A warning, however. It's illegal to use photographs intended for non-commercial use in an advertisement without the consent of the people pictured. To be safe, you should use only photographs with models or those for which you have the written permission of the people involved.

As we discussed in Chapter 5, photographs are the single highest readership item in the editorial section of a newspaper. It's safe to say that they attract high levels of attention in advertisements, too. Photographs normally have more impact than illustrations. They usually are heavier graphically and are more credible. Photographs without any special treatment are the strongest, but in some situations, special screens may produce an appropriate image. Illustrations sometimes are easier to tailor to the specific advertising message. Advertisements with illustrations also attract more advertising readership than those without illustrations, and the bigger the illustration, the higher the readership.

Both photographs and illustrations can help direct the reader's eye. If someone in the visual is pointing, the copy or headline ought to be at the end of the finger. If the people are looking down, put the headline underneath.

Using color

Color sells. And color in newspapers is probably even more effective than color in magazines. One reason is contrast. In the newspaper's black-and-white world, editorial and advertising color stand out. How much varies widely with the study. Some have shown readership almost twice as high; others at 40 to 50 percent higher. Either way, it's significant. Although the specific numbers are debatable (though not to the advertiser, who's trying to decide whether the premium price is worth it), the trend is consistent. Readers will buy newspapers with color on the front more consistently than the same paper in black and white. Advertiser returns, as measured by such things as coupon redemption, always increase with color.

Color also affects eye flow. Readers move from color to black and white. Designers should use color to influence the sequence of readership. When color appears in an advertisement, either the signature should be in color, or color should appear close to it to complete the sale.

Designers should also be conscious of the colors chosen. Different colors have different messages (see Chapter 11). In one study, 200 people were asked to comment on coffee. The respondents didn't know it, but different colored coffee pots were used to serve different groups the same coffee. Of those served from a brown pot, 73 percent said the coffee was too strong. Of those from a red pot, 84 percent said it was rich and full bodied. This illustrates the power of color to influence perceptions, and that's why color choices in advertising are important. Because darker colors recede and brighter colors come to the front, colors can be used to emphasize some points over others.

Sometimes a dab of color may be more effective than the whole paint can. When television was mostly black and white, color drew attention to advertisements in color. Soon, all commercials were in color. The networks wouldn't even permit black-and-white commercials. However, when competitive pressures finally forced them to rescind the rule, Dr Pepper jumped at the chance. Its black-and-white ads drew a disproportionate amount of attention because they appeared in a sea of color. Soon, other advertisers began using black and white in all or parts of commercials. Contrast is a powerful weapon in video and print.

Putting it all together

Effective advertisements have strong headlines and, usually, a strong visual. There are several categories of headlines, but four of the most common are:

1. The benefit headline. Sell the sizzle, not the steak. Sell the free time, not the lawnmower. Sell acceptability, not deodorant. Sell safety, not tires. If it's free, say so (Fig. 16.5).

2. The news headline. The advertiser has a new product. Timeliness makes it news, and the news becomes a sales tool.

3. The how-to headline. The advertiser hooks onto the service journalism trend by promising the customer the solution to a problem. It may be a home-repair problem or a sex-appeal problem. The headline concentrates on the how-to aspect.

4. The testimonial headline. Other customers or celebrities testify on behalf of the product.

The headline combined with the illustration attracts the eye because of size and placement, and the content should focus the reader on the benefits of the product or products. The headline on car loans (Fig. 16.6) is a rhyme that, if reinforced, may echo in customers' minds. The typeface is playful; the illustration is playful; and the white space buffers both from the adjoining advertisements or editorial copy.

The headline and illustration together create the focus or lead for the ad. The most successful are those that have a dominant element. The four items that lead the Byrd's grocery ad (Fig. 16.7) are larger than the others, but because there are four, they compete with each other. Nothing has

16.5 "Free" attracts attention. Putting it in the headline emphasizes the benefit and attracts scanners.

16.6 The title is a catchy turn of words that will echo is some readers' minds.

16.7 This multiple-element ad organizes the items but does not emphasize any of them.

16.8 By contrast with the ad in Fig. 16.7, this grocery ad offers one element that's larger and, therefore, more important than the others. With a dominant element, the page looks more organized.

16.9 A grid alone won't organize an ad if too many rules, borders and decorative elements are added.

dominance. Compare that with the Schnucks' grocery ad (Fig. 16.8). One module is dominant, and so is the type. The ad has a focus. It also has unity. Each element is presented with the same graded screen. In the original, the name of each item appears in red.

The Schnucks' design also illustrates another important principle: organization. On multiple-element ads, designers should create grids and work in modules to organize. Large modules are devoted to the most important product or products; smaller modules sell other items. The grid helps organize elements and show the relationship among them. But the grid alone doesn't remove clutter. Even ads with clearly defined grids can suffocate the content with too many bells and whistles (Fig. 16.9).

The reader's eye moves from left to right, top to bottom, big to small, dark to light and color to black and white. Designers should take advantage of these natural patterns. For instance, the lead headline will be big. The gradation in type size and weight will lead readers to the punch line, product or price, which should be larger and bolder than the copy. The reader moves from large and dark to small and light to medium and bold.

Every advertisement should give the customers the information they need to take action. That information usually includes address, phone and fax numbers, store hours, whether customers can order by phone, which credit cards are accepted, whether the store takes checks, date the sale ends, etc. It doesn't do any good to create an advertisement that falls short of critical information.

Designing accessories

Here are some other things to keep in mind in advertisement design:

1. Rules and borders should define the advertisement, not draw attention to themselves. Heavy rules may emphasize a small ad on a broadsheet page, but they also can obscure the content. Decorative borders occasionally help create the proper environment, but more often, they simply clutter the ad. Use restraint.

2. Used correctly, white space isn't wasted space. It's used correctly when it is to the outside of the type and illustrations. It buffers the ad against other advertisements or editorial copy. Surround a 2 x 5 ad with other ads, build white space into it and it will stick out of the crowd. Don't trap white space inside the elements, however, or you'll draw attention to the white space instead of the content. Let the signature breath by building in white space around it.

3. Align elements in the ad with other elements. This is easier to do if you have a grid. For instance, once you locate your lead headline and illustration, the copy block might align vertically with the headline or illustration.

4. Create a "look" for an advertiser. There should be aspects of the design—the typeface, the signature, the use of white space, the grid—that identify the frequent advertiser.

V.

BEYOND THE BASICS: NEWSPAPER DESIGN

17. THE PROCESS OF REDESIGN

At the Waco Tribune-Herald, staff members eagerly awaited response from readers to the redesigned paper. What would they think of the new typeface? The teasers below the flag? The new section formats? The new content?

What did the readers call about? Favorite comic strips that had been dropped. And one reader complained that she couldn't find Ann Landers. "But it is where it has always been," the editor told the reader. Actually, it had been moved—about 3 inches down the page.

This is the reality of redesign. Move something and you will get complaints. The first wave of reactions often is from loyal readers who have well-rehearsed habits. Habit is a powerful force when dealing with consumers. Just ask the Canadian marmalade company that produced three flavors. The labels were color-coded to the flavors. In a redesign of the labels, the color-coding system was eliminated. Sales dropped dramatically. The field marketing staff identified the problem, the colors were put back on the labels and sales were restored.

Change is uncomfortable for many readers. But it can be anticipated and managed. In Waco, the management, which had set a goal of attracting more younger readers without alienating the older, loyal readers, was uncomfortable with changing the newspaper's traditional Old English flag. But when the older, loyal readers in a focus group enthusiastically supported the change, it was accepted.

Change is also uncomfortable to many people in the newsroom.

183

When a redesign is properly defined as an examination of process and content as well as organization and appearance, it strikes at the heart of everyone's work. A redesign takes time and commitment. It requires the involvement of readers and staff members throughout the newspaper. When it is done right, it is one of the most rewarding jobs in your career.

Getting others involved

Just as tapping the creative resources of people in the newsroom results in a better product, so will tapping the resources of a wide variety of the newspaper's employees. The person who has final authority to accept or reject the redesign plans, whether it be the editor or the publisher, should be on the redesign committee. In addition, the committee should include the staff member primarily responsible for graphics; departmental editors and representatives of the copy desk; reporters; and personnel from the production, advertising and circulation or marketing departments.

Why should non-news people be on the committee? The news or editorial department may be responsible for content and form, but the marketing or circulation department has to sell it. Unfortunate as it may be, the people in marketing often talk to more customers than editors do. And no design is going to be successful unless the production department has the opportunity to point out mechanical possibilities and limitations.

Advertising representatives are equally important. Column widths can't be changed in any publication without involving advertising and management. Other policies that may come out of a redesign, such as restrictions on reverse ads and on small editorial holes at the top of inside pages, also require involvement of the advertising department.

There is yet another important reason to include all these people: It's good management. A broadly based committee offers a variety of perspectives and experiences, and because the members are responsible for the formulation of the plan, they will be more enthusiastic about implementing it. A committee can't design a paper, but it can establish the goals and provide feedback. The designer translates those goals to the paper.

Predesign questions

Design, as we have seen, involves process, content and form. The process is how the newsroom is organized and how its members interact to generate ideas and stories and how they determine the means to tell those stories (see Chapter 12).

Because form follows content, questions about content must be answered before a redesign is ordered. Susan Clark, then editor and publisher of the Niagara (Niagara Falls, N.Y.) Gazette, emphasized this point in a report on her paper's redesign: "The reader survey has not meant just a redesign of our newspaper. It has meant, most importantly, an examination of what we write and how we write it."

Every publication should answer the following questions before undergoing a redesign:

1. What content changes should be made? Readers can help make decisions about content changes, and newspapers can determine relatively cheaply what readers think. Some newspapers use focus-group sessions. The newspaper invites groups of readers and non-readers (perhaps to separate sessions) to a roundtable discussion. If possible, the editors watch through one-way windows. Otherwise, they can listen to a tape recording or watch a videotape. Another approach, sometimes used in addition to focus groups, is to survey a scientifically selected group of subscribers and possibly non-subscribers. What you ask depends on what you have identified as potential problem areas: content, personality, organization, credibility, usefulness. A semantic differential scale such as that used by Click and Stempel (1974) to test readers' reactions to the front pages is useful to check their perceptions of personality and credibility factors. Respondents are asked to rate the newspaper on a scale of 1 to 10 with word pairs at either end. You can see from the categories and word choices below that the scale is also useful for testing design prototypes and the redesign after it is published:

Evaluative: pleasant/unpleasant, valuable/worthless, important/unimportant, interesting/boring.
Ethical: fair/unfair, truthful/untruthful, accurate/inaccurate, unbiased/biased, responsible/irresponsible.
Stylistic: exciting/dull, fresh/stale, easy/difficult, neat/messy, colorful/colorless.
Potency: bold/timid, powerful/weak, loud/soft.
Activity: tense/relaxed, active/passive, modern/old-fashioned.

It is enlightening to have readers, editors and staff rank the present paper on these factors. The staff often has a perception quite different from management, and readers may respond differently than either the staff or management. However, the scale provides only guidelines, not answers. Important questions about content and organization can't be answered with this kind of scale.

Another important method of examining content is by gathering staff members from all departments and posing this question: What do your readers and non-readers do with their time and money? The question will produce hundreds of answers. The next step is to ask which beats cover these activities. The exercise illustrates the gap between what newspapers cover and where people's interests lie. From there, the staff can select the most important of the uncovered items and find ways to include them in the beat system.

Related questions are "what's in the paper that shouldn't be?" and "what's not in the paper that should be?" The first question forces the staff to look critically at what's there. Like a ship picking up barnacles, a newspaper picks up content that may have been important 10 or 20 years earlier but may not meet readers' needs now. The second question is another way of asking what readers want.

2. What are your marketing goals? How many editions do you have, and who are the audiences of each? How many newspapers are sold in vending machines? What is the potential growth? Who sub-

We are in a liberated age where technology permits newspaper people to produce newspapers we could once only dream about. The only constraints are those concerned with knowing what to do and how to do it; not with who is to do it.
Bob James
NEWSPAPER CONSULTANT, ENGLAND

There is nothing as awakening for the staff as being exposed to what their readers think about them.

Vikki Porter
EXECUTIVE EDITOR
The Olympian

scribes to your paper and why? Who doesn't and why not?

3. What are the characteristics of your market? Is it highly competitive? Does the competition come from other newspapers, shoppers and broadcast or home-delivery information systems? What is the white collar/blue collar mix? What time do people go to work and get home? What kind of a mass transportation system exists? Are you near lakes, mountains or forests where people spend hours in recreation? Are you in an urban area where movie rentals, theater, dining out and sports are important recreational activities? Is there a mix of religions or does one denomination dominate? How would you describe the community—retirement? financial? agribusiness?

4. How will the paper be organized? In survey after survey, market after market, readers repeat that their primary design concern is with the organization of the paper. Beyond the basic divisions for news, what additional sections do you have for your particular audience? For instance, Dallas is a fashion center, so the Morning News has a big fashion section. The St. Petersburg Times offers a tabloid called "Seniority" for its retirement community. The Miami Herald prints a Spanish-language edition. The New York Times has an outstanding books section. Each market has its own peculiarities, and each newspaper ought to reflect them. When answering questions about organization before a redesign, some newspaper managements, especially if they are consulting with the advertising and marketing departments, may find potential sections that will broaden the newspaper's appeal. Organization also means anchoring all regularly appearing features, ranging from advice columns to editorial columns, in the same place in every issue.

5. What personality do you want to project? Type used in combination with other devices creates a personality. Ask key management personnel to describe the personality they want the paper to have and compare the responses. If they agree, the management team has a common goal. However, there probably will be differences of opinion. Agreement must be reached on the personality desired before the designer can select the elements to achieve that personality. Although readers get their first impression from the typography of a newspaper, the content must be consistent with the rest of the message. The Eugene, Ore., Register-Guard, set three goals that affected the personality of the paper: "Keep the traditional look and feel of the Register-Guard and make changes without shocking our readers; maintain an elegant and pleasing appearance; increase the entry points on the page, offering more 'at-a-glance' devices."

6. What are your personnel limitations? Is the newspaper large enough to have a design editor? How many staff members will be responsible for the daily implementation of the design? Who are they? Is the staff capable of carrying out the design? Will someone watch for variation in the design and make the necessary adjustments as problems arise? Does the staff have artists to create illustrations, maps and charts? If the staff is limited, should you consider a formatted design?

7. What are the limitations of the management system? If the editorial management doesn't include a strong graphics voice, the design

can't be executed no matter how well-intentioned the editor may be. The format can change, but lack of visual thinking will not produce good word and picture combinations or a paper that explains with graphs, maps and charts.

8. What are the limitations of the production system? If color is to be used daily, is there a photo staff capable of producing it, a production staff capable of processing it and enough press capacity to print it? Is the paper printed on an offset press? What limitations does the production process impose on the design?

The content and organization of the newspaper can be determined largely by the answers to these questions. That is important because design is the proper organization of the content in an artistically pleasing and technically legible package. The way to design is through long-term planning to establish the newspaper's goals and short-term planning to produce the stories and illustrations that appear in the newspaper daily.

Implementation

Using the responses to the above questions, the designer can begin to organize and label the content of the newspaper and select the elements to achieve the personality desired. If a modern functional look is desired, the popular Helvetica, Univers or Franklin Gothic typefaces may be appropriate. If management wants to emphasize the newspaper's tradition, one of the classic faces such as Caslon or Century may be more appropriate. If the newspaper wants to build a reputation for local coverage, the second section, clearly labeled, could lead off with local news. However, the front-page story selection is also vital to that image. Decisions about the packaging, placement and location of columnists must be determined by how hard the editors want to sell them. If the paper has large amounts of record copy (real estate transactions, court news and police blotter material), material must be gathered efficiently and presented coherently.

As the designer tries to solve each of these problems, the redesign committee, or a smaller group representing it, needs to see and respond to proposed changes. Incorporating some of the committee suggestions into the redesign will be helpful in getting their support and will save the designer a great deal of time. Problems or disagreements that surface early in the process can be solved much more easily than those that surface at the last minute. A designer who is deeply involved in the project may find it difficult to compromise or separate ego from practicality. If the committee members have seen the various parts of the redesign, they are more likely to approve the whole.

Once the committee has approved the project, it must be sold to both staff and readers. If the staff has been kept informed during the course of the project, the results will not be a surprise. However, the committee and the designer must have enough flexibility to adjust the plan when the staff members find weaknesses.

One of the first questions editors ask is whether to phase in the redesign or to introduce it entirely in one issue. The answer lies in the local market conditions. Introducing all or most of it at once allows the

> *I'm positively thrilled! Don't let any belly-bitchers tell you otherwise. This is something worth getting up for!*
>
> **Jackson Sun reader**
> **COMMENTING ON REDESIGN**

17.1 This prototype shows three ways to handle round-ups of different categories of news for inside pages.

17.2 At a focus group, participants were first asked to talk about the paper that they were already reading.

17.3 Then the focus group was asked to react to a prototype of a front page format under consideration. They liked most of the changes, but they suggested that less space be devoted to the teasers.

17.4 The focus group participants had an impact. The redesigned paper incorporated several suggestions, including handling of the promotional items.

newspaper to use the redesign in a circulation promotion campaign. Many newspapers introduce it to advertisers a few days before readers see it. A phase-in takes away much of the impact of the changes, but depending on your readership, that might be necessary. The New York Times has phased in a number of changes. A look behind its news section reveals a variety of well-designed sections. The Times changed a section at a time, quietly and steadily. Its readers, like those of the Wall Street Journal, are consumers of the newspaper's traditions, credibility and authority. Any dramatic change in format or content could have been disastrous.

Remember that a redesign won't resurrect a failing newspaper. Peter Palazzo redesigned the New York Herald Tribune and Chicago Daily News as they lay on their deathbeds. The diagnosis was terminal before the transfusion. The time to redesign is when things are going well. A newspaper that is constantly updating is responding to changing market conditions.

Prototype phase

The designer or designers translate ideas into concrete examples in the prototype phase. Designers should be willing to produce several suggestions for each page and to listen closely to reactions (Fig. 17.1). Prototypes first are directed to an in-house group. When general agreement is reached on one or two approaches, it's time to take the prototypes to a reader focus group. When the pages are taken to readers, they should be printed on the newspaper's press to make it look as realistic as possible. In Waco, three

17.5 This prototype drew favorable comments on the promotional items across the top and the flag, which reflected the arch for the St. Louis community.

17.6 The headline treatment on the lead story confused many focus group participants, in part, because it was a question.

17.7 The pullouts giving times and places drew rave reviews from the focus group participants.

17.8 This was one of the most popular pages with the focus group participants. Few papers marketed to a black audience offer summaries of national and international news of interest to them.

17.9 The participants loved the content, and endorsed the trivia quiz. They said the quiz would help draw younger readers to the page.

17.10 The results of the focus groups were summarized by reproducing the pages and offering comments from the participants.

groups of readers were convened to represent different demographic and readership segments. First they were asked questions about the paper as it was (Fig. 17.2). Then they were shown prototypes of several pages (Fig. 17.3). They liked the more modern look, selected preferences from a sampling of new nameplates and expressed concern about the amount of space devoted to the teasers. The designer reduced the size of the teasers and added the new flag for the final product (Fig. 17.4).

The Sears Foundation, in research that has implications for the majority press as well as the minority press, sponsored a study by the author of content and design changes on behalf of African-American papers. The study appears to show that minority readers are interested in many of the same content categories as majority readers but react more positively when they are written with their interests in mind. African-Americans like lively presentation of the material. Some of the prototypes appear in Figures 17.5 through 17.10.

The results

Design changes at newspapers are sometimes dramatic and sometimes subtle. In Raleigh, N.C., the paper hadn't been redesigned for years. The change is dramatic (Fig. 17.11 through 17.16). By comparison, at the Orange County Register, the change was less noticeable because of more recent redesigns (Fig. 17.24 and 17.25). A sampling of some redesigns follows (Figs. 17.11 through 17.28).

17.11 This is how the Raleigh, N.C., paper appeared before the redesign.

17.12 The redesigned flag gives the paper a more classic look, and the typography and vertical emphasis change the presentation of the news.

17.13 The Sunday edition looks different from the daily because of the treatment of the flag and promo boxes.

17.14 This is how the News & Observer's sports page looked before the redesign.

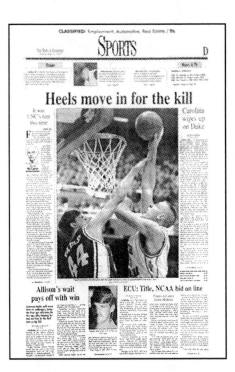

17.15 The redesigned sports section offers color and promotional elements.

17.16 The feature section headers change with the day of the week.

17.17 The Times had Futura headlines and traditional deck formats.

17.18 The redesign introduced a new headline face, flag and conversational decks.

17.19 Sectional pages offer a distinctive look with their vertical labels.

17.20 Prior to the redesign, the Oregonian was already offering conversational decks and an aggressive presentation of the news.

17.21 The redesign introduced bold conversational decks and a new promotional format. The frontpage grid consists of a 14-pica vertical digest and a nine-column, six-pica grid for the rest of the page.

17.22 The Seattle Times' look before the redesign was about 15 years old. The sans serif heads and the boxcar teasers looked tired.

17.23 Rather than just running the flags of the Times and the Post-Intelligencer in the combined Sunday edition, the paper is named "Sunday." The typography changes lightened the look of the paper.

17.24 The Register wasn't far behind the Times when it redesigned.

17.25 The redesign offers a fresh format above the flag, a sans serif with more personality and weight contrast in the conversational decks.

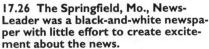

17.26 The Springfield, Mo., News-Leader was a black-and-white newspaper with little effort to create excitement about the news.

17.27 The redesign extended into the newsroom planning process. With planning, designers have the tools and the time to create exciting displays. The designers knew the decision was coming and planned the presentation accordingly.

17.28 Designers take advantage of the best way to tell a story to create impact. The map showing the overall movement of the story is an effective story-telling device. Spot blue has been added to the flag and the bar at the bottom of the page. Pictures and graphics also appear in color daily.

The stylebook

Like the editing stylebook, the purpose of the design stylebook is to enforce consistency and arbitrate disputes. It should not restrict creativity. Stylebooks should concentrate on what is or should be, not on what should not be.

The length and detail of a stylebook vary according to the size of the newspaper and the staff. Small newspapers, which don't have many sections, may get by with a few pages; papers with several sections and a huge staff need a stylebook that will probably run 50 or more pages. Formats alone often take another 10 to 20 pages.

Every stylebook should include information on how the paper is to be organized, the grid, typography, spacing, rules, photography, color, and design accessories such as logos, cutlines and jump lines. By the time the staff receives the stylebook, members should be well briefed on the contents.

Besides receiving the new stylebook and getting to know it, staff members should have enough training with the new formats to become familiar with them, to work out the bugs and clear up ambiguities. The training schedule must account for advance sections.

Education and promotion

A good newspaper belongs to the readers, not to the staff or publisher. That's why it's important to talk to the readers when you're ready to introduce the redesign. You're changing their newspaper; they deserve the courtesy of knowing ahead of time what is coming and why.

17.29 The Portland, Me., newspaper introduced its redesign by creating an information graphic to explain new features.

17.30 The News of Boca Raton, Fla., extensively promoted its radical redesign with in-house pages selling and telling about the redesign before it was introduced.

17.31 The Sun-Times introduced one of its redesigns by showing the evolution of the nameplate.

17.32 The Raleigh News & Observer published a fat tabloid section to promote its redesign. The tabloid featured articles and pictures of many of the staff members.

17.33 The tabloid, which appeared before the redesign was introduced, showed prototypes of the new pages and explained new features.

The newspaper can communicate through stories and advertisements. The Portland (Me.) Press Herald explained some of the features coming in the redesigned newspaper (Fig. 17.29). The News in Boca Raton, Fla., published a four-page section explaining the changes (Fig. 17.30), and the editor wrote a column about the benefits to the readers. The Chicago Sun-Times underwent a modest change and promoted it by showing the evolution of the newspaper's nameplate (Fig. 17.31). The Raleigh News & Observer published a tabloid explaining the changes and introducing staff members (Figs. 17.32 and 17.33). Every newspaper that introduces a redesign should talk to its readers, and then let the readers talk back. Some have staff members take phone calls. Others ask readers to fill out comment sheets. Some invite faxes. All of the methods involve engaging the community in a conversation.

> *The design of a daily newspaper is a difficult undertaking. Compromise on the niceties of typography is inevitable, control of layout minimal, and perfection unobtainable.*
>
> **Alan Fletcher**
> **DESIGNER**

18. DESIGNING SECTIONS

"Sometimes I feel that they [the local paper] are out to hassle me," a participant in a readership study said. "You can't find things, you're always turning pages, and the whole paper begins to fall apart."

Enter the designer with the tools to keep the paper from falling apart. The tools include organizational talents, labels and unifying devices. Like a carpenter constructing a house, the designer constructs the newspaper from the solid footings of sections. When the designer is finished and the occupants move in, they soon become familiar with every nook and cranny. It's hoped they will also feel at home.

The designer approaches the job with an understanding of how people go through a newspaper, why they read it and what competes for the their time and attention. Most of all, the designer appreciates the function of a newspaper. Designers should be more concerned about reader reaction than peer reaction.

Readers bring different expectations to different parts of the paper. Let's look at those differences.

The front page

Many design challenges are common to all sections, but each section has its own personality. More than any other, the front page is the paper. It's the first thing the reader sees; it sets the tone; it announces what's important. Through its structure, typography, visuals and element count, it proclaims the newspaper's personality.

18.1 The Des Moines Register looks modern because of its typography and color, but it retains a traditional touch with its vertical emphasis.

Vertical/horizontal. The Wall Street Journal is defined by its vertical format and its light typography. The Des Moines Register (Fig. 18.1) is also primarily vertical, but its bolder typography, pictures and color give it a different feel. Because a vertical format offers the opportunity to run more stories than a horizontal format, many newspapers have become more vertical in the last few years.

Most papers use a combination of horizontal and vertical elements. The combination approach is the most flexible, the most responsive to the news and the one most suited to offer a surprise each day.

Story and element count. Whether the paper is vertical or horizontal, a key factor in the paper's personality is the element count. Some editors count stories, but a more important factor is the number of elements for the window-shopper. Readers scan visuals and display type. Each story is an element because it has a headline, but each visual, each promo, each brief is also an element. USA Today and the Wall Street Journal have high element counts. Even the New York Times often has as many as 15 elements on the front page. The La Crosse (Wis.) Tribune also offers a high element count but looks significantly different from USA Today and the Journal (Fig. 18.2). The Maine Sunday Telegram has a much lower element count—and a different personality—on the front page (Fig. 18.3).

Readers of the 1990s have told researchers they want more activity on pages. Teasers or promotional items, color and briefs increase the element count and thus the activity.

Teasers. Most newspapers have teasers stripped above the flag; some have them below the flag (Fig. 18.4). Readers look at teasers. In the Poynter Institute for Media Studies' "Eyes on the News" study, readers looked at the teasers in the Minneapolis and Orange County papers even more than in the St. Petersburg paper, where the teasers were more quiet (Fig. 18.5). No study has yet been published to show whether readership of the teasers translates into higher readership of the stories they promote. Some newspapers also say they use them to increase street sales, but there is little evidence of any correlation between promos and sales. In fact, most customers know which newspaper they're going to buy from a machine or newsstand before they even see them.

Nonetheless, people who have the papers look at promotional items. That's another point of

18.2 The LaCrosse Tribune has a horizontal element, but uses pullouts and summaries to create a high element count.

18.3 On Sundays the Telegram lowers the element count slightly from the daily pace. The page always looks quieter because of the typography.

sale, and it also means newspapers can consider running them vertically or across the bottom to open up the top of the page again. Regardless of where they run, designers should change the format of the teasers often. Familiarity breeds boredom (see Chapter 19).

The grid. Most grids range from five to 10 columns. The narrow columns are usually used for decks and pullouts. In Figure 18.6, the narrow columns show up in the grid for the election graphic, in the pullout on the left of the feature package and in the deck for the lovelorn story. USA Today is seven columns. Most newspapers are six. Many have five. Usually, the narrower the columns, the higher the element count. Photos usually benefit from wider columns. In a five-column format, a three-column picture is about 46 picas wide. In a six-column format, it's about 39 picas wide.

Photographs. The trade-off for higher element counts often is less space to display pictures. The familiar battle in newsrooms across the country is between the news and photo editors. The news editor often argues for two or three stories above the fold. The photo editor argues that a large picture or pictures will attract more readership. Compromises often are made. The picture is run a column smaller; the picture is pushed down and disappears over the fold. Given the high readership of photographs, it's surprising how often they are misused. Good design starts with the photograph.

Digests. Many papers are running digests on the front. Digests are the easiest way to increase the element count and are at the heart of the page 1 presentation in the Wall Street Journal and USA Today. Digests are a reaction to people who say they don't have much time. A front page with a digest offers a more extensive menu of important information.

Framing. Often, the higher the element count, the more framing there is. The frame defines the built-in features; in Figure 18.7, you see the progression from teasers over the flag to teasers and briefs, run either vertically or horizontally. The x indicates the space available for the display news. As framing increases, flexibility decreases. Severe framing impinges on good photographic display. Even a vertical column of briefs can restrict photo display.

Jumps. Also affecting the front-page look is the policy on jumps. Readers hate jumps, but most newspapers continue to use them. A

18.4 Some designers believe that putting the teasers below the flag may increase the readership, but no studies have been conducted on it yet.

18.5 The more modest promotional treatment at St. Petersburg resulted in lower readership than in Minneapolis and Orange County.

18.6 The Oregonian has nine six-pica columns alongside its 14-pica digest column.

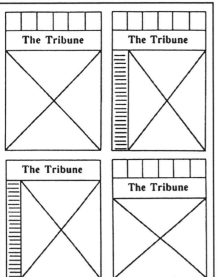

18.7 Framing defines the space for standing features. The X is the space is left for the daily report.

paper that jumps stories generally will have more stories on the front page than a paper that has a no-jump or low-jump policy. Pioneered by the News in Boca Raton, Fla., the "Boca jump" is a story that stops on page 1 and refers to a related story inside, which can be a sidebar or even the main story. If stories are jumped, consider using "please," as in "Please see KEYWORD, p. X." One researcher found that readers appreciated the simple courtesy (Pipps 1985).

Continued stories should also be located on the same page and in the same place each issue if possible. Some newspapers, including the New York Times, jump stories from one section to another, a practice that is inconvenient if not maddening to a reader who might not be able to find the section. Ideally, jumps from page 1 or a section front should be located on the back page of the section. However, that is a highly coveted advertising page and often is not available to editorial. Page 2 is a questionable location for jumps because it's sometimes difficult to clip stories that appear on both sides of a page. Wherever continued stories are located, they should be there consistently so subscribers learn where to look.

What they see when they arrive is often a one-word label over the jumped story. That's not enough. The advantage of a label jump head is that it is easily recognized by the reader who is following the story from the cover. However, few readers go directly to a jumped story. Most of them continue scanning the cover and may even read through the section before picking up a continued story. Others will not have seen the original story when they encounter the jump. A headline will attract more readers than a label. However, a headline that reflects the

18.8 This jump head style integrates the label format with a new headline. That combination appears to serve readers best.

18.9 The lead headline in a black sans serif stands out from the Bodoni used on all the other headlines.

18.10 The creative use of type gives the feature story a distinctive look and identifies it as special.

new material in the jump may not be recognized immediately as the same story. A combination of headline styles emphasizes the strengths of the two approaches.

One solution is a combination of a label and a new headline. There are several typographic ways of handling this combination. One is a mini-hammer head that serves as a keyword in identifying the story. The deck sells the new information (Fig. 18.8). Another is to isolate the keyword typographically:

Keyword: The rest of the headline tells the story

Keyword: *The rest of the headline tells the story*

Headline treatment. Many newspapers use a bolder head, sometimes even a different typeface, on the lead story (Fig.18.9). Metros routinely use bolder, larger headlines for early street sales editions. Many of those same papers tone down for home delivery. As explained in Chapter 10, headline formats should offer type contrast in weight, form (roman and italic) or combinations of weight and form.

Type excitement. Many newspapers also use a special weight, form or format on feature or offbeat stories on Page 1. Special treatment is needed to differentiate special stories from the news (Fig. 18.10).

Color. Readers like color, but that doesn't mean you have to use a paint brush. If spot color is designed into the format, designers don't have to invent a new way to use it each day. You design color into the format by locating it in standing elements, such as teasers and digests. If you don't have process color photography, it becomes more important to locate spot color at the top and bottom of the page for page balance. If you have color pictures, the secondary photo usually takes care of the balance problem.

The big event. Editors and designers could learn a lot about their potential to create excitement if they studied how they handle the big events. Creativity is born of the excitement. Editors are willing to ignore the rules that restrict day-to-day presentation (always have seven stories on Page 1; always have three stories above the fold; always promote three stories above the flag; always run a digest, etc.). As newspapers look to their standing in the media mix in the year 2000, perhaps some of the techniques they use for big-event coverage should be incorporated into daily presentation. San Jose cleared out the front page for the start of the Gulf War (Fig. 18.11); Waco had its own war to cover when the Branch Davidian compound went up in flames (Fig. 18.12); Orange County was ablaze, and the Register reflected it (Fig. 18.13); the Chicago Tribune reflected the happy news when the Bulls won their third straight title (Fig. 18.14); and the Detroit News reflected the unhappy news when the state team lost in the national championship (Fig. 18.15). Lessons for everyday presentation? Big pictures. Explanatory graphics. No formatting. Designers and editors use formulas as crutches. If you have to have seven stories, you'll find them, whether they belong on Page 1 or not. Some days the front page could tell the news better with pictures than with words. Sometimes with

18.11 The Persian Gulf War brought out large type and exciting displays in newspapers across America. Many editors were willing to drop the usual number of Page 1 stories to accommodate the lead story.

18.12 In Waco, the Branch Davidians was a local story, and the newspaper display reflected that importance.

18.13 The Register devoted the entire front page to the fires that were sweeping through their circulation area. This page led a special section that wrapped around the main paper. The more traditional Page 1 appeared inside.

18.14 Good news is big news, too. When the Chicago Bulls won its third consecutive championship, the Tribune reflected the city's excitement.

18.15 Sports dominated the front page of the Detroit News, even in a losing effort. The large type and picture creates a dominant element. The promo item on GM is larger than usual because the story got pushed off the front by the sports drama.

graphics. Sometimes it could pull together three or four stories on the same subject from different locations. Custom keeps us from applying the lessons daily. The last newspaper ever published will probably have three stories teased across the top, a vertical column of digests down the left, two pictures and six stories.

Inside news

Just as the front should reflect the unpredictability of the flow and intensity of the news, the inside pages should be organized to provide stability. News should be organized by categories and labeled. Readers should know the order of the packaging and become accustomed to the consistency. They should know where to find everything from the weather to the national news because it's

18.16 The Tennessean offers the world in five minutes on Page 2A daily. It's one of many industry efforts to create a newspaper within the newspaper.

18.17 The Seattle Times' unusual grid creates a feeling of a newsletter for its briefing page.

18.18 The Detroit News offers a Page 2 that combines a table of contents with a daily briefing ranging from serious to the fluff.

in the same sequence each day. The order in which you find the departments in Time magazine is the same each week; the space devoted to the departments expands and contracts to reflect the content. The cover story appears in the logical department. The consistency helps the subscriber; the excitement is created by the surprises found within the departments.

Page 2. One of the more interesting innovations in the last few years is the development of a newspaper within a newspaper. Reacting to readers who say they don't have time to read the entire newspaper, editors have created summaries of the paper, which serve as both a quick read and a promotion of inside stories (Figs. 18.16 through 18.18). Page 2 also is a favorite location for celebrity briefs and weather. Regardless of the size of the paper, there will always be a Page 2, so it's a logical place to anchor standing features.

Briefs packages. Compared with the typical story, packages of briefs get good readership. Packaging is the key, however. Some newspapers even run maps and keys to locate each story (Fig. 18.19). A more typical digest combines pictures and copy (Fig. 18.20). The Seattle Times runs an extensive digest aimed at suburban readers (Fig. 18.21). Designers should build in weight contrast and carefully control the white space to make the packages more pleasing. Some newspapers run digests in sans serif to differentiate them from the serif type in the longer stories.

Records pages. In smaller communities, a records page is a familiar sight. It is the heart of the newspaper. On it, you find everything from fire calls to birth announcements to real estate transactions (Fig.

18.19 The Akron, Ohio, paper uses a map to locate its digest stories.

18.20 A standard digest often runs in a column wider than those on the rest of the page. Such treatment gives the page a much-needed vertical element.

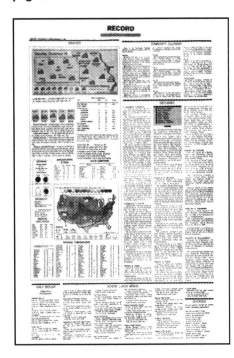

18.22 Many smaller newspapers publish popular records pages. For the designer, the challenge is to build in areas of relief from the columns of gray text. The weather maps, which appear in color, offer a standing visual element for the page.

18.21 The Seattle Times devotes more than half a page to a regional round-up.

18.22). If the advertising stack permits, this is a good place for a seven-column format because you can get more listings into the same amount of space. It's important to provide typographic contrast and white space on these text-intensive pages. Bold or black headlines, sometimes even in a different but complementary typeface, permit a smaller size without sacrificing effect. Extra white space between the end of a listing and the next headline airs out the digest. If you have extensive records copy, consider building a window on the page in which you can run a standing feature or a stand-alone photograph or graphic. The weather map serves the same purpose at many newspapers.

Obituaries. Like any item you expect some readers to clip and save, present obituaries in vertical formats. This minimizes the number of wraps from one column to the next and makes it easier for readers to clip. Other items in the same category: school lunch menus, weddings, engagements and recipes.

Other news pages. On the rest of the news pages, remember these points:

1. Work off the edge of ads to create modular spaces.

2. Try to keep photos and graphics as far away from the ads as you can. If the ads pyramid right, place the photo at the left.

3. Don't box a story on top of an ad. It looks too much like advertising.

4. Run briefs vertically if possible. On short stories, the fewer breaks to the next column, the better.

5. Vary the rhythm on a page containing two or more stories by using a wider setting on one.

6. Pages 2 and 3 are important for establishing readership. Fight to keep these pages as open as possible.

7. Consider creating a table of contents. Magazine editors have discovered that a table of contents attracts high readership and that people who see a story listed in a table of contents are more likely to read the full story than those who don't. Newspapers have many more articles each day than a magazine, yet few make an effort beyond an index to help the reader find anything, let alone encourage them to read it. The table of contents is both a map and a tease for the stories (Fig. 18.23).

FEATURE SECTIONS

Lifestyle, Food, Entertainment, Arts and Travel often have separate staffs and separate sections. However, they share the same problems.

The poster or billboard (one-subject pages) was popular in lifestyle sections until the mid-1980s. Then the move to create more active pages reached many feature sections. The impact is illustrated at the Detroit Free Press (Fig. 18.24) and Raleigh News & Observer (Fig. 18.25). Detroit builds quick reads across the top; Raleigh runs them across the bottom. Both approaches make sure that there is more than one subject to keep readers on the page. The St. Paul Pioneer Press is even more active across the top and down the left with its inverted L framing (Fig. 18.26).

Here are some suggestions for section fronts:

1. There is still room for one-subject pages, but segment the package to make it look less daunting.

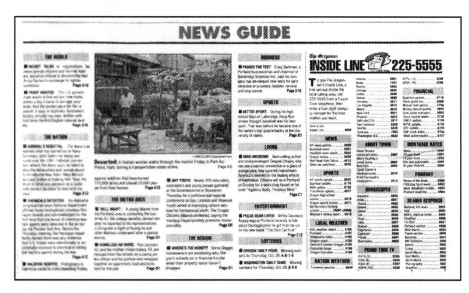

18.23 The Oregonian offers a table of contents that also can be read as an element itself. Magazines have known for years that contents pages attract high readership.

18.24 Feature pages have become more active. Researchers have found that in multi-section newspapers, many scanners make decisions about reading by looking only at the top half of the page.

18.25 If you fold this page in half, the reader still sees pictures, the main headline and the headline for a secondary story.

18.26 A typical feature page at the St. Paul Pioneer Press offers dozens of elements above the fold.

2. To increase the element count, establish a frame (Fig. 18.27). Designers tire of the formats a long time before readers do. Nonetheless, the frame shouldn't be a straitjacket. That might sometimes mean making a vertical digest into a horizontal element. Or even moving it inside.

3. You have more opportunity because of time and subject matter to use the range of storytelling devices available. Make the best of them. Your pages should use maps and charts, illustrations and photography.

4. Design with type. Manipulate the letters and stack the words. Use type appropriate to the content if your stylebook permits (Fig. 8.28).

5. Even if you don't design with type, make use of alternate headline formats. A banner headline on a feature page is as out of place as shorts at a formal wedding. Regularly use titles, labels, readouts and blurbs (Fig. 18.29).

6. Let the grid reflect your content. Use wider settings for your feature stories and narrower settings for your quick reads and listings.

7. Use white space in inventive ways. The Chicago Tribune, for instance, uses more white space between elements in its Tempo section than in its news section. That helps establish a section personality (Fig. 18.30).

8. Tease stories that are inside. Be aggressive. Sell.

9. Surprise the reader. Make it readable but make it different (Fig. 18.31).

18.27 The frame on this page is an inverted "L". It includes the page header and column down the left. Frames can increase the element count.

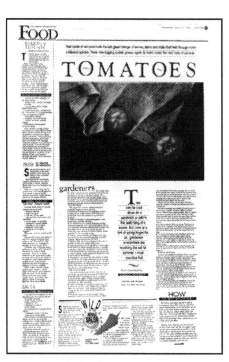

18.28 If your stylebook permits it, distinctive typography used distinctively can enhance your feature pages.

18.29 This page has a newsier feel than many feature pages, but even here, the lead headline treatment varies from the traditional news presentation.

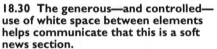

18.30 The generous—and controlled—use of white space between elements helps communicate that this is a soft news section.

18.31 The silhouette treatment on the wooden utensils offers the readers a surprise.

18.32 The screened box offers readers phone numbers and addresses so they can order the catalogs discussed in the story. This is a service journalism technique: It gives readers the information they need to act.

10. Offer the service-journalism angle. Tell readers what they need to know and tell them how to act on it. Pull out phone and fax numbers and addresses (Fig. 18.32). Show them how to make something with illustrations.

11. Think about how readers are supposed to use the information and present it accordingly. If you want them to clip it, don't wrap the information from one column to the top of the next. Put it in clipable modules (Fig. 18.33).

12. If you don't have process color, think twice about food pictures. Instead of concentrating on the food, you might have to concentrate on the people making the food in black and white.

INSIDE FEATURES

Many feature-section editors have to deal with calendars, columnists, weddings and engagements. Each presents special challenges. Probably what they have most in common, however, is that journalists dislike dealing with these items and readers enjoy reading them. They're too important to be overlooked.

Just as creating a records page is important in the news section, creating a good calendar is important in many feature sections. The calendar should appear in the same place and at the same time. The typography should be legible and offer type contrast in weight, form or both (Fig. 18.34). Any listing, calendar included, usually works better in a vertical format than horizontal because the vertical minimizes breaks in the copy.

18.33 Editors want readers to clip recipes. That's why they should be in easily clipped units. Recipes shouldn't jump from one column to the next.

18.34 Calendars are one of the most popular features in an newspaper. They should appear in the same place. Color contrast needs to be built into the typography to provide visual relief and to direct the reader.

18.36 The Des Moines Register's presentation is quieter and more restrained throughout the paper. The sports section reflects the overall design philosophy.

18.35 This type of presentation is reader friendly. The pictures and stories can be clipped in one unit. The arrangement makes it easy to identify the relationship between story and picture.

Space or lack of it is the arbiter of whether or not advice columns are packaged. If possible, do it. If advice columnists can't be printed on the same page, they at least should appear in the same place every issue. Like calendars, they should appear in the same place at a regular time.

Numerous short stories cause one problem common to feature sections. Grouping them under common subject headings creates a larger graphic element, which is easier to handle, rather than running them as small stand-alone stories.

Weddings and engagements present another challenge to designers. To make these items useful to readers, keep the copy with the photograph. Readers should be able to cut them out in one piece (Fig. 18.35). Another solution is to create clusters of photographs and run copy beneath the related photograph. If the copy runs short, leave the white space.

SPORTS

A hybrid, sports offers the timeliness of news, the interest of features and compelling photographs. The section design should reflect that integration of content. Most do. Sports pages can be quiet and reflective (Fig. 18.36) or loud and excited (Fig. 18.37).

Regardless of the pacing, all sports sections have available to them action pictures, reams of statistics waiting for a chart to happen and good quotes. The section should reflect that content by bold photo editing, generous sizing and frequent use of pullout quotes, charts, tables and diagrams. For instance, the Times-Picayune uses a diagram to follow the Saints' progress on offense and defense (Fig. 18.38).

Sports agate is the ultimate in record keeping. Designers must present a huge body of statistical data with the least amount of space and the highest amount of legibility the paper can afford. Many newspapers are using 7-point type. At that size, and considering the kind of information in the scoreboards, designers save space and increase legibility by going to a seven- or eight-column format with gutters of about 6 points. The narrow format holds the word count per line at a reasonable level and leaves fewer unfilled lines. In 12- or 13-pica columns, items such as standings are spread out just to fill space. The Providence Journal Bulletin uses an eight-column grid but doubles up on it as necessary (Fig. 18.39).

18.37 Game day offers editors an opportunity to combine exciting photography with big type to reflect the excitement of the content.

18.38 The Times-Picayune used a creative information graphic to chart some key plays. Pictures don't tell the whole story.

Designers of sports agate should also do the following:

1. Build in a variety of medium and bold type. Readers need the visual relief.

2. Use sans serif type. It is more legible in small sizes than type with serifs, which often disappear. A slightly condensed face will save significant amounts of space. Little or no leading is needed.

3. Use a combination of bold type and rules to break up the mass of agate gray. Some newspapers use icons, but be careful; it's easy to clutter the listings.

4. Use column rules. Narrow columns with narrow gutters need column rules to separate the type.

5. Consider using a window on the agate page for relief. A window is a space, usually carved into the top middle of the page, that contains anything from briefs to television listings (Fig. 18.40).

BUSINESS

Unlike sports, business sections have to create most of their visuals because what they cover doesn't lend itself to action photography. In addition, because most people take money seriously, the tone of the business section is also less flippant than sports.

But that doesn't mean the presentation needs to be dull. Some people think information graphics were invented with business editors in mind. That's not true, but business editors certainly benefit from them. So do readers. The daily grist of the business section is num-

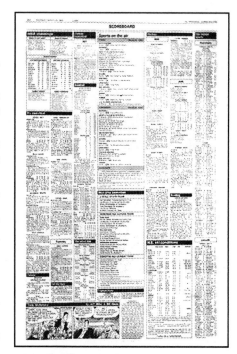

18.39 Sports agate should be in narrower columns to increase legibility and get more items on the page. This is an eight-column page. Two-column sets are used as needed.

18.40 At the Examiner in Independence, Mo., a window offers visual relief on the agate page.

18.41 The Seattle Times offers a newsletter in the vertical column instead of the more common digest. The typography is quiet.

18.42 The Orange County Register's business page is bolder because its type is heavier and its pictures and graphics are in color.

18.43 Graphics are an important part of the Chicago Tribune's business pages.

bers. Charts and tables are not only useful but also essential. Diagrams help explain how the economy works better than long blocks of text do. In fact, charts and tables are so useful that business editors must resist the temptation to fill the pages with boilerplate graphics—syndicated graphics with no local angle and often questionable connections to the story they accompany.

Just because information graphics are so obvious doesn't mean that other forms of storytelling aren't available. Editors can use illustrators to draw the people they are writing about, or they can do photographic portraiture. Good portraiture photography goes far beyond the usual newspaper head-and-shoulders shot. Although editors should use all these forms of storytelling, one should come to dominate the pages and establish the personality of the section. Pages from Seattle, Orange County and Chicago (Figs. 18.41 through 18.43) use both graphics and photographs to help tell stories.

One problem business and sports sections have in common is dealing with agate. To relieve the intensity of the text, the designer can build a window on the stock page. Such a window usually is a collection of market statistics; its placement with the stocks airs out an otherwise dense page (Fig. 18.44). Advertisements also create windows—and bring in revenue. Advertisements floating on stock pages don't intrude on the readership flow because readers pick out stocks; they don't read columns of listings (Fig. 18.45). Some newspapers, including the Chicago Tribune, offer a useful graphic on how to read the listings (Fig. 18.46).

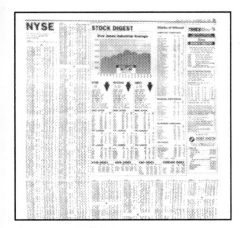

18.44 On stock pages, as on sports agate pages, a window effectively provides visual relief to the gray text.

18.45 Many newspapers are selling an ad that appears on the stock page. It takes the place of the window. Even if it floats in the center of the page, the ad does not interfere with readership.

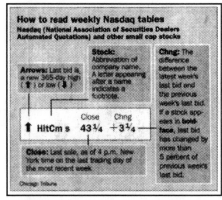

18.46 Many newspapers assume people who look at stock listings know all the symbols. The Chicago Tribune doesn't take it for granted and provides a valuable reader service.

Column widths for agate depend on the amount of data your newspaper includes. Those that publish only the name of the stock and highs and lows can use a 10-column grid. Those that run the stock name and six classes of data use a nine-column grid. Vertical rules can be used to separate columns.

Stock listing pages don't need to be pretty; they need to be functional. That means that stocks should be easy to find. Some papers put the letters of the alphabet in bold; others use a rule to help organize and segment the table.

EDITORIAL

The editorial or opinion pages are the last of the great untouched pages in most newspapers. Editorial pages haven't changed much in 40 years, even at many papers that have had significant redesigns. The editorial page content generally consists of opinions from the newspaper editors, columnists, cartoonists and readers. A few newspapers use photographs to support an editorial point; some use photos or drawings to illustrate the concerns in readers' letters. These are admirable improvements. Photographs, especially, are strong editorial devices that increase readership and add impact. Another area that tradition rather than logic dominates is the signatures on letters. Readers will look to see who the writer is before reading; why not put the signature at the beginning of the letter?

In most newspapers, the editorial page's format is the same each day by tradition. Most newspapers prefer to create an environment in which issues are discussed rationally. Credibility could be damaged by flashy display, but that doesn't mean the pages have to be dull. The appropriate use of photographs, illustrations and charts can help here as well as anywhere else in the paper.

The designer's first goal to create the proper editorial personality, which should be noticeably different from the news pages. Once the personality has been identified, there are two other major concerns:

18.47 A nine-column grid offers the designer opportunities to provide white space and place pullouts.

18.48 The Springfield, Mo., paper actively encourages readers to participate in its editorial pages by prominently displaying fax and phone numbers and devoting space to letters.

providing contrast to differentiate between the newspaper's opinion and the opinion of others, and anchoring the standing elements. Because form is part of the message, contrast usually is used to separate the newspaper's opinion from the rest of the page. This can be achieved by setting the editorial column significantly wider than the rest of the copy, using larger type or using a different text face. When the contrast is missing, the readers have to guess whose opinion they are reading. Labeling is important too.

The St. Paul Pioneer Press and the Springfield, Mo., News-Leader are two of the many papers that have introduced some innovations to the editorial page (Figs. 18.47 and 18.48). Among them: narrow columns to let the pages breathe and editorial summaries. Some argue that the summaries will hurt readership; oth-

18.49 The narrow column builds in white space to a text-intensive page.

18.50 A quiet feature approach gives this college paper's opinion page a distinctive look and feel.

18.51 The appropriate illustration is integrated with the text seamlessly.

ers say that people who read the editorials will read them for the reasoning. Unfortunately, we don't have any readership studies on summaries yet.

Editorial and op-ed (opposite-the-editorial) pages are logical places to use a four- or five-column format. With no advertising, the designer has an opportunity to create a grid that reflects the content. The Des Moines Register uses a narrow column for the columnist's picture and a quote (Fig. 18.49). This opens the page and gives the scanner another reason to read. Designers should also think about the visuals. In addition to the editorial cartoon, will there be photographs? Line art? Caricatures? Some of the most innovative work has appeared in the student newspaper at the University of California—San Diego. The use of illustrations and ample white space gives the page a sense of presence not often found in daily newspapers (Figs. 18.50 and 18.51).

18.52 The Chicago Tribune's Kidnews page tries to attract young readers with plenty of color and exciting content.

18.53 The design of the Freep, a shortened form of Free Press, is like the pages found in many teen magazines.

YOUTH PAGES

Newspapers have tried to reach out to youth by creating special pages for them. Some are aimed at sub-teens; others at teens. As always, the designs should reflect the market. All four of the examples do this in their own way (Figs. 18.52 through 18.55). Two are papers in big markets; one is from a medium-sized market; and one is from a small market. Despite the size differences, the papers present lively pages calculated to appeal in content and presentation to a young audience. However, more readership studies need to be done to see whether these pages are successful. Teenagers who aren't opening the paper aren't going to see the pages, no matter what the content or presentation.

WEATHER PAGES

Ever since USA Today produced its full-page weather presentation in color, newspapers have devoted more time and attention to the weather. Some of it is simply emulation of USA Today without much thought for the local market. USA Today's market is national. Many of its readers are traveling. Other newspapers' markets are local or regional. Readers can get more recent weather information from the television or radio. For instance, editors of a 60,000-circulation paper listening to readers at a focus group decided to reduce the weather to a

18.54 The Tennessean involves the teens in their page and reflects that involvement with the head shots.

18.55 The 40,000-circulation Tribune in LaCrosse, Wi., produces a teen page with local content. Its design is consistent with the rest of the paper.

quarter page in black and white after they heard readers say they didn't use the newspaper for weather information. On the other hand, many newspapers in winter vacation areas such as Florida and Arizona hear their readers complain about incomplete temperature tables. All of the snowbirds want to know the temperature and weather conditions back home. Newspapers can give detailed, historical weather data for the area and temperatures and weather conditions worldwide. Although some of that is available on television, it's much more difficult to get when it's wanted.

Once you have determined what your market wants, the challenge is to present it with maps and tables that are readable and use as little space as necessary. The Oregonian uses about two-thirds of a page and focuses on the regional weather in black and white (Fig. 18.56). The Orange County Register, covering a broader-circulation area, offers information about tides and coastal, inland and mountain temperatures. It's all presented in color (Fig. 18.57). Designers should be sure to include explanations of the symbols on the weather maps.

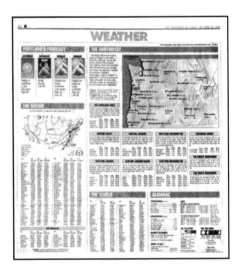

18.56 The Oregonian offers a comprehensive weather report in black-and-white. Several newspapers have discovered that color on weather doesn't make any difference to readers in their market, but in some parts of the country, the color is popular.

18.57 In Orange County, California, where so many residents are from somewhere else, the national weather is a popular feature. The paper runs it in color.

19. DESIGNING ACCESSORIES

 Accessories are, by definition, secondary. In a newspaper, the design accessories include the nameplate, teasers, labels, bylines, logos and icons. Readers don't buy a newspaper to look at accessories, but these accessories help readers find their way through the publication. Like a king's aide, accessories should be seen and not heard. They do their job when they direct readers to the content, not to themselves. Prefer simplicity to clutter.

NAMEPLATES

The nameplate, or flag, sets the tone for the newspaper. Its design is important because it is usually the first thing the reader sees. In designing the nameplate, you should consider seven factors: (1) personality, (2) flexibility, (3) importance of each word in the name, (4) insignia, (5) spacing, (6) customizing and (7) subordinate elements.

PERSONALITY

The nameplate can say to the reader, "this is an old-fashioned newspaper" or "this is an up-to-date newspaper." The difference between traditional and old-fashioned is a thin line that often involves the elements included in the flag. When it's unnecessarily cluttered, it can communicate an amateurish quality. The type in the nameplate of the Baca County (Colo.) Plainsman Herald has a weak personality and is surrounded by clutter that detracts from the credibility of the newspaper. One solution would be a visual pun that makes the nameplate

213

19.1 The clutter around the flag offers an ironic comment on the name. An alternative plays off the name.

as simple and "plain" as the name (Fig. 19.1).

The type chosen to convey the name can be old without being old-fashioned. Compare the Des Moines Register, Detroit Free Press and Seattle Times (Fig. 19.2). The Register uses the traditional old English typeface; the Free Press has altered it slightly to eliminate some of the flourishes; the Times has used it as a starting point but created a modern version. Other newspapers have completely severed ties with the traditional nameplate. Some, like the Sun in Biloxi, Miss., had little past. When the Sun was started in 1973, the nameplate conveyed the message that the newspaper was a young, bright product. However, when it was merged with its sister paper, the Herald, the symbol disappeared (Fig. 19.3). Waco looked at several possibilities—and asked for responses from focus groups—before selecting the last one (Fig. 19.4). Color, as a background, on the type or on insignia with the nameplate, also is important in creating an image.

Personalities don't change overnight, and neither should nameplates. Proposed replacements should be allowed to simmer in the newsroom. Determining the connotation of a type is an inexact science at best, and editors should get as many reactions as possible to the proposed replacement before making a decision.

FLEXIBILITY

Some editors like nameplates that can run the entire width of the paper or can be used in a narrower format. Newspapers with short names may be able to run either a five- or six-column flag by adjusting the amount of white space at both ends. Editors should be reluctant to vary the flag width more than one column because it is the major identifier each day. Flexibility is less important than familiarity.

IMPORTANCE OF WORDS

Because all the words in a newspaper's name are not of equal importance, the designer can subordinate some words to others by changing the size and boldness of type. This gives the designer a chance to use larger type for the main part of the name (Fig. 19.5). Changing the emphasis on words, however, is wrapped up in a newspaper's marketing. Some downplay the name of the city to market

19.2 All three papers use a variation of Old English. Des Moines is most faithful to the original; Seattle has made the flag look more modern.

19.3 By using large and small capital letters, the designer was able to create one word out of three.

19.4 Participants in focus groups were asked to comment on several flag designs. They helped pick the one on the bottom.

themselves as regional newspapers; others want to be closely identified with the city where they are published. Designers have to create nameplates consistent with the newspaper's marketing mission.

INSIGNIA

It's easy to clutter a nameplate, but a simple insignia can help establish the identity of the paper. The insignia can reflect the area or a major landmark, or it can be a trademark for the newspaper. Whatever the insignia, it should be simple and fit neatly into the nameplate. The Gazette in Montreal has an orange rising sun integrated neatly behind the nameplate (Fig. 19.6). The News in Kingstree, S.C., uses the pine so familiar to the state to shade its letters (Fig. 19.7).

SPACING

As a rule, the spacing between letters should be tight. Kerning and even ligatures should be considered. Horizontal spacing should also be minimal. Spacing should be optical, not mechanical.

CUSTOMIZING

Some nameplates can be easily duplicated by anyone with access to typesetting equipment, others are hand drawn, and some use standard type in an individualized manner. It is impossible and unnecessary to design a nameplate that can't be duplicated, but it is desirable to customize it. The Detroit News has a simple nameplate, but notice how it was customized (Fig. 19.8). The Th is run together as a ligature; the ear of the r overlaps the o; the e and s sit under the serifs of the w. As already mentioned, an insignia, especially when neatly integrated, individualizes the nameplate.

SUBORDINATE ELEMENTS

The design of the nameplate includes the name of the paper and all those elements that surround it—insignia, folio lines, cutoff rules, weather blurbs. Too many elements cause clutter. The weight of cutoff rules should be selected carefully so there is a clear delineation to show where the nameplate ends and the news begins. When this isn't clear, the lead headline often sits uncomfortably close to the type in the nameplate. If the flag is ever dropped to permit promotional boxes or a story to run above it, at least a 1-point rule should be placed between the flag and the material above. Generally, the weight of type in the flag dictates the weight of the cutoff rule: bold type, bold rule.

Labels

Section logos, or identifiers, are labels to tell readers where they are in the paper. They're read differently than headlines and text. They merit only a glance, like the sign on a restroom door. Large section logos, such as the ones used by the Orange County Register (Fig. 19.9), make a bold statement at the beginning of each section. The name of the paper appears below the section name. The Dallas Morning News uses a 14-point gray-bar cutoff rule, a 24-point reproduction of its nameplate and a 2-point cutoff rule (Fig. 19.10). The Pittsburgh Post-Gazette gives its feature section a distinctive look by running the page

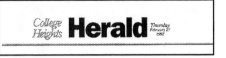

19.5 By subordinating College Heights, the designer was able to give Herald more emphasis.

19.6 The color on the original creates a rising sun over the Gazette in Montreal.

19.7 The state tree is expertly integrated into the flag of the Kingstree, S.C., newspaper.

19.8 At first glance it may not be obvious, but the Detroit News has a customized nameplate.

19.9 The large, condensed type signals a section. The name of the paper appears on the folio line underneath, and the teases to inside material is modest.

19.10 The Morning News uses its flag in small type in the folio line under the section head.

19.11 The Pittsburgh Post-Gazette used large type for its vertical section front, but the screen lowers the noise level. The black would have competed too much with the content.

19.12 St. Petersburg sometimes alternates the teaser format among sections.

19.13 The Providence Journal-Bulletin uses a significantly different section header design for its "lifebeat" section.

label vertically (Fig. 19.11).

With space at a premium, some newspapers have looked at page labels as one place to conserve. This can be done by using variations of a typeface. For instance, bold type can be run smaller without losing impact. Condensed or extended variations might be appropriate, although extended would save more space than the more vertical condensed type. If the type in the nameplate is not customized, using a variation of it in the sectional logos provides unity and contrast at the same time. Screening the type produces the same effect.

Refers or teasers to inside stories can be built into the sectional logos. The page headers of the St. Petersburg Times are consistent, but the teaser formats change from section to section (Fig. 19.12). The teasers should be handled carefully to avoid clutter.

Consistency in typeface has been a tradition, but it's one that's crumbling, and probably properly so. Some newspapers have introduced section labels that reflect the content of that section. The Providence Journal Bulletin, for example, uses distinctly different labels for its Lifebeat section and Style page, but the Providence section head is the standard for the rest (Fig. 19.13). Designers who choose this path might want to consider incorporating the name of the paper or the paper's icon into the section head.

Labeling extends beyond the tops of the pages, however. Designers create categories of information; each category has a different-sized label. For example, working from large to small, category 1 would be section fronts; category 2 would be inside page labels; category 3 would be the label for standing features such as Daily Records or Newsmakers; and category 4 would take us into labels within the category 3 feature. By establishing categories, the designer can achieve consistency throughout the paper. Editors adding features later can identify the correct label by identifying the category.

Teasers

Selling the content of the paper is a popular as well as necessary function of the editorial department. Teasers are usually placed across the top, down the side or anchored at the bottom of Page 1. Some newspapers have teaser packages that expand and contract. The location depends on how the newspaper is trying to market itself. Papers that have significant newsstand sales often run the teasers over the top; those located in smaller communities with less significant newsstand sales may move the teasers to the bottom of the page.

Despite the popularity of teasers, there is little research on whether they sell papers or increase readership of the inside stories that they promote. Media General, in fact, found that three-fourths of the people who bought a newspaper from a rack did so out of habit, rather than for what was in the paper that day (Mauro 1986). The Poynter Institute color study found that if there is color below the flag but none on the teasers above the flag, few people look at the teasers (Garcia and Fry 1986). However, readership of teasers is high (Garcia and Stark 1991).

Designers and editors are faced with a series of trade-offs with teasers. They increase the element count and excitement of the page, but they crowd out stories and pictures. They attract high levels of readership at the top of the page, but they force pictures and stories below the fold. Newspapers that have art and graphics departments usually offer the best and most dynamic teasers (Fig. 19.14). Newspapers with smaller staffs also have to find a way to promote the content dynamically without devoting as many staff hours to it each day. One way is to create a half dozen formats. The designer can select one that best reflects the promotional items for that day (Fig. 19.15). The typical three boxes

19.14 **Newspapers with art departments such as the Detroit News can create teaser boards that are different and visually arresting on a deadline basis.**

19.15 **The space remains the same, but the way it is divided changes from day to day as the content changes. This kind of variety may increase readership.**

across the top belong in the design history books. Whatever approach is used, bold, extra-bold and bold condensed type are effective in teasers because they offer impact with less size. Use lighter faces for the details. And as is always the case, the design starts with the content. Too many teasers consist of a two- or three-word title with a refer to the page. That's a waste of space. Use smaller type to set the hook in a snappy copy block.

Bylines

Bylines help readers make the transition from the headline type to the text. There are several possibilities (Fig. 19.16), but the byline style selected should be harmonious with the overall style of the paper. For instance, you wouldn't want to use a thick and thin line over and under a byline unless the overall design involved thicks and thins. Unity is the controlling principle. There are two general guidelines for all bylines: (1) Flush left is best because people read from left to right; however, if headlines are centered, it would make sense to center bylines. (2) Byline type and/or size should contrast with the text. If you choose the same type as the text, then the weight and size can provide contrast. If you choose sans serif to contrast with the text, you can add weight as additional contrast.

Logos

If you opened your local paper every day and saw a variety of column logos, you would probably wonder if anybody at the newspaper was reading it. Designers rely on column logos (also know as sigs and standing sigs) to achieve unity, create a personality for writers and help readers locate standing features. Because these three functions are critical to the success of a newspaper, designers spend a lot of time working on logos.

Good logos reflect the marketing philosophy of the newspaper. If the newspaper is trying to develop and sell personalities, the logos should contain a picture of the writer.

By GARY ROETS
Staff Writer

By GARY ROETS
Staff Writer

By GARY ROETS
Staff Writer

By GARY ROETS
Staff Writer

By Gary Roets
Staff Writer

By Gary Roets
Staff Writer

by Gary Roets
staff writer

19.16 **Besides identifying the author, bylines serve as a transition from display to text type. The typography should reflect the philosophy used elsewhere in the paper.**

Good logos used correctly help guide the reader through the newspaper. They should be used as locators, not headlines. Headlines attract the casual and infrequent reader to the content of a specific column; logos identify the feature for the faithful reader. The phenomenon is not unlike highway travelers who look for the billboard of a specific motel chain. For some, the billboard is sufficient; others take a look at the motel itself before they decide whether to stay.

Good logos also unify the newspaper. A consistent logo style identifies the paper to subscribers no matter which section they pick up. This consistency is one more indication that the editors are in control of the product. Inconsistency, whether in writing, editing or graphics style, damages credibility. Some newspapers, particularly large ones, have different logo styles in different sections. Varying a logo theme may be a better approach than completely changing the style.

When designing column logos, you should keep five considerations in mind:

1. Size. Logos should be compact. They have more in common with the Izod alligator than a neon sign.

2. Flexibility. Are they proportioned so they can be set in one, one-and-one-half, and two columns? Normally, one-column logos are slightly wider than they are deep, and larger ones should be horizontal rectangles.

3. Marketing. If you are trying to sell the name of the column, emphasize it. If you are trying to sell the author, use a photograph. Column logos without pictures are not as warm or personal as those with them. Even artists' renderings of authors are less personal than pictures. Caricatures convey humor and informality.

4. Personality. Design of the column logos should be consistent with the design of other standing elements (such as the nameplate and sectional logos) and the tone of the publication.

5. Cropping. Crop tight, but be careful not to amputate. Several newspapers have tried to use pictures with parts of heads cut off in logos only to redo them because of reader complaints.

The column logos shown in Figure 19.17 illustrate the variety of approaches.

Logos on one-column features should be placed above the headline to keep them from interfering with the reader. Logos on horizontal features normally appear at the top of the second column. Smaller logos with type wrapping around the logo are also effective.

Story logos

A package of stories on a single day or a story that runs more than one day should have a graphic identifying element. Logos help editors get around the problem of labeling something as a series, which readers generally avoid unless the content is gripping. It's easy to scare off readers, who don't want to make a long-term commitment or may have missed one or more parts, by labeling related stories as a series. Each story should stand alone; the graphic logo provides the continuity (Fig. 19.17). Space for a teaser line for the next day's story can be built into

19.17

the logo.

Icons

Iconography is the use of drawings, or icons, to represent objects, actions and qualities. Linguists have found that most people interpret certain drawings or symbols the same way. One team of linguists found 620 concepts common to the 26 language-culture communities they studied. By combining icons with words, designers should be able to eliminate much of the ambiguity in messages (Fig. 19.18). Designers don't have to invent these symbols. Several books are available that show international and other useful symbols (see Additional Readings).

Column logos

ALICE KAHN

ON THE REBOUND

— Tim Gallimore —

CITYSIDES

ALICE KAHN

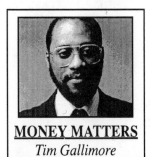

MONEY MATTERS
Tim Gallimore

ALICE KAHN

19.18 Column logos that contain pictures are more personal than those without.

GLOSSARY

Agate—Traditionally, 5 1/2-point type, although now commonly used for type up to 7 points; agate line is an advertising space measurement 1/14 of an inch deep.

Ascender—The part of a letter that extends above the body of the type.

Balance—Placement of elements to produce a harmoniously integrated page.

Banner—A large headline that extends across the top of the front page above the most important story of the day.

Bar—In type, a horizontal or slanted line connected at both ends.

Baseline—Line on which the center body of type rests.

Base maps—Maps showing the outline of a political subdivision, ranging from a continent to a city ward.

Bastard type—Type set a different width than the standard column setting.

Black letter—*See* Text letter.

Bleed—An illustration filling one or more margins and running to the edge of the page.

Blurb—A quote or a small part of a story displayed in type larger than text, usually 14 to 18 points.

Body type—*See* Text type.

Boldface—Type that has thicker, darker lines than the medium or lighter weights of the same face.

Border—An ornamental rule.

Bowl—In type, the curved line that creates a hollow space in a letter.

Broadsheet—Full-sized newspaper, as opposed the smaller tabloids.

Burn—To transfer type and images to a sensitized photographic plate.

Byline—Line crediting the writer, photographer or designer. Most commonly, it refers to the writer's credit at the top of the story.

Characters per pica (CPP)—Measurement of the width of a typeface, computed by counting the average number of letters that will fit in a given horizontal space and dividing by the number of picas.

Cold type—Type produced by a photographic or digitized process rather than by pressing inked metal forms against paper.

Color filter—Filter that absorbs all but one color.

Color separation—The product of a method of separating a color print or transparency into its three primary colors and black.

Concord—Blending of typographic elements to form a uniform impression.

Contrast—Effect achieved by varying shapes, sizes and weights of the elements on a page.

Contrast and balance—Layout technique in which a page is balanced by using contrasting shapes and weights.

Counter—White space within the letter.

Cursive—Race of type that is a stylized reproduction of formal handwriting. Also known as script.

Cutline—Information under a picture or artwork. Also known as a caption.

Cutoff rule—A line used to separate elements on a page.

Deck—One or more lines of display type that are smaller than the main headline.

Descender—The part of a letter that extends below the body of the type.

Design—A system of planning in which the person who arranges the elements on the page has some influence over the collection and selection of those elements.

Display type—Type larger than that used for text. In newspapers, display type ranges upward from 14 points.

Double truck—Facing pages in which the space between the pages is also used.

Dummy—The page, usually half the size of the page being produced, on which the editor shows where all the elements are to be arranged; the blueprint of the page.

Duotone—One color plus black, achieved by shooting two halftone negatives of the picture and producing two plates for the page.

Dutch wrap—Extending copy beyond the headline; also called a raw wrap.

Ear—The distinctive stroke at the top right of the letters *g* and *r*.

Em—a unit of space equal to the space taken by the capital *M* of the type size being used.

En—Half an em, or half the size of the capital M of the type being used.

Family—In type classification, typefaces that are closely related in design and share a common name. They differ in width, weight and form.

Flag—*See* Nameplate.

Flush-left—Type that begins at the left-hand edge or border of the column.

Flush-right—Type that ends at the right-hand edge or border of the column.

Focus—Starting point on the page, achieved by selecting a dominant element or elements.

Font—A complete set of type in one style and size.

Frame—Those elements of the page that are the same each issue. Teasers or a column are often part of a page frame.

Gutter—The vertical white space between columns of type.

Hairline—The thin stroke of a letter.

Halftone—Reproduction in which tones have been photographed through a screen to break up the areas into dots whose size determines the dark and light areas.

Hammer—One- or two-word headlines in large type, usually over a deck.

Hues—Pure colors such as red, yellow, green and blue.

Inset—Photograph or copy contained within the borders of a photograph.

Inter-letter spacing—applying principles of kerning to display type.

Italic—Serif type sloped to the right.

Jim dash—Cutoff rule that does not cross the entire column.

Justified type—Type set so that the lines are all of equal length by hyphenating words and placing more or less space between words.

Kerning—Selective reduction of white space between irregularly shaped letters to create even optical spacing.

Key plate—Printing plate that puts the first image on the paper.

Kicker—Three or four words that are set about half the size of the main headline and usually appear flush left above the main headline.

Layout—Arrangement of elements on the page, usually done without any voice in the preparation or selection of those elements.

Leading—Sometimes written "ledding," this is the space between lines of type.

Leg—A column or wrap of type in a story.

Legibility—Measurement of the speed and accuracy with which type can be read and understood.

Letter fitting—inter-letter space adjustments in display type.

Letterpress—Method of printing in which raised letters are inked and pressed against paper.

Ligature—Two or more characters designed as a single unit. Common ligatures include the combinations of *ff, ffi, fi, ffl* and *fl*. A ligature has to be created by design, not by kerning.

Logo—An insignia of type, art or both

that ties together stories in a series or identifies a regular feature such as a columnist.

Loop—The curved part of letters such as *o*, *c* and *e*, which is often drawn distinctively.

Masthead—A listing of the publication's managers and editors, name of the paper, date, volume and sometimes the publication's creed.

Modern—Sometimes used to differentiate among types in the roman race. The type is geometric and symmetrical.

Module—A rectangular or square shape on a page. To run a story in modules means that each column of type is the same depth.

Mortise—Overlapping of two or more photographs or of a headline and a photograph.

Nameplate—The newspaper's name as it appears at the top of Page 1. Also know as the flag.

Novelty—*See* Ornamental.

Nut graph—A conversational headline deck; it includes subject, verb and articles.

Oblique—Sans serif type slanted to the right.

Offset—A printing method in which the inked image transfers from plate to rubber blanket to paper. It is based on the principle that grease and water do not mix.

Old style—Sometimes used to differentiate among typefaces in the roman race. The type is asymmetrical and less-formal looking than other roman faces.

Optimum format—The layout in which columns are set at the most legible line length.

Ornamental—Race of type designed to create such a specific mood or emotion that it is not useful for other uses. Also known as novelty.

Pagination—System of producing pages from a typesetting machine, thus eliminating the need for a composing room.

Photocomposition—Method of producing type by exposing negatives of the characters on film or paper or reproducing them digitally.

Pica—A unit of measurement; 6 picas equal 1 inch.

Plate—The metal on which the photographic image of a page is developed by exposing it to a negative. The plate is then placed on the press.

Point—A unit of measurement; 12 points equal 1 pica. Headlines are measured vertically in points.

Poster—The space on the page left after framing to be used for display. A poster or billboard page is one devoted to a single subject. A miniposter is a small space, about tabloid size, devoted to a display.

Process color—Full- or four-color reproduction achieved by separating each color on individual pieces of film and burning them on separate printing plates. The process colors are yellow, magenta, cyan and black.

Proportion—Proper size and spacing relationships among the elements on the page.

Pullouts—Any typographic devices pulled out of a story and displayed in a form other than text. Pullouts include blurbs, summary boxes, fact boxes and quotes.

Pyramid format—Arrangement of advertisements in a stack up the right or left side of the page.

Quad—An empty printing unit for spacing. An em quad is the square of the type size.

Race—The broadest category of type classification. Type is divided into six races: roman, square serif, sans serif, text letter, cursive and ornamental.

Ragged right type—Type set with a fixed left starting point but with an irregular ending point at the right of the line.

Read-in—Type subordinate in size to the main head and placed above it. The main head completes the thought started in the read-in.

Read-out—A deck that reads directly out of the main head. Unlike the main head, it is written in a conversational tone.

Roman—A race of type characterized by serifs and thick and thin strokes. Also used to mean straight-up-and-down type as opposed to italic or oblique.

Rule—A plain line that ranges upward in width from 1/2 point. *See* Border.

Sans serif—A race of type without serifs and with uniform strokes. Also referred to as gothic.

Scanner—Electronic or laser machine that reads one color of a photograph at a time and transfers the image to a separation.

Screen—Glass or film used in cameras to break copy into halftone dots. The number of lines per linear inch of the screen determines the fineness of the reproduction; the higher the number, the better the reproduction.

Script—*See* Cursive.

Segmenting—Dividing a story into smaller bites.

Separation—A negative containing elements to be printed in one of the process colors. A full-color picture normally requires four separations.

Series—The range of sizes in a typeface. With photocomposition and digital typesetting, the range of sizes includes fractions of points.

Serif—The cross-stroke at the end of the main stroke of a letter.

Shades—Color formed by mixing pure colors with black (*see* Hues).

Sidebar—A secondary story intended to be run with a major story on the same subject.

Sidesaddle—Placement of type to the left side of the story rather than over it. Also called side head.

Slug—One-word designation for a story as it moves through the production system.

Spot color—Any color printing other than process.

Square serif—A race of type with monotone strokes and squared-off or blocked serifs.

Stereotype—A flat or curved metal plate cast from a papier-mâché mold or the process.

Stress—The thickness of a curved stroke; the shading of the letter.

Stroke—The primary line of the letter.

Tabloid—A publication whose pages are approximately half the size of a broadsheet or full-sized newspaper and usually printed on newsprint.

Teaser—A graphic written and designed to draw readers' attention to something in the publication, usually on an inside page.

Terminal—The distinctive finish to the stroke on sans serif type.

Text letter—Face of type that has a medieval appearance of early European hand lettering. Also known as black letter.

Text type—Also referred to as body type; used in newspaper stories and editorials.

Tints—Color formed by mixing pure colors with white.

Tombstoning—Bumping of two or more headlines or unrelated graphic elements.

Tones—Color formed by mixing pure colors and white and black.

Tracking—Fixing the spacing between letters in a block of type to achieve a certain color or density. Kerning applies to pairs of letters or a character and punctuation; tracking applies to a block of text.

Transitional—Sometimes used to differentiate among types in the roman race. The type has characteristics of both old and modern faces.

Transparency—A color photograph on slide film.

Typography—The arrangement and effect of type.

Unity—Harmony among the elements on a page and among the parts of the publication.

Value—The degree of lightness or darkness of a color.

Well format—Arrangement of advertisements in the shape of a U on a page.

Wrap—A column or leg of type. Type set over six columns would have six wraps.

x-height—Height of the lowercase x, the standard for measuring type.

References Cited

Aaronson, Bernard. 1970. Some affective stereotypes of color. *Int. J. Symb.* 2(2):15–27.

Ashe, Reid. 1992. What readers really want. *Nieman Reports*, Spring: 7-10.

Bain, Chic, and David H. Weaver. 1979. Newspaper design and newspaper readership. Paper presented to the Graphics Division, Association for Education in Journalism, Houston.

Becker, D., J. Heinrich, R. Von Sichowky, and D. Wendt. 1970. Reader preferences for typeface and leading. *J. Typogr. Res.* 1(Winter):61-66.

Benton, Camille. 1979. The connotative dimensions of selected display typefaces. Paper presented to the Association for Education in Journalism, Houston.

Birren, Faber. 1961. *Creative Color.* New York: Reinhold, p. 48.

Clark, Ruth. 1979. Changing needs of changing readers. American Society of Newspaper Editors Newspaper Readership Project, May.

Click, J. W., and Guido H. Stempel III. 1974. Reader response to modern and traditional front page make-up. ANPA News Res. Bull. 4, June.

Curley, John. 1979. PILOT research tailored to unique needs of each newspaper. *Gannetteer* March:8.

Curley, Thomas. 1979. Readers want latest news, consistent and complete newspapers. *Gannetteer* March:6-8.

David, Prabu. 1992. Accuracy of visual perception of quantitative graphics: An exploratory study. *Journalism Q.* 69:272–92.

Dowding, G. 1957. *Factors in the Choice of Typefaces.* London: Wace.

Fabrizio, R., L. Kaplan, and G. Teal. 1967. Readability as a function of the straightness of right-hand margins. *J. Typogr. Res.* January:90-95.

Fiquette, Larry. 1993. Story was a hit and miss. *St. Louis Post-Dispatch.* October 17:2.

Fitzgerald, Mark. 1993. Controversial photo. *Editor & Publisher*, October 23, pp.14–15.

Garcia, Mario, and Don Fry, eds. 1986. *Color in American Newspapers.* St. Petersburg, Fla.: Poynter Institute for Media Studies.

Garcia, Mario, and Pegie Stark. 1991. *Eyes on the News.* St. Petersburg, Fla.: Poynter Institute for Media Studies.

Gentry, James K., and Barbara Zang. 1989. Characteristics of graphics managers at metropolitan dailies. *Newspaper Research Journal* 10(4): 85-95.

Hartley, James, and Peter Barnhill. 1971. Experiments with unjustified text. *Visible Language* 5(3):265–78.

Haskins, Jack. 1958. Testing suitability of typefaces for editorial subject matter. *Journalism Q.* 35:186–94.

Haskins, Jack P., and Lois P. Flynne. 1974. Effect of headline typeface variation on reading interest. *Journalism Q.* 51:677–82.

Hilliard, Robert D. 1990. What power rests in the 'Big Chair?' *The Journal of the Society of Newspaper Design.* October/November:10-12.

Holmes, Grace. 1931. The relative legibility of black print and white print. *J. Appl. Psychol.* 15(June):248—51.

Hurley, Gerald D., and Angus McDougall. 1971. *Visual Impact in Print.* Chicago: American Publishers Press.

Hvistendahl, J. K., and Mary R. Kahl. 1975. Roman v. sans serif body type: Readability and reader preference. ANPA News Res. Bull. 2, January.

Itten, Johannes. 1964. *Design and Form.* New York: Reinhold.

Kalfus, Marilyn. 1991. Photos often pose dilemmas. Santa Ana, Ca.: *Orange County Register.* March 24:30-31.

Kochersberger, Robert C. Jr. 1988. Survey of suicide photos use by newspapers in three states. *Newspaper Research Journal* 9(4):1–11.

Lewis, Wayne. 1989. Readership of buried ads versus ads placed beside reading material. *Newspaper Research Journal* 10(2):67-74.

Lott, Pam. 1993. "A Study of the Use of a Small Non-Lead Informational Graphic on a Newspaper Page." Unpublished master's thesis. Ohio University, Athens, Ohio.

Mauro, John. 1986. Survey of Front Page Color vs. Black and White. Richmond, Va.: Media General.

McDougall, Angus, and Veita Jo Hampton. 1990. *Picture Editing and Layout.* Columbia, Mo.: Viscom Press, pp. 132–61.

Moen, Daryl. 1989. Unpublished study. University of Missouri, Columbia, Mo.

Pipps, Val Steven. 1985. "Measuring the effects of newspaper graphic elements on reader satisfaction with a redesigned newspaper using two methodologies." Doctoral diss., Newhouse School of Mass Communications, Syracuse, N.Y.

Poindexter, Paula M. 1978. Non-readers: Why they don't read. ANPA News Res. Rep. 9, January.

Poulton, E. C. 1955. Letter differentiation and rate of comprehension of reading. *J. Appl. Psychol.* 49:358–62.

Reaves, Sheila. 1987. Digital retouching. Is there a place for it in newspaper photography? An examination of ethics. *News Photographer* January:23-33.

___. 1992/1993. "What's wrong with this picture?" *Newspaper Research Journal* 13/14:131–53.

Robinson, David O., Michael Abbamonte, and Selby Evans. 1971. Why serifs are important: The perception of small print. *Visible Language* 5 (Autumn):353—59.

Roethlein, B. E. 1912. The relative legibility of different faces of printing type. *Am. J. Psychol.* 23(January):1–36.

Ruel, Laura. 1993. "The effect of information graphics on reading comprehension in newspapers." Unpublished master's thesis. University of Missouri–Columbia.

Sharpe, Deborah T. 1974. *The Psychology of Color and Design.* Chicago: Nelson-Hall, pp. 91–92.

Siskind, Theresa G. 1979. The effect of newspaper design on readers preferences. *Journalism Q.* 56:54–61.

Sissors, Jack Z. 1974. Do youthful college-educated readers prefer contemporary newspaper designs? *Journalism Q.* 51:307–13.

Stark, Pegie. 1992. Information and Graphics. St. Petersburg, Fla.: *Poynter Report,* pp.8-10.

Tannenbaum, Percy, Harvey K. Jacobson, and Eleanor L. Norris. 1964. An experimental investigation of typeface connotations. *Journalism Q.* 41:65—73.

Terry, Art. 1980. "Photography for editors." Unpublished master's thesis. University of Missouri–Columbia.

Thornburg, Ron. 1986. The ethics of the controversial photo. APME Photo and Graphics Committee Report, pp. 2–11.

Tinker, Miles A. 1963. *Legibility of Print.* Ames: Iowa State University Press, pp. 88–107.

Tinker, Miles A., and D. G. Paterson. 1929. Studies of typographical factors influencing speed of reading: III. Length of line. *J. Appl. Psychol.* June:205–19.

Tufte, Edward R. 1983. *The Visual Display of Quantitative Information.* Cheshire, Conn.: Graphics Press.

U&lc. 1983. What's new from ITC? August:27–33.

Vessey, Iris. 1991. Cognitive fit: A theory-based analysis of the graphs versus tables literature. *Decision Sciences* 22:219–40.

Ward, Douglas B. 1992. The effectiveness of sidebar graphics. *Journalism Q.* 69:318–28.

ADDITIONAL READINGS

Arnold, Edmond C. 1969. *Modern Newspaper Design*. New York: Harper & Row.

——. 1981. *Designing the Total Newspaper*. New York: Harper & Row.

Bain, Eric K. 1970. *The Theory and Practice of Typographic Design*. New York: Hastings House.

Baird, Russell N., Arthur T. Turnbull, and Duncan McDonald. 1987. *The Graphics of Communication*, 5th ed. New York: Holt, Rinehart and Winston.

Beach, Mark. 1992. *Graphically Speaking*. Cincinnati: North Light Books.

Berry, W. Turner, and A. F. Johnson. 1953. *Encyclopedia of Type Faces*. London: Blandford Press.

Best of Newspaper Design. Annual. Reston, Va.: Society of Newspaper Design.

Birren, Faber. 1969. *Principles of Color*. New York: Van Nostrand Reinhold.

Black, Roger. 1990. *Roger Black's Desktop Design Power*. New York: Bantam.

Bohle, Robert. 1990. *Publication Design for Editors*. Englewood Cliffs, N.J.: Prentice-Hall.

Burt, Sir Cyril. 1959. *A Psychological Study of Typography*. Oxford, U.K.: Cambridge University Press.

Conover, Theodore E. 1985. *Graphic Communications Today*. St. Paul: West.

Craig, James. 1981. *Designing with Type*. New York: Watson-Guptill.

Dair, Carl. 1982. *Design with Type*. Toronto: University of Toronto Press.

Evans, Harold. 1973. *Newspaper Design, Book Five*. New York: Rinehart and Winston.

Finberg, Howard I., and Bruce D. Itule. 1990. *Visual Editing: A Graphic Guide for Journalists*. Belmont, Calif.: Wadsworth.

Garcia, Mario R., and Pegie Stark. 1990. *Eyes on the News*. Ed Miller, ed. St. Petersburg, Fla.: Poynter Institute for Media Studies.

Gregory, D. L. 1970. *The Intelligent Eye*. New York: McGraw-Hill.

Harrower, Tim. 1992. *The Newspaper Designer's Handbook*, 2nd ed. Dubuque, Iowa: William C. Brown.

Holmes, Nigel. 1984. *Designer's Guide to Creating Charts and Diagrams*. New York: Watson-Guptill.

——. 1985. *Designing Pictorial Symbols*. New York: Watson-Guptill.

Hurlburt, Allen. 1977. *Layout: The Design of the Printed Page*. New York: Watson-Guptill.

——. 1982. *The Grid*. New York: Van Nostrand Reinhold.

Johnson, A. F. 1966. *Type Designs*. Norwich, England: Jarrold and Sons.

Lieberman, J. Ben. 1978. *Type and Typefaces*, 2nd ed. New Rochelle, N.Y.: Myriade Press.

Machlup, Fritz, and Una Mansfield, eds. 1983. *The Study of Information*. New York: John Wiley & Sons.

Merrinian, Frank. 1965. *A.T.A. Type Comparison Book*. New York: Advertising Association of America.

Modley, Rudolf. 1976. *Handbook of Pictorial Symbols*. New York: Dover Publications, Inc.

Muller-Brockman, Josef. 1981. *Grid Systems in Graphic Design*. New York: Hastings House.

Nelson, Roy Paul. 1983. *Publication Design*, 3rd ed. Dubuque, Iowa: William C. Brown.

———. 1985. *The Design of Advertising*, 5th ed. Dubuque, Iowa: William C. Brown.

Ovink, G. W. 1938. *Legibility, Atmosphere-Value and Forms of Printing Types*. Leiden: A. W. Sijfhoff.

Polk, Ralph W., and Harry L. Gage. 1953. *A Composition Manual*. Washington, D.C.: Printing Industry of America.

Rehe, Rolfe. 1979. *Typography: How To Make It Most Legible*. Carmel, Ind.: Design Research International.

———. 1985. *Typography and Design for Newspapers*. Carmel, Ind.: Design Research International.

Rooklege, Gordon, and Christopher Perfect. 1983. *Rookledge's International Typefinder: The Essential Handbook of Typeface Recognition and Selection*. New York: Beil.

Rosen, Ben. 1967. *Type and Typography*, 2nd ed. New York: Van Nostrand Reinhold.

Roszak, Theodore. 1986. *The Cult of Information*. New York: Pantheon Books.

Smith, Charles. 1965. *Color-Study and Teaching*. New York: Van Nostrand Reinhold.

Solomon, Martin, 1986. *The Art of Typography*. New York: Watson-Guptill.

Spencer, Herbert. 1969. *The Visible Word*. New York: Hastings House.

Wheatley, W. E. 1985. *Typeface Analogue*. Arlington, Va.: National Composition Association.

West, Suzanne. 1990. *Working with Style*. New York: Watson-Guptill.

Wurman, Richard Saul. 1990. *Information Anxiety*. New York: Bantam Books.

Zachrisson, Bror. 1965. *Studies in Legibility of Printed Text*. Stockholm, Sweden: Almquist and Wiskel.

CREDITS

The author and publisher wish to thank the following publications and individuals for permission to reprint their material as well as others who graciously granted permission but did not request a credit citation.

Fig. 1.1: Reprinted by permission of the Shreveport Journal Publishing Co.

Figs. 1.2, 1.5, 1.6, 13.9, 15.19, 17.24, 17.25, 18.13, 18.34, 18.42, 18.57:Reprinted with permission of The Orange County Register, Copyright @ 1986, 1992, 1993

Figs. 1.3, 1.4, 12.5, 12.6, 12.7, 12.8, 15.14, 15.15: Used with permission of The Miami Herald.

Fig. 1.7: Courtesy of The Morning Call, Allentown, Pa.

Figs. 1.8, 1.9, 12.1: The Hartford Courant

Figs. 1.10, 16.2: Reprinted by permission; The Globe and Mail.

Figs. 1.11, 10,12, 18.31: The Dallas Morning News

Figs. 1.12, 8.2, 18.35, 18.55: LaCrosse Tribune

Figs. 1.13, 3.13, 5.14, 10.11, 13.4, 17.20, 17.21, 18.6, 18.23, 18.45, 18.56: Reprinted with the permission of The Oregonian.

Figs. 2.4, 17.11, 17.12, 17.13, 17.14, 17.15, 17.16, 17.32,17.33,18.25: Reprinted with permission from The News and Observer of Raleigh, North Carolina.

Figs. 3.1, 3.29, 5.30: The Register-Guard

Figs. 3.11, 9.8, 10.2, 13.2, 18.44: Reprinted with permission of the St. Petersburg Times.

Figs. 3.12, 15.16, 15.17: Reprinted with permission of The Virginian Pilot.

Figs. 3.14, 3.15: Courtesy of the Wichita Eagle

Figs. 3.17, 3.23, 3.24, 4.15, 4.16, 4.18, 5.1, 5.10, 5.15, 5.16, 5.25, 5.26, 5.27, 13.1, 16.5, 16.6, 16.8, 16.9, 18.28, 18.29, 18.32, 18.33: Courtesy of the Columbia (Mo.) Missourian

Figs. 3.21, 10.5, 15.23: Permission granted by Ft. Lauderdale Sun Sentinel.

Fig. 3.31: Copyright 1987, Los Angeles Times

Figs. 4.1, 4.5, 17.22, 17.23, 18.17, 18.21, 18.41: Reprinted with permission of The Seattle Times.

Fig. 4.4: Reprinted by permission; Albany (N.Y.) Times-Union

Fig. 4.6: Reprinted by permission of the Reston (Va.) Times

Figs. 4.10, 4.17, 18.20: The Herald-Sun, Durham, N.C.

Figs. 4.11, 5.8, 5.13, 6.2, 13.3, 13.7, 13.8, 18.14, 18.30, 18.43, 18.46, 18.52: The Chicago Tribune.

Figs. 4.12: Reprinted with permission from The Atlanta Journal and The Atlanta Constitution.

Figs. 4.13, 5.3, 6.5, 6.10, 6.13, 15.24: @1989, 1991, 1992, 1993, USA Today. Reprinted with permission.

Fig. 4.19: Durham Daily Sun

Figs. 4.20, 10.4, 10.6, 18.1, 18.36, 18.49: Copyright @ 1993 The Des Moines Register and Tribune Company. Reprinted with permission.

Fig. 4.25: St. Albert (Canada) Gazette

Fig. 5.2: News Photographer

Figs. 5.4: Reprinted courtesy of The Boston Globe.

Fig. 5.7: Reprinted with permission of the San Antonio Express News.

Fig. 5.11, 5.28: Columbia (Mo.) Daily Tribune

Figs. 5.17, 18.27, 18.39: The Providence Journal-Bulletin

Figs. 5.18: Copyright @ 1986, The Tampa Tribune.

Figs. 5.19, 5.20, 5.21: The Topeka-Capital Journal.

Fig. 5.22: Courtesy of Brian Kennedy, Hungry Horse News

Figs. 5.23, 5.24: Courtesy of Bill Sikes

Fig. 5.29, 18.38: Courtesy of the Times-Picayune Publishing Co.

Fig. 6.14: On Money Talk; by permission of Dean Witter InterCapital, Inc.

Figs. 6.18, 6.19, 18.11: The San Jose Mercury News.

Figs. 6.22, 18.9: The St. Louis Post-Dispatch.

Figs. 6.23, 17.26, 17.27, 17.28, 18.48: The Springfield (Mo.) News-Leader and Greg Branson.

Figs. 6.24, 13.6, 18.26, 18.47: Reprinted with permission from the St. Paul Pioneer Press.

Figs. 7.11, 7.12, 7.15: Reprinted by permission of Loren Needles, Analytic Inc.

Fig. 8.1: Frankfurter Allgemeine

Figs. 10.3, 13.5, 15.18: Reprinted with permission of The Baltimore Sun Co.

Figs. 10.8: The Kansas City-Star.

Fig. 10.10: The Daily Texan, University of Texas

Figs. 11.1: The Spokesman Review.

Figs. 11.12, 13.11, 18.24, 18.53: Courtesy, Detroit Free Press.

Figs. 13.10, 18.15, 18.18, 19.14: Reprinted with permission of The Detroit News.

Fig. 14.1: Reprinted with permission of The Volante

Figs. 14.3, 14.21:The News and Record

Figs. 14.4, 14.14, 14.20, 14.33, 14.35: Reprinted with permission of The Sagamore.

Figs. 14.5, 14.12, 14.13, 14.22, 14.23, 14.24, 14.28, 14.29, 14.30, 14.37, 14.38, 14.44, 14.45, 18.50, 18.51: Reprinted with permission of The Guardian.

Figs. 14.6: Reprinted with permission of the Minnesota Daily

Figs. 14.7: Reprinted with permission of Fourth Write and San Antonio College

Figs. 14.8: Reprinted with permission of The Sower, printed twice a year by the Daily

Nebraskan at University of Nebraska-Lincoln.

Figs. 14.11: Reprinted with permission of The Daily Illini, University of Illinois

Figs. 14.15, 14.16, 14.31: Reprinted with permission of The California Aggie

Figs. 14.19: The Sentinel

Figs. 14.26, 14.41: Collegian

Figs. 14.27, 14.36, 14.40: Reprinted with permission of College Heights Herald of Western Kentucky University.

Figs. 14.39: Courtesy of the Marquette Tribune.

Figs. 14.34: Jeff Paslay/ Design Editor, Photo Essay by Michael Shindler/ Oregon Daily Emerald, University of Oregon.

Figs. 15.1, 15.10, 15.11: Copyright New York Daily News, used with permission.

Figs. 15.2, 15.9, 15.13: Reprinted with permission of The Rocky Rocky Mountain News.

Figs. 15.3, 15.7, 15.8: The Leader.

Fig. 15.4: The Atlanta Tribune.

Figs. 15.5, 15.12: Reprinted by permission of the author and The Village Voice.

Fig. 15.6: The Riverfront Times.

Figs. 15.21, 15.22: BEGA and the Universidad de Navarra (Spain)

Figs. 16.3, 16.4; Courtesy of the Chicago Defender.

Figs. 16.7: The Daily Herald.

Figs. 17.2, 17.4, 18.4, 18.8, 18.10, 18.12: Copyright Waco Tribune-Herald.

Figs. 17.17, 17.18, 17.19: Santa Maria Times; Wayne Agner, Mark Craddock, Chris Gotsill, designers.

Figs. 17.29, 18.3: Courtesy of the Portland (Maine) Newspapers.

Figs. 17.30: Boca Raton News.

Figs. 17.31: Reprinted with per-

mission of Chicago Sun-Times.

Figs. 18.16, 18.54: From The Tennessean.

Figs. 18.19: The Beacon Journal

Figs. 18.22, 18.40: Reprinted with permission of The Independence Examiner.

Figs. 18.37: Reprinted with permission of the Gazette Telegraph.

Figs. 18.38: Courtesy of The Times-Picayune Publishing Corporation.

Figs. 19.11: The Pittsburgh Post-Gazette

INDEX